The United Nations Secretariat

The United Nations Secretariat

The Rules and the Practice

Theodor Meron

Lexington Books
D.C. Heath and Company
Lexington, Massachusetts
Toronto

Library of Congress Cataloging in Publication Data

Meron, Theodor, 1930–

    The United Nations Secretariat.

    Includes index.

    1. United Nations. Secretariat. I. Title.

JX1977.A362M47   341.23'2   76–53920

ISBN 0–669–01299–8

Copyright © 1977 by D.C. Heath and Company

Published simultaneously in Canada

Printed in the United States of America

International Standard Book Number: 0–669–02199–8

Library of Congress Catalog Card Number: 76–53920

Contents

List of Tables

Preface

My interest in the administration of the United Nations dates back to the early sixties when, from the vantage point of a representative on the Fifth (Administrative and Budgetary) Committee of the General Assembly, I could observe the fascinating process of interaction between administrative, budgetary, political, legal, economic, and social factors.[1]

In recent years I, like many others, became increasingly concerned with the trends and the developments in the Secretariat of the United Nations. It is my belief that the future success or failure of the United Nations will be determined not only by the wisdom and sense of responsibility or lack of it—of its political and legislative organs and particularly the General Assembly and the Security Council—but also by the type and the quality of the Secretariat that will carry out the work of the Organization.

I felt, therefore, that there is a need for a study of the United Nations Secretariat focusing on the examination of its personnel policies in the light of the United Nations Charter and the subsequently developed law of the United Nations. I am extremely grateful to the Rockefeller Foundation—and particularly to Messrs. Elmore Jackson and John Stremlau—for making it possible for me to take a year's leave of absence from the Foreign Service of Israel in order to carry out this study.

I am truly grateful to Dean Norman Redlich and to the New York University Law School, where I served as Visiting Professor of Law, for providing me with facilities and secretarial help.

I am also greatly indebted to many officials of the United Nations Secretariat who helped me with material, advice, guidance, and encouragement. While not naming them individually, I wish to thank them all through Mr. George F. Davidson, Under-Secretary-General for Administration and Management.

Special thanks go to Mr. Alfred G. Moss and Mr. Harry N. M. Winton whose mastery of United Nations documents and kind help have made my task much easier. Very special thanks go to Mrs. Teresita N. Alfonso who has patiently and ably typed and retyped the manuscript. Without her intelligent help this work would not have seen light. Last but not least, I wish to thank Mr. William C. Hitchcock, of the California Bar, for so meticulously proofreading the manuscript.

While expressing my gratitude to all these persons and to all those unnamed who have given me help and support, I wish to stress that the re-

---

[1] MERON, *Administrative and Budgetary Coordination by the General Assembly,* in UNITED NATIONS ADMINISTRATION OF ECONOMIC AND SOCIAL PROGRAMS (COLUMBIA U. PRESS, MANGONE Ed., 1966), *The United Nations "Common System" of Salary, Allowance, and Benefits: A Critical Appraisal of Coordination in Personnel Matters,* 21 INT'L ORG. 284(1967); *Budget Approval by the General Assembly of the United Nations: Duty or Discretion?* 36 BRIT. Y.B. INT'L. L. 91(1967).

sponsibility for the contents of this book is, of course, mine alone and that neither the Rockefeller Foundation nor any other institution share in any way the responsibility which I alone must bear.

An article based on Chapter 4 has originally appeared in *The American Journal of International Law*. I express my appreciation to its Editor-in-Chief, Professor R. R. Baxter.

New York, August, 1976

Introduction

The Secretary-General of the United Nations has recently referred to the goal of building up an international staff of the highest standard of efficiency, competence, and integrity, responsible only to the Organization and with as wide a geographical basis as possible. He acknowledged that the fact that the United Nations is a predominantly political organization inevitably exposes the Secretariat to pressures from many quarters although "Governments have generally made great efforts to respect the terms of Article 100, paragraph 2, of the Charter..."[1] He expressed the belief that it has been widely recognized that an objective, independent Secretariat[2] is in the long run in the best interest of all Member States.

It is, however, not at all certain that the values held in 1945 by the majority of the 51 states that signed the Charter at San Francisco are shared today by the majority of the 144 Member States of the United Nations. What is clear is the fact that the Secretariat is under considerable pressure from without and from within with regard to recruitment, to promotion, and in broader terms with respect to its international character and independence. The Secretariat suffers from considerable malaise, which is due to a wide spectrum of causes such as the decline—in the United States and in some other countries—in the centrality and in the prestige of the United Nations and in its ability to attract outstanding talent for service in the Secretariat. Among other causes are doubts about the relevance and the significance of the tasks assigned to the Secretariat as a whole and to a great many members of the staff; uncertainty about tenure, career prospects; and unhappiness about the increasing politicization of personnel procedures. Rightly or wrongly the staff is under the impression that permanent missions to the United Nations have an important influence on promotion procedures relating to their nationals in the Secretariat. This results in greater vulnerability to national influences. There is also concern about the filling of a growing percentage of senior posts through recruitment from outside, which has an adverse effect on the advancement prospects of the existing staff, and that nationality and other political considerations overshadow the principle of merit.

Problems relating to the professional staff of the Secretariat are usually considered in political, administrative, and budgetary terms. The author feels that time has come to discuss them in legal terms too or, rather,

---

[1] INTRODUCTION TO THE REPORT OF THE SECRETARY-GENERAL ON THE WORK OF THE ORGANIZATION, 30 GAOR, Supp. No. 1A (A/10001/Add. 1) at 9.

[2] See, in general, Schwebel, *International Character of the Secretariat of the United Nations*, 30 BRIT. Y.B. INT'L L.71 (1953). Jenks, *Some Problems of an International Civil Service*, 2 REPORT OF THE SPECIAL COMMITTEE FOR THE REVIEW OF THE UNITED NATIONS SALARY SYSTEM, 27 GAOR, Supp. No. 28 (A/8728), at 132.

in the light of the purposes and the requirements of the Charter. Indeed, given the political and social stresses to which the staff is exposed, it is imperative to focus on, to reinvigorate the role of law, and to develop proper procedures, counterbalances, safeguards, and due process. The object of this study is to make a contribution toward these ends.

A few words about the scope of this study may be appropriate. It will focus on the professional and higher categories of staff financed under the regular (assessed) budget of the United Nations and working in the Secretariat of the United Nations in New York and in Geneva, the regional economic commissions, the United Nations Conference on Trade and Development, the United Nations Industrial Development Organization, and the United Nations Environment Programme. The author hopes, however, that this study may also be of some relevance to the professional and higher categories of staff of other United Nations programmes and of the specialized agencies.

The professional and higher categories of staff comprise the following: Under-Secretary-General (USG), Assistant-Secretary-General (ASG), Director (D–2), Principal Officer (D–1), Senior Officer (P–5), First Officer (P–4), Second Officer (P–3), Associate Officer (P–2), and Assistant Officer (P–1). In addition, the United Nations staff includes general services (secretarial, technical, and clerical staff) and other categories such as security service, field service, and manual workers with which this study is not directly concerned.[3]

The statistical data were obtained by the author from a number of sources in the Secretariat. They do not all refer to the same time and sometimes are based on differing definitions. The author has included such statistical data in this study only in order to indicate general phenomena and trends.

---

[3] For a list of established posts, as approved by the thirtieth session of the General Assembly (1975), and for a list of the organizational units of the Secretariat, see A/10500, at 74–77.

Table of Principal Abbreviations

A and M	Department of Administration and Management
ACC	Administrative Committee on Co-ordination
AMS	Administrative Management Service
CCAQ	Consultative Committee on Administrative Questions
CS	Department of Conference Services
ECA	Economic Commission for Africa
ECE	Economic Commission for Europe
ECLA	Economic Commission for Latin America
ECWA	Economic Commission for Western Asia
ESA	Department of Economic and Social Affairs
ESACDP	Centre for Development Planning, Projections and Policies, ESA
ESADHA	Centre for Social Development and Humanitarian Affairs, ESA
ESAOTC	Office of Technical Co-operation, ESA
ESAPAF	Division of Public Administration and Finance, ESA
ESARET	Centre for Natural Resources, Energy and Transport, ESA
ESASCT	Office for Science and Technology, ESA
ESASTO	Statistical Office, ESA
ESAWFC	World Food Council
ESCAP	Economic and Social Commission for Asia and the Pacific
FICSA	Federation of International Civil Servants' Associations
GAOR	General Assembly Official Records
GE COD	Conference of the Committee on Disarmament, Geneva
HABITAT	United Nations Conference on Human Settlements
ICSC	International Civil Service Commission
JAC	Joint Advisory Committee
JIU	Joint Inspection Unit
LEGAL	Office of Legal Affairs
LEGALC	Codification Division

LEGALG	General Legal Division
OFS	Office of Financial Services, A and M
OGS	Office of General Services, A and M
OPI	Office of Public Information
OPS	Office of Personnel Services
PATD	Department of Political Affairs, Trusteeship and Decolonization
PSCA	Department of Political and Security Council Affairs
SGCLS	United Nations Conference on the Law of the Sea, Offices of the Secretary-General
SGEOSG	Executive Office of the Secretary-General
SGIAAC	Office for Inter-Agency Affairs and Co-ordination
SGPGAA	Office of the Under-Secretary-General for Political and General Assembly Affairs
SGSPA	Office of the Under-Secretaries-General for Special Political Affairs
SGSPQ	Office of the Assistant Secretary-General for Special Political Questions
TARS	Technical Assistance Recruitment Service
UNAT	United Nations Administrative Tribunal
U.N.C.I.O.	United Nations Conference on International Organization
UNCTAD	United Nations Conference on Trade and Development
UNDOF	United Nations Disengagement Observer Force
UNDRO	Office of the United Nations Disaster Relief Co-ordinator
UNEF	United Nations Emergency Force
UNEP	United Nations Environment Programme
UNFICYP	United Nations Peacekeeping Force in Cyprus
UNHCR	Office of the United Nations High Commissioner for Refugees
UNICEF	United Nations Children's Fund
UNIDO	United Nations Industrial Development Organization
UNITAR	United Nations Institute for Training and Research
UNMOGIP	United Nations Military Observer Group in India and Pakistan
UNOG	United Nations Office at Geneva

UNRWA United Nations Relief and Works Agency for Palestine Refugees in the Near East

UNTSO United Nations Truce Supervision Organization in Palestine

**The United Nations
Secretariat**

1

The Legislative History

The question of the future composition of the Secretariat was not one of the main preoccupations of the authors of the several drafts of the Charter prepared in the Department of State. Nor was it one of the main concerns of the Dumbarton Oaks Conference or of the San Francisco Conference. The powers of the Secretary-General, and the method of his appointment attracted more attention,[1] as did one of the related questions, whether to appoint deputies to the Secretary-General.

Department of State Drafts

As pointed out by Russell, one of the basic decisions that had to be taken by the Department of State was whether the Secretariat would be national or international in character: national in the sense of being staffed by officials temporarily detached from service in governments, paid by their governments and serving in "a quasi-representative capacity," or international, staffed by appointees of the Organization, paid from its budget and responsible solely to it. Following the precedent of the League of Nations, the decision taken by the officials of the Department of State was to support the principle of the international character of the Secretariat.[2]

The Draft Constitution of International Organization, of July 14, 1943, provided in Article 7(2) that "[t]he secretaries and the staff shall be appointed by the General Secretary with the approval of the Council. In making appointments the widest distribution among nationalities shall be made that is compatible with technical efficiency." Paragraph 3 established the principle of the international character of the Secretariat.[3] Paragraph 6 provided that all positions were to be open equally to men and women.[4]

---

[1] See, in general, RUSSELL & MUTHER, A HISTORY OF THE UNITED NATIONS CHARTER 369–77, 431–32, 854–62 (1958).

[2] *Ibid.*, at 369–70.

[3] Text in POSTWAR FOREIGN POLICY PREPARATION 1939–1945 at 476 (1950), Department of State Publication 3580.

[4] Russell observes that the omission of this principle from certain drafts "was due more to the thought that such protection against discrimination was no longer necessary than to any anti-feminist bias." *Op. cit., supra* note 1, at 370, n. 2. It is instructive to note that at the San Francisco Conference during the discussion of proposals to appoint deputies to the Secretary-General, the delegate of Brazil made the comment that to say "his deputies" implied "that the Secretary-General must be a man, and that should not at all be implied. You should say 'and the deputies' ". Verbatim minutes of 29th meeting of Committee I/2, June 17, 1945.

1

The Charter of the United Nations of August 14, 1943 (as written by the research staff) followed, in Article 5, the general approach of the Draft Constitution of International Organization.[5]

The concise Plan for the Establishment of an International Organization for the Maintenance of International Peace and Security, of December 23, 1943, stated only that the "various component organs and agencies of the organization should have appropriate administrative staffs."[6]

The Possible Plan for a General International Organization of April 29, 1944, contained more detailed provisions on the staffing of the Secretariat. According to section X, the Director-General was to appoint deputies and principal officers of the central administrative staff, subject to confirmation by the General Assembly; directors of commissions and agencies created by the Executive Council or the General Assembly subject to confirmation by the creating organ, and (himself) such other personnel for which he was responsible. Section X(5) provided that "[o]fficers appointed to the central administrative staff should be selected on the basis of technical or administrative competence and experience, and of the widest practicable distribution among nationalities." Such officials should "be constituted as a continuing international civil service." The officials were to undertake to perform their duties in the impartial manner and spirit necessary to advance the interests and purposes of the Organization, and Member States were to impose no obligations upon their nationals, officials of the international Organization, that would be inconsistent with the performance of their duties.[7]

The [United States] Tentative Proposals for a General International Organization of July 18, 1944, followed, with some minor modifications, the language of the provisions on the composition of the Secretariat which appeared in the Plan of April 29, 1944.[8]

Dumbarton Oaks

A different approach was followed by the Dumbarton Oaks Proposals for the Establishment of a General International Organization. Although the United States and the Chinese proposals went into some detail with regard to the staff of the Secretary-General and the general view was that he should have whatever staff would be considered necessary, there was no

[5] POSTWAR FOREIGN POLICY PREPARATION *op. cit., supra* note 3, at 528.
[6] Text in RUSSELL & MUTHER, *op. cit., supra* note 1, at 992.
[7] Text in POSTWAR FOREIGN POLICY PREPARATION, *op. cit., supra* note 3, at 590–91.
[8] *Ibid.*, at 605.

detailed provision for staff.[9] The sole general reference to the staff of the Organization was included in Chapter X, which dealt with the Secretariat to the effect that "[t]here should be a Secretariat comprising a Secretary-General and such staff as may be required. The Secretary-General should be the chief administrative officer of the Organization."[10]

San Francisco

In San Francisco, the principal controversy pertaining to the staff of the Secretariat related to the question of the deputies to the Secretary-General.[11] Although the question of the composition of the Secretariat beyond that of the deputies was hardly discussed, it was at least addressed by several of the amendments. Thus, Mexico proposed that the staff should be selected with a view to making it as fully internationally representative as possible.[12] Uruguay proposed that the staff should be made up through broad international representation and open to men and women alike.[13] Brazil, the Dominican Republic, and Mexico jointly suggested that all positions on the staff should be open equally to men and women.[14] Czechoslovakia observed that the choice of personnel would certainly be effected with the utmost care and that there was every reason to believe that the best people would be available.[15] Of particular importance were the amendments presented by Canada and by New Zealand. The Canadian amendment proposed the addition to the Dumbarton Oaks text of a provision whereby a truly international civil service should be established. The personnel was to be selected by the Secretary-General under rules to be established by the General Assembly, positions being open equally to men and women. "Subject to the paramount importance of seeking the highest standards of efficiency, competence and integrity, due regard shall be paid to the importance of recruiting personnel on as wide a geographical basis as possible."[16]

A similar amendment was proposed by New Zealand.[17]

[9] RUSSELL & MUTHER, *op. cit., supra* note 1, at 431–32.

[10] Text in POSTWAR FOREIGN POLICY PREPARATION, *op. cit., supra* note 3 at 618. 3 UNITED NATIONS CONFERENCE ON INTERNATIONAL ORGANIZATION (hereinafter "U.N.C.I.O.")22.

[11] RUSSELL & MUTHER, *op. cit., supra* note 1, at 854.

[12] 7 U.N.C.I.O. 505.

[13] *Ibid.*

[14] *Ibid.*, at 507.

[15] *Ibid.*, at 508.

[16] *Ibid.*, at 510.

[17] *Ibid.*, at 511.

4

The "sponsors' amendment," submitted by the United States, United Kingdom, Soviet Union, and China, provided that the Secretariat should comprise a Secretary-General, four deputies, and such staff as may be required. The Secretary-General and his deputies were to be elected by the General Assembly on recommendation of the Security Council for a period of three years, the Secretary-General being eligible for reelection.[18] The proposal for the election by the General Assembly of deputies to the Secretary-General was said to be designed "to increase the international prestige of the Secretariat." The delegate from Canada to Committee II/1 objected on grounds of principle, however, pointing out that, if the deputies were to be directly elected by the General Assembly, this would make it extremely difficult for the Secretary-General as the chief administrative officer to carry out the duties assigned to him under the Charter, and it was to be feared that decisions on important administrative matters would have to be taken by a committee of five. Moreover, such an election of the deputies "would be inconsistent with the establishment of a truly international civil service."[19]

The chairman of Committee I/2 appointed a special subcommittee (I/2/D) to consider Chapter X dealing with the Secretariat. The subcommittee considered the Canadian amendment in a revised form, and unanimously recommended a text (Chapter X, paragraph 6) virtually identical to that contained in Article 101 (3) of the United Nations Charter.[20]

The subcommittee also unanimously agreed that positions in the Secretariat, as one of the principal organs of the Organization, would be open to men and women on an equal basis, but that such a provision had already been incorporated elsewhere in the Charter. [21]

It is of interest to observe that during the discussion several delegations expressed the view that the Canadian amendment was concerned with minor technical details and should accordingly not appear in the Charter. Other delegates contended that the amendment contained general principles that were to guide the General Assembly when it established detailed regulations governing the staff of the Secretariat.[22]

---

[18] *Ibid.*, at 507. See in general RUSSELL & MUTHER, *op. cit.*, *supra* note 1, at 854–62.

[19] 8 U.N.C.I.O. 332. For the story of the rejection of amendments by the sponsoring governments and by the Soviet Union, respectively, see 7 U.N.C.I.O. 106–07, 280–81, 333, 390–91. The New Zealand delegation to the San Francisco Conference observed, in its report, that deputies could hardly be expected to work as a team under the Secretary-General. Being appointed for only three years in the first instance, they would feel that their careers lay much more with their governments than with the Secretariat. They would not constitute an efficient and loyal administration. UNITED NATIONS CONFERENCE ON INTERNATIONAL ORGANIZATION: REPORT ON THE CONFERENCE HELD AT SAN FRANCISCO 25 April–26 June 1945, by the RT. HON. PETER FRASER, CHAIRMAN OF THE NEW ZEALAND DELEGATION 35–36 (1945).

[20] 7 U.N.C.I.O. 558. Following an amendment by the Netherlands, the word "appointed" was subsequently introduced to replace the word "selected." *Ibid.*, at 394–95.

[21] *Ibid.*, at 558, 395.

[22] *Ibid.*, at 395.

In the course of the consideration of the Charter provisions pertaining to the Secretariat, the members of Committee I/2 quickly and unanimously agreed that given its central importance to the work of the entire Organization the Secretariat "should be of the highest quality and should be organized on a truly international basis."[23]

Subcommittee I/2/D was also seized of amendments submitted by Canada, New Zealand, and by the sponsoring governments, respectively, establishing the principles of the international responsibility of the Secretary-General and his staff, their obligation not to seek or to receive instructions from any external authority, and the obligation of the members to respect the international character of the responsibilities of the Secretariat and not to seek to influence the Secretary-General and the staff in the discharge of their responsibilities.[24]

Members of the subcommittee felt that such a provision would strengthen the position of the Secretariat and unanimously recommended for adoption a text, the language of which was based on the amendment of Canada and on that of the four sponsoring governments. This text eventually became Article 100 of the United Nations Charter.

During the Nineteenth Meeting of Committee I/2 held on June 4, 1945, however, the delegation of the USSR expressed opposition to the inclusion in the Charter of paragraph 6 of Chapter X of the report of the subcommittee, arguing that it dealt with technical questions pertaining to the recruitment of personnel. The discussion of the Soviet position as reflected in the unpublished and uncorrected verbatim minutes of the committee throws some light on the meaning and scope of the phrase "due regard shall be paid to the importance of recruiting staff on as wide a geographical basis as possible."

The delegate of Belgium replied to the delegate of the USSR that the paragraph concerned important points of principle that should be mentioned in the Charter itself. Referring to the importance of recruiting staff on a wide geographical basis, the delegate of Belgium said "that the Secretary-General in selecting his staff should call on the citizens of different countries, because what we want is an efficient international staff." The delegate of Greece, too, regarded this principle as an important one. But, in his view, it reflected the principle of equitable geographical distribution laid down in the provisions of the Charter pertaining to the election of the nonpermanent members of the Security Council (Article 23 of the Charter). The staff of the Secretariat should, therefore, be recruited on this basis. The delegate of the Ukraine stated that he had no objection on substantive grounds to the principle of geographical distribution of the

---

[23] *Ibid.*, at 387. See also the REPORT OF THE CANADIAN DELEGATION ON THE UNITED NATIONS CONFERENCE ON INTERNATIONAL ORGANIZATION, HELD AT SAN FRANCISCO, 25 April–26 June, 1945, at 58–60 (1945).

[24] 7 U.N.C.I.O. 510–12, 393–94, 557–58.

personnel. Smaller nations should have as large a representation in the Secretariat as possible, but the rights would not be equal for all. Although it was desirable and necessary to allow as many nations as possible to participate in the work of the Organization, the great powers had greater obligations and should have greater rights.

The delegate of the USSR strongly objected to the analogy drawn by the delegate of Greece between the principle of equitable geographical distribution with regard to the election of nonpermanent members to the Security Council, which he regarded as "a paramount consideration," and the geographical basis in the recruitment of staff. In the elections to the Security Council the primary objective was to make the Security Council representative of the major areas of the world. But would people appointed to the Secretariat represent regional interests? In his view it was "obvious that the same principle of geographic distribution cannot apply if we strive to found a technical organization of international character underlining the national character and not the fact that it would be based on any regional consideration."

The motion of the USSR to suppress paragraph 6 was decisively defeated.

Thus, although the principle of regional representation was implicit in the comments of Greece, Belgium, the Ukrainian SSR, and the Soviet Union all interpreted "geographical basis" as referring to individual states.

What conclusions can be drawn from the preceding survey of the legislative history of Article 101 of the Charter?

Obviously, the Founding Fathers were intent on establishing a truly international Secretariat and were anxious to assure its international character. They were against the proposal that senior officials be appointed or confirmed by the political or legislative organs of the Organization. They insisted on the authority of the Secretary-General to appoint even the most senior officials of the Secretariat, subject only to the general regulations to be established by the General Assembly and—of course—subject to the Charter.[25] It appears that they wanted a continuing, career international civil service. It is clear that they desired the staff of the Secretariat to have the highest possible qualifications, efficiency, competence, and integrity. Indeed, it is clear that the principle of merit was paramount and prevailed over the importance given to recruiting staff on as wide a geographical basis as possible. But the Founding Fathers gave no thought to the exact relationship of merit to geography, beyond the establishment of the paramountcy of the former. Neither did they clarify what was meant

---

[25] Compare with Article 6(3) of the Covenant of the League of Nations, according to which the staff of the Secretariat was to be appointed by the Secretary-General with the approval of the council.

by "geographical basis." The simplest and probably the most plausible interpretation of this term would be that the Founding Fathers desired the widest possible "representation" of nationalities in the Secretariat. They wanted a Secretariat organized on a truly international basis. There is no evidence that the Founding Fathers have ever intended the "geographical basis" to mean a broad cultural basis, regional basis, and so on, theories advanced *post hoc* by various interested parties. Nor did they consider any system of weighted "representation" in the Secretariat, such as that based on assessments to the budget of the Organization or on population. We must also assume that the words "geographical basis" in Article 101(3) mean something different from the words "equitable geographical distribution" in Article 23, that is, representation of states, rather than of regions.

Preparatory Commission

It is of special interest to examine how the Preparatory Commission of the United Nations, convened in London shortly after the San Francisco Conference, envisaged the future organization and composition of the Secretariat. The commission observed that the manner in which the Secretariat would perform its tasks would determine the degree to which the objectives of the Charter would be realized. To enjoy the confidence of the members of the Organization, the Secretariat must be truly international. It could not be composed, even in part, of national representatives responsible to governments. Indeed, the Preparatory Commission assumed that those appointed for two years or more must resign from any position they might hold in public or private employment.

The Preparatory Commission was of the view that unless members of the staff could be offered some assurance of being able to make their careers in the Secretariat, many of the best candidates would inevitably be kept away. It observed that "members of the staff [cannot] be expected fully to subordinate the special interest of their countries to the international interest if they are merely detached temporarily from national administrations and remain dependent upon them for their future."[26] Although it was important that officials from national services should be enabled to serve in the Secretariat so that personal contacts between the Secretariat and national administrations might be strengthened and a body of national officials with international experience created, they could serve for periods not longer than two years under a system of secondment or leave without pay.[27]

---

[26] REPORT OF THE PREPARATORY COMMISSION OF THE UNITED NATIONS, PC/20, at 92 (1945).

[27] *Ibid.*, at 93.

In the light of the above considerations, and given the importance of securing the advantages of experience and of establishing sound administrative traditions, the bulk of the staff should, in the view of the Preparatory Commission, consist of persons who would make their career in the Secretariat. They should be given contracts for an indeterminate period subject to review every five years. An appointment should not be terminated to make way for the appointment of a person of another nationality or for other reasons which are not connected with the work of the staff member. But not the entire Secretariat should be recruited on a permanent basis. Certain senior officers should be appointed under contracts not to exceed five years, subject to the possibility of renewal.[28] The Secretary-General would be free to offer temporary appointments to specialists in technical fields, to persons with special political qualifications likely to be required for the performance of urgent and exceptional tasks, and to candidates from geographical regions inadequately represented if suitable candidates from that region were not readily available for permanent appointment.

The Preparatory Commission thus spoke of geopraghical regions inadequately represented rather than of states inadequately represented. The commission expressed the belief that the principle of merit in recruitment "can in large measure be reconciled" with that of recruiting staff on as wide a geographical basis as possible.[29]

According to the Preparatory Commission, every member of the staff should have an opportunity for promotion to even the highest posts. Where candidates of equal merit were available, and subject to the requirements of service and to "the maintenance of equitable geographical distribution," it expressed preference for filling "vacancies for long-term appointments" by promotion rather than by appointment from outside.[30] By "vacancies for long-term appointments," the Preparatory Commission probably meant posts requiring considerable experience and continuity. It may be observed that the Preparatory Commission applied to the staff the term "equitable geographical distribution" (as in Article 23 of the Charter), thus significantly rephrasing the second part of Article 101(3) of the Charter. This term was to become a household term of the Organization, the expression of a principle steadily growing in importance in relation to, and at the expense of, the paramount principle of merit.

The Preparatory Commission also proposed the establishment of an international civil service commission,[31] a proposal which, although ac-

[28] *Ibid.*, at 92–93. Compare, REPORT BY THE EXECUTIVE COMMITTEE TO THE PREPARATORY COMMISSION OF THE UNITED NATIONS, PC/EX/113/Rev.1, at 81 (1945).
[29] REPORT OF THE PREPATORY COMMISSION OF THE UNITED NATIONS, PC/20, at 85 (1945).
[30] *Ibid.*, at 91.
[31] *Ibid.*, at 92.

cepted by the General Assembly by Resolution 13 (I), only became reality some 30 years later.[32]

One particular proposal made to the Preparatory Commission deserves special mention. The delegation of Yugoslavia proposed, first, that the staff of the Secretariat "shall be selected from nationals belonging to Members of the United Nations," and, secondly, that, to better ensure that the candidates were qualified, "the appointment of officials of the Secretariat should be made with the consent of the Member Government of which the candidate is a national."[33]

The delegate of Yugoslavia was willing to insert the words "as a general rule" in the first part of his proposal, so that in exceptional circumstances victims of fascist oppression might become eligible for international service, regardless of nationality. Delegates were, nevertheless, against the insertion of any such restrictive provision, or felt that it was unneccessary since the Secretary-General would in fact recruit citizens of the United Nations. This part of the proposal did not obtain the necessary two-thirds majority.

As regards the second part of the proposal, the delegate of Yugoslavia explained that in many cases the governments were in the best position to assess the qualifications of the candidates. The United Nations was an intergovernmental organization and persons appointed to the Secretariat must command the confidence of their governments if they were to be of real value to it. Of course, once they were appointed, governments would respect their exclusively international responsibilities. Yugoslavia further argued that its proposal could be properly adopted as regulations established by the General Assembly under Article 101 of the Charter. A large number of delegations opposed the proposal as impinging on the exclusive responsibilities of the Secretary-General under Article 101, as threatening the freedom, independence, and truly international character of the Secretariat, and as defeating the spirit and infringing the letter of Article 100. Although it made common sense that the staff should, as far as possible, be acceptable to member governments and that the Secretary-General would often request from them or from private bodies information regarding candidates, it would be extremely undesirable to write into the text anything that would "give national governments particular rights in this respect, or permit political pressure on the Secretary-General." [34] Moreover, governments were not always qualified to pronounce on a candidate's suitability and might find it embarrassing to recommend a candi-

---

[32] By Resolution 3042 (XXVII) the General Assembly decided in principle to establish an International Civil Service Commission. The commission's statute was approved by General Assembly Resolution 3357(XXIX) in 1974. The commission began to function on 1 April 1975.

[33] PC/AB/54.

[34] 22nd Meeting of the Preparatory Commission, PC/AB/66, at 51.

date belonging to a political opposition. It was wiser, therefore, to rely on the discretion and the good sense of the Secretary-General. This part of the Yugoslav proposal was defeated by a large majority.[35]

---

[35] *Ibid.*

2 Trials and Tribulations of the Geographical Distribution: The Evolution of the System

In February, 1946, the General Assembly expressed the wish that appropriate methods of recruitment be established to assemble a staff that would be characterized by the highest standards of efficiency, competence, and integrity, with due regard being paid to recruitment on as wide a geographical basis as possible. The Secretary-General was asked to follow the suggestions concerning recruitment outlined in the report of the Preparatory Commission.[1]

Initially, the Secretary-General's urgent task was to assemble staff so as to make the organization of the Secretariat a reality. Urgency, rather than broad geographical distribution, was the order of the day. And, although in theory merit was clearly established as the paramount principle governing recruitment, the haste that characterized recruitment to the Secretariat did not make it possible to ensure that the qualifications mentioned in Article 101(3) of the Charter were fully met. The picture of the staff that began to emerge was a very lopsided one. Thus, in 1946, the nationals of the 11 most substantially represented nations comprised 83.8 percent of the professional internationally recruited staff. In August, 1947, 13 nations[2] had 721 staff members out of a total of 902 in professional and higher grades (international recruitment), other than those in posts requiring special language qualifications. In 1947, 31 Member States were clearly underrepresented including the Soviet Union, India, and the regions of Latin America and the Middle East.

Desirable Ranges

It became obvious that the Secretary-General had to take steps rapidly to introduce a greater measure of geographical balance. For the first time, therefore, in September, 1948, Trygve Lie proposed a formula to translate the principle of geographical distribution, enunciated in Article 101 (3) of the Charter into practical administrative terms for the use of the Secretariat in its recruitment of staff. Thus, the Secretary-General stated, *ex ca-*

---

[1] General Assembly Resolution 13 (I).

[2] Belgium, Canada, Czechoslovakia, Denmark, Ecuador, France, Greece, Haiti, Netherlands, Norway, Poland, United Kingdom, United States of America. A/652, 3 GAOR, Plenary Meetings 155, at 158–59.

11

thedra, that the cardinal principle of geographical distribution meant not that nationals of a particular nation should have a specified number of posts at a particular grade or grades, or that they should receive a particular percentage of the total outlay in salaries, but that, in the first place, the administration should be satisfied that the Secretariat be enriched by the experience and culture which each member nation can provide and that each member should be satisfied that its own culture and philosophy make a full contribution to the Secretariat. The Secretary-General felt that any rigid mathematical formula, whether related to national income, literacy, financial contributions to the United Nations budget, or any other criterion, would reduce the necessary administrative flexibility. Nevertheless, in contradiction to the cultural content interpretation of the principle of geographical distribution, he concluded that, since financial contributions to the United Nations budget had been fixed in relation to a combination of pertinent criteria, it would be reasonable to take these contributions as a basis for a weighted system, with upward and downward variations within 25 percent of the budgetary contributions. This was designed to introduce a degree of flexibility (but not admitting an upward deviation in the number of nationals from countries contributing more than 10 percent of the budget, so as to ensure that no nation would have an undue proportion of staff in the Secretariat).[3] A national minimum quota, however, not dependent on budgetary contributions, was introduced, whereby no country would be regarded as overrepresented if the number of its nationals in the Secretariat was less than four.[4]

As time went on it became obvious that the Secretariat had become to a considerable extent a body of tenured officials. There was little possibility of change and great difficulty in correcting the imbalance in its geographical structure. In December, 1956, Hammarskjöld observed that in view of the high degree of staff stability that had been reached, opportunity for change in the nationality pattern was limited. The process of ensuring the wide geographical basis prescribed in the Charter required, therefore, a continuous, long-term effort.[5] Hammarskjöld was of the view that in order to have a first-class Secretariat, the majority of the staff would have to serve on a career basis. Although the Secretariat could not offer people a reasonable career unless it had a stable overall establishment, it was important to provide the Secretariat with an adequate proportion of posts that would be filled by way of fixed-term appointments of people made available from national services and other institutions. In fact,

---

[3] A/652, 3 GAOR, Plenary Meetings, at 157. See also A/652, 3 GAOR, General Assembly Resolution 153 (II).

[4] Secretary-General's Bulletin No. 77, 3 GAOR, Plenary Meetings, at 160. Regarding the implementation of this policy, see *ibid*, Plenary Meetings, at 156; General Assembly Resolution 233 (III).

[5] A/C.5/689, 11 GAOR, Annexes, Agenda Item 43, at 71.

Hammarskjöld envisaged the use of fixed-term appointments as a way of creating a quicker turnover which would help in the creation of greater geographical balance without sacrifice to the stability provided by a career service. He also advocated a greater administrative freedom for the movement of staff within the approved budget. He argued that, since the Secretariat was one and indivisible, the Secretary-General should be able to transfer both posts and staff between departments and offices so as to use that staff to its best advantage and where the individuals were most needed. This policy of Hammarskjöld's, which was expressed in the so-called "Consolidated Manning Table," gave him the flexibility to promote staff by moving posts around within the Secretariat.[6] It also enabled him to obviate situations in which key posts in a unit were held by staff members of the same nationality. Thus, interdepartmental and intersectional transfers of staff created both opportunities for promotion and for better geographical balance within the various departments of the Secretariat.[7]

Although the principle of geographical distribution requires the maintenance of a balance in the Secretariat as a whole, rather than within each individual department, it is obvious that the Secretary-General has a legitimate interest in avoiding a situation in which particular units of the Secretariat would be staffed or dominated by persons of one particular nationality, or even one particular region or group of countries. In practice, there has been a tendency, therefore, to establish a "mini" geographical distribution in the various departments.

In the Fifth Committee, the pressure grew for more rapid improvement of the geographical balance. As could have been expected, the new states admitted to membership since 1955 were dissatisfied not only with the slow rate of improvement of the geographical balance, but also with the substance of the 1948 formula, which, pegged as it was to the scale of assessments, inadequately reflected, in their view, the principle of equality of states and, indeed, the differences in population. During the twelfth session of the General Assembly (1957) delegates from underrepresented countries argued that a political organization such as the United Nations could not attach only a secondary importance to the principle of geographical distribution in the composition of a principal organ. [8]

In 1958 the Secretary-General began to use the term "desirable range of posts"[9] in tables showing the nationality and the number of staff in posts subject to geographical distribution. The minimum desirable range of posts was one to three for each Member State whose rate of assessment

---

[6] A/3041, 10 GAOR, Agenda Items 38 and 47, at 41–42.

[7] A/3797, 12 GAOR, Annexes, Agenda Item 51, at 4.

[8] *Ibid.*

[9] See e.g., A/C.5/750, 13 GAOR, Annexes, Agenda Item 53, at 2–3.

was less than 0.14 percent. The Secretary-General stressed that analyses of the geographical distribution of the staff in comparison with the desirable ranges were offered as useful tools but that the questions involved could not be dealt with in mathematical terms nor with mathematical precision.[10]

A resolution was adopted by the General Assembly in 1959 (1436 [XIV]) that stated that vacancies in posts at higher levels should be filled, as far as possible, by qualified candidates who were representative of geographical areas and main cultures either not represented or not adequately represented in such posts. Thus, the General Assembly by resolution started stressing the greater representation at senior posts of "geographical areas and main cultures."

Georges-Picot Committee, Troika, and Demands of New Member States

In December, 1959, the General Assembly, by Resolution 1446 (XIV), appointed the Committee of Experts whose mandate was to work together with the Secretary-General to review the activities and organization of the Secretariat. Its purpose was to bring about maximum economy and efficiency. Guillaume Georges-Picot, former Permanent Representative of France to the United Nations and former United Nations Assistant Secretary-General, was appointed chairman of the committee. Although the initial terms of reference of the Committee of Experts did not include questions pertaining to the geographical distribution of the staff, in 1960 the General Assembly decided, by Resolution 1559 (XV), to request the committee to study the categories of posts subject to geographical distribution and the criteria for determining the range of posts for each Member State with a view to securing a wide geographical distribution. The decision to revise the original terms of reference of the Committee of Experts was related to two developments. In the first place, the Soviet Union had come out with its proposals for introducing the "troika" arrangement into the Secretariat. The Soviet Union argued that the United Nations could not fulfill its obligations unless the various regions, with distinctive political characteristics, were adequately represented in the Secretariat. The Secretariat should equally represent three groups of Member States described as the "socialist" states, the "neutralist" states, and the "United States and its Allies." Opposing the "troika" concept, delegates of the Western countries argued that, under Article 101 of the Charter, geography was subordinate to the paramount consideration of merit and that,

[10] A/C.5/784, 14 GAOR, Annexes, Agenda Item 54, at 1–2.

moreover, under Article 100, staff members could not seek or receive instructions from governments. Member States undertook to respect the exclusively international character of the responsibilities of the Secretary-General and his staff. Insistence on the notion of "representation" of Member States in the Secretariat, they claimed, might defeat the essential purpose of geographical distribution, which was meant to enrich the Secretariat with personnel of the highest standard reflecting the broadest crosssection of differing experiences and differing cultures.

In the second place, the newly admitted Member States argued that the method for determining a desirable range of posts for each Member State was at variance with the Charter, which accorded equality to each Member State without reference to material resources.[11]

The Committee of Experts on the Activities and Organization of the Secretariat submitted its report, in June, 1961,[12] at a time when the membership of the United Nations had already increased to 99 states. Most of these new members were the newly independent states of Asia and Africa. The committee enumerated the arguments advanced by critics of the formula for the calculation of desirable ranges: the system was at variance with the Charter principle of equality of states; it gave a preponderant influence in the Secretariat to certain countries; it was faulty in that it treated all posts equally and it did not give sufficient weight to the population factor. In view of this criticism, the majority of the committee proposed a new formula that would take into acount not only financial contributions but also the factors of equality of states and population, and which would introduce an element of flexibility by allowing for the allocation of a certain number of posts on a regional basis. A minimum of two staff members from each Member State was to be adopted as the basis in order to reflect the membership in the Organization. To reflect the population factor, from each Member State one staff member was to be recruited for each 10 million population up to 150 million, and one additional staff member would be alloted for each 30 million population in excess of 150 million. The remainder of the posts available under geographical distribution would be allocated to Member States in accordance with their contributions to the regular budget of the United Nations. For the most senior posts in the Secretariat (D–2 and higher) the committee proposed a similarly constructed formula for distribution on a regional basis.[13]

While opposing the Soviet demands (troika) as contrary to the Charter, the Secretary-General supported the inclusion of population as a factor on the ground that any formula based exclusively on the contribu-

---

[11] See also A/4642, 15 GAOR, Annexes, Agenda Item 60, at 22–23.
[12] A/4776,16 GAOR, Annexes, Agenda Item 61, at 1.
[13] *Ibid.*, at 10–11.

tions of Member States to the budget would have the effect of penalizing countries that might be economically weak but that could make a good contribution to the work of the Secretariat.[14]

The report of the Georges-Picot Committee gave rise, during the sixteenth session of the General Assembly, to a debate in the Fifth Committee that focused on conflicting interpretations of the Charter. Western delegates argued that, since the principle of merit was the paramount consideration under Article 101(3), it inevitably followed that the geographical consideration was subordinate. It was argued that the term "geographical distribution" was not to be found in the Charter (except in Article 23, in relation to the composition of the Security Council), which provided that the staff should be recruited on the basis of certain prescribed qualifications. The Charter did not even stipulate that candidates must be nationals of any particular country as a condition of their recruitment into the Secretariat. Therefore, it was erroneous to interpret "geographical basis" as meaning nationality. While some interpreted nationality in a regional sense, others gave it an ideological twist. The Secretariat was composed of individuals rather than nationals of Member States and its staff must be protected by Article 8. The correct way of interpreting Article 101 was, according to this view, to give it a broad cultural interpretation.

Other delegations maintained that the word "geographical" should be interpreted in its literal sense and certainly not in any political sense. The idea of "representation" of countries or groups of countries within the Secretariat was contrary to the Charter and staff members could not be recruited on the basis of political or ideological considerations.

The Soviet Union, however, continued to insist that the term "geographical" had been used by the authors of the Charter mainly in its political sense, since the Charter was a political document and that the contemporary reality of three main groups of nations must be reflected in the composition of the Secretariat. Moreover, according to the Soviet thesis, it rested with the Member State alone to decide whether or not a given person was one of its nationals and whether or not he was qualified to "represent" his country in the Secretariat.[15]

The Fifth Committee, confronted with two competing draft resolutions, was unable to reach agreement and asked the Secretary-General for a statement of his views, to be presented to the seventeenth session of the General Assembly.

In a report presented to the seventeenth session (1962), the Secretary-General endorsed the view that membership in the Organization—expressing the principle of universality—should be one of the basic factors in the hiring of its staff.[16] The factor of contributions would also continue

[14] A/4794, 16 GAOR, Annexes, Agenda Item 61, at 47–48.
[15] A/5063, 16 GAOR, Annexes, Agenda Item 64, at 20.
[16] A/5270, 17 GAOR, Annexes, Agenda Item 70, at 4 *et seq*.

to be applied. As regards the population factor, the Secretary-General drew attention to the great disparity in population between the largest and the smallest states. The effect of this disparity could be mitigated by the adoption of a floor and ceiling, similar to those applicable to the scale of contributions to the budget.

Population had a bearing on the determination of the scale of assessments. Of two countries with the same total national income, the country with the larger population would have a lower assessment rate and thus might be considered to have lost entitlement for posts in relation to the country with a smaller population. He preferred the use of a reserve or a "float" of a number of posts for corrective action rather than the adoption of a separate population factor, even if such a factor were moderated by a floor and a ceiling.

As regards the scope of application of the geographical distribution formula,[17] the Secretary-General was of the view that bodies financed by voluntary contributions should not be formally subject to the principle of geographical distribution. They were designed to give assistance to countries requesting it. It was not in the interest of such programmes to be bound to a rigid formula, even if it were based on contributions. Given their relatively small staff and the importance of technical competence, serious consequences could result from the rigidity in administration and the restrictions in choice of staff that a fixed formula could introduce. It was, of course, desirable to have the staff of such bodies as broadly based as possible.

In conclusion, the Secretary-General stressed that no statistical formula could be considered a practical substitute for the discretion and good sense of the chief administrative officer. He proposed that for professional posts in the Secretariat (excluding those with special language requirements), equitable geographical distribution should account for a minimum range of one to five posts attributable to membership; a reserve of 100 posts was to be allocated on a regional basis to take account of such differences in sizes of population as do not receive sufficient weight in the other two factors; and the balance of posts should be distributed on the basis of the ratios of assessed contributions. The General Assembly endorsed the Secretary-General's recommendations in its Resolution 1852 (XVII). That resolution also called for a more balanced regional composition of the staff at the D–1 level and above.

It is interesting to observe that the Georges-Picot report would have given the factor of population a weight of about 15 percent in the formula. The draft resolution presented during the sixteenth session of the General Assembly by Afro-Asian and Latin American countries would have given the factor of population an even greater weight—one-third—based on the Secretariat's strength at the time. There was a strong, though unarticulat-

[17] Regarding groups not subject to geographical distribution, see *infra* note 19.

ed, feeling among the Western countries that either proposal would have given too great a representation in the Secretariat to the highly populated Asian countries.[18]

The formula adopted in Resolution 1852, modified by some variations in the relative weight of various factors, still forms the basis of the present system. At present, the principle of geographical distribution is expressed in desirable ranges calculated for each state as follows: A range of one to six posts is assigned to each state by virtue of its membership in the Organization; out of 2,400 professional and higher level posts,[19] financed under the regular budget, in the Secretariat proper, 200 posts are distributed among the geographical regions, taking into account the population factor. The remaining posts are allocated to each state on the basis of its assessment to the budget.[20] Obviously, as the number of Member States increases, the number of posts attributed to the membership factor increases, while the number of remaining posts attributed to the factor of contributions to the budget declines.[21]

There were considerable differences in the representation of states from the same geographical region up to and including the senior levels.[22] It could have been expected, therefore, that there would be a renewed emphasis on distribution of posts within each region. And, indeed, General Assembly Resolution 1928 (XVIII) (1963) requested that the Secretary-General in future recruitment of staff take into special account the equitable distribution of posts among Member States of each region, especially at the levels of D–1 and above.

Language Balance and Additional Guidelines

Various General Assembly resolutions adopted since then not only called for preference to be given to candidates from underrepresented states, but also superimposed on the system of the desirable ranges, additional recruitment guidelines or criteria that are not rendered in mathematical terms.

[18] 17 GAOR, Annexes, Agenda Item 70, at 4.

[19] Excluded from the geographical distribution are professional posts requiring special language qualifications (such as interpreters and translators), general service category posts (as well as manual labor and security posts), posts filled after interagency consultations, expert posts in the technical cooperation programmes, and posts in programmes financed by voluntary contributions.

[20] A/10184, at 6 (1975).

[21] Periodic changes in the scale of assessments affect not only the allocation of posts to the factor of contributions, but also the weight of the population factor, which is calculated on the basis of the allowance made for states where the *per capita* income is below a certain level.

[22] See e.g., the cases of India and Pakistan, A/C.5/987, 18 GAOR, Annexes, Agenda Item 66, at 7.

Thus, during the twenty-first session of the General Assembly (1966), following an initiative by France, criticism was levelled at the Secretariat for practising an apparent differentiation in its recruitment policy as between French-speaking and English-speaking candidates. It was argued that the former were often rejected on the ground that they did not have a sufficient command of English but that knowledge of French was not a requirement for English-speaking candidates. Although French was a working language of the Organization, French-speaking staff members were judged on the quality of their work in another language. The Secretariat should therefore improve its recruitment practices, so as to reflect more accurately the various cultures of the members of the United Nations. The French initiative was, of course, rather Gaullist and political. It was abetted by lagging representation of Francophone Africa, which could be attributed, in part, to a better civil service experience in English-speaking African countries. In order to corral the Latin American votes, at a late stage it was decided that the same consideration should be given to the Spanish language and no hierarchy among the several working languages of the Organization should be established. It was proposed that a linguistic factor should be introduced into the guidelines for recruitment. In light of such views,[23] the General Assembly requested the Secretary-General, by Resolution 2241B(XXI), to study the methods that should be used to ensure a more equitable use of the working languages of the Organization and a better balance among those languages in the recruitment of staff.

As regards the desirable ranges, some delegates in the General Assembly emphasized again the desirability of introducing a weighted point system that would reflect the level of posts. The Secretary-General repeatedly stated that there was no advantage in introducing such a further complication.[24]

In his report to the twenty-fourth session of the General Assembly (1969), the Secretary-General reported that he interpreted Resolution 1852(XVII) to mean that candidates from overrepresented countries should not be considered for appointment except in a number of exceptional circumstances, including the case where the candidate, although a national of an overrepresented country, came from a region that was itself substantially underrepresented. Here the Secretary-General interpreted the term "region" as "designating a geographical or linguistic grouping."[25]

During the debate, which took place in the Fifth Committee, doubts

---

[23] A/6605, 21 GAOR, Annexes, Agenda Item 81, at 27–28. See also Report of the Committee on the Reorganization of the Secretariat, A/7359, at 36–37 (1968); A/7334, 23 GAOR, Annexes, Agenda Item 81, at 14.

[24] See *ibid*. See also A/6860, 22 GAOR, Annexes, Agenda Item 82, at 8, 11.

[25] A/7745, 24 GAOR, Annexes, Agenda Item 83, at 2–3.

were expressed regarding the appropriateness of recruiting nationals of overrepresented countries from underrepresented regions, particularly if this were done at the expense of underrepresented countries. Indeed, the principle of balanced regional composition had been introduced by Resolution 1852 (XVII) only for certain senior posts, given the fact that the limited number of senior posts would not lend itself to distribution on a basis of country. Moreover, linguistic balance and equitable geographical distribution were separate matters, and linguistic groupings should not be included in the term "region" as defined for the purpose of attaining geographical balance.[26] By Resolution 2539 (XXIV) the General Assembly reaffirmed the need for an equitable geographical distribution of the staff as between regions and within regions, in particular at the level of senior posts, and the need for a better linguistic balance in the Secretariat and, once more, renewed its invitation to the Secretary-General to give preference to nationals from countries unrepresented or underrepresented. In view of the growing percentage of fixed-term appointments, the General Assembly also stressed that long-term service was conducive to greater efficiency in certain posts entailing complex duties and responsibilities.[27]

In its Resolution 2736 (XXV) (1970), the General Assembly laid down as regards recruitment for the regional economic commissions that, if qualified candidates of comparatively underrepresented countries could not be found within a reasonable period, preference should be given to qualified candidates from other countries of the same region that were not fully represented. As regards posts involving complex duties and responsibilities, the General Assembly considered that preference should be given to those who were willing to accept a career appointment or a fixed-term appointment of not less than five years. Given the rising age structure of the Secretariat, the General Assembly also provided that special efforts were to be made to recruit young men and women for service with the United Nations through the development of more objective selection methods and, wherever appropriate, open competitive examinations.

During the twenty-sixth session (1971), Colombia moved an amendment designed to give preference to nationals of developing countries.[28] During the twenty-seventh session (1972), the Fifth Committee agreed to include in its report a text proposed by Costa Rica, according to which greater attention should be given at the time of recruitment, especially to senior management policy posts, to candidates from underrepresented countries, "particularly the developing countries."[29]

---

[26] A/7851, 24 GAOR, Annexes, Agenda Item 83, at 30.
[27] For the interpretation of Resolution 2539(XXIV) by the Secretary-General, see A/8156, 25 GAOR, Annexes, Agenda Item 82, at 2–3.
[28] A/8604, 26 GAOR, Annexes, Agenda Item 84, at 3.
[29] A/8980, 27 GAOR, Annexes, Agenda Item 81, at 9.

The Secretary-General pointed out that the Costa Rican text raised difficult questions of interpretation. It suggested that the principle of geographical distribution should be applied to a particular kind of post, namely, management policy posts, to distinguish them from senior posts generally. Moreover, it introduced a distinction between candidates of underrepresented developing countries and those who came from other underrepresented countries. Previously preference was to be given to candidates from underrepresented countries regardless of the degree of their development.[30] The Secretary-General suggested that the balance established in 1962 had been altered by the introduction of additional guidelines. The fitness of a candidate for appointment had to be assessed against such additional criteria as: (a) the proportion of regional staff to be provided in each of the regional economic commissions (the policy was aimed at the staffing of regional economic commissions by a "desirable mix" of 75 percent from the region and 25 percent from other regions); (b) the need to improve the composition of the staff by working language, by age, and by sex; (c) the share of appointments to be assigned to those who were willing to serve on a career or long-term basis and those who could only serve for a relatively short period; and (d), as regards candidates for senior posts, the appointment was to be assessed against the further criterion whether the appointment would bring about a better distribution among the regions and within the regions. It was not clear what the relationship was between the various criteria and what weight should be given to each of them. Moreover, given the growing emphasis on adherence to quantitative guidelines, there was a greater reluctance to exercise the administrative discretion that was necessary to determine the qualitative fitness of a candidate if his appointment appeared to fall outside those guidelines.[31]

During the twenty-ninth session of the General Assembly (1974) the Secretary-General presented initial recommendations regarding a revision of the formula for calculating the desirable ranges so as to raise the minimum allowed for the membership factor.[32] The General Assembly endorsed a decision of the Fifth Committee which, once more, paid lip service to the principle that the use of national and regional desirable ranges was designed to be only a flexible tool of management. The Fifth Committee maintained the request that, in recruiting staff for the senior categories that participate directly in the administrative policymaking of the United Nations, greater attention should be given to candidates from countries inadequately represented in such categories, particularly candidates from the developing countries. The committee stressed that the principle of

---

[30] A/9120, at 10 (1973).
[31] Ibid., at 35–36.
[32] A/9724, at 6.

equitable geographical distribution should be applied to the Secretariat as a whole and that no post, department, division, or unit should be considered as the exclusive preserve of any individual Member State or any region.[33]

In 1975 the [Gardner] Group of Experts on the Structure of the United Nations System proposed that countries within a region or within a subregion agree among themselves to pool the number of posts allocated to them for purposes of satisfying the requirements of equitable geographical distribution.[34] The Secretary-General supported this concept of regional pooling since it would give him a greater measure of flexibility in the recruitment of nationals in a given region, as long as the region itself were not overrepresented.[35] This would amount, of course, to a shift of emphasis from a national to a regional balance in the composition of the Secretariat.

It should, however, be observed that such a regional approach to recruitment does not appear to be acceptable to the many underrepresented countries in various regions that view with jealousy the overrepresentation of certain countries within their regions. Indeed, during the thirtieth session of the General Assembly, various underrepresented states made it abundantly clear that they would not be satisfied with the improvement of the representation of their regions and would insist on a full attainment of their own national ranges.

In his 1975 report on the composition of the Secretariat, the Secretary-General drew attention to the practice of excluding various categories of staff from the principle of geographical distribution,[36] and raised the question whether the Organization should not take into account the advantages accruing to those Member States whose language was an official or working language, or those Member States on whose territory United Nations offices have been established. In both cases, such states had considerable numbers of nationals working for the United Nations apart from those recruited under the "quota" system.[37]

---

[33] It is of interest to observe that one of the departments in which a cultural balance is necessary (between the common law and the civil law) is the Office of Legal Affairs. For additional guidelines, see Fifth Committee Report A/9980, para. 45, approved by the General Assembly at its 2324th plenary meeting. 29 GAOR, Supp. No. 31 (A/9631), at 139.

[34] A NEW UNITED NATIONS STRUCTURE FOR GLOBAL ECONOMIC CO-OPERATION, E/AC.62/9, para. 93(b).

[35] A/10184, at 8, 10.

[36] Ibid., at 8.

[37] Moreover, the 1975 Sixth Annual [Stanley Foundation] Conference on United Nations Procedures, in which a number of senior officials from the Secretariat participated, expressed the view that there was less justification to entirely excluding the growing number of language posts from the application of the principle of geographical distribution. STANLEY FOUNDATION, REPORT OF THE SIXTH ANNUAL CONFERENCE ON UNITED NATIONS PROCEDURES 14 (1975).

In the view of the author, the inclusion of posts with special language requirements, now filled on the basis of objective competitive examinations, among those subject to geographical distribution would make the staffing of such posts extremely difficult. It is also obvious that, if the language staff from countries such as the United Kingdom, the USSR, and France were added to their nationals serving in posts subject to geographical distribution, the national representation of these countries would be greatly inflated by staff performing basically a servicing function, and those countries would find it more difficult to claim substantive or policy-making posts. Such a proposal would thus be unacceptable to the countries that already have many nationals working in language posts in the Secretariat.

In the same report, the Secretary-General made suggestions for a further increase in the weight of the membership factor. He proposed that the number of posts subject to geographical distribution be raised from 2,400 to 2,600. The minimum range allowed for each Member State by reason of membership alone would be raised from one to six to two to eight. According to this formula measured by the median of the desirable range, the membership factor would represent 26.5 percent of the total (in comparison to 20.1 percent in August, 1975), the weight of the population factor would be raised to 8.5 percent (8.3 percent in August, 1975) and the weight of the contributions factor would be lowered to 65.0 percent (from 71.7 percent in August, 1975). These figures related to a membership of 138 Member States. A flexibility factor of 15 percent (but not less than three staff members) could be added to or subtracted from the precise figure—the median of the range—for each Member State. These tentative suggestions of the Secretary-General aroused, however, concerted opposition on the part of the larger contributors who argued, in the course of the thirtieth session of the General Assembly, that, as a consequence of the admission of new Member States, the number of posts allocated to the factor of membership was quickly rising at the expense of the number of posts remaining to be allocated to the factor of contributions, and that there was no justification, therefore, for changing the formula in favour of the membership factor.

Following the debate in the Fifth Committee, the Secretary-General was asked to present recommendations to the thirty-first session of the General Assembly. Given the absence of consensus in the Fifth Committee and without clear guidance from the committee, the Secretary-General may find it difficult to propose far-reaching reforms. It is likely that, despite objections on the part of the larger contributors, the trend will continue inexorably in favour of a greater weight being given to the factor of membership—reflecting the principle of equality of states—at the expense of the factor of contributions.

The increasing emphasis on the principle of geographical distribution as regards not only senior posts but also all posts in the Secretariat has resulted to a considerable extent from the claims of the largely underrepresented developing countries. Some of these countries have regarded the principle of merit as an excuse for delaying or obstructing the improvement of their nationals' representation in the Secretariat.

Thus, a draft resolution proposed in 1975 by a number of underrepresented countries led by Japan requesting the Secretary-General to take all necessary measures to recruit the staff members subject to geographical distribution from the countries unrepresented or underrepresented in the Secretariat[38] was amended by adding the words "in particular from the developing countries" and adopted as Resolution 3417B (XXX). Thus, preference for nationals of developing countries over nationals of other underrepresented Member States was introduced with regard to recruitment to all posts in the Secretariat, not only to senior posts, as provided under earlier Fifth Committee reports. Although this resolution—which was to be implemented in accordance to Article 101(3)—was adopted by the Fifth Committee without objection, another draft resolution pushed by the powerful voting group of the developing countries aroused considerable opposition on the part of the developed countries. The debate on this draft was of particular interest because it focused on Article 101(3). The developing countries, led by Iran, proposed a draft resolution that noted, in its preambular paragraphs, that, although 73 percent of the Member States were developing countries, 64.5 percent of the staff members occupying senior positions in the Secretariat were nationals of developed countries and that the achievement of the objectives and the goals of the United Nations, especially with respect to the developing countries, required that the latter be appropriately represented at policymaking levels. The draft resolution requested the Secretary-General to take appropriate steps to increase the number of staff members recruited from among nationals of developing countries for senior posts in the Secretariat. Although this draft did not contain any novel elements (except that principles previously expressed in Fifth Committee reports were now elevated to the more formal status of General Assembly resolutions), it was opposed by the representative of the United States who stressed that the principle of merit was to be paramount in recruitment, and that, in the formula for determining the desirable ranges, financial contributions were the overriding factor. He argued that the representation of developing countries at policymaking levels was somewhat higher than the midpoint of their assigned range. He was opposed to putting pressure on the Secretary-General to increase the number of officials from developing countries

---

[38] A/C.5/L.1271.

in senior posts when the Secretary-General was already complying with the formula approved by the General Assembly.[39]

The delegate from New Zealand proposed to insert in the operative paragraph the words "taking into consideration Article 101, paragraph 3, of the Charter,"[40] but the sponsors rejected the amendment on the ground that the provisions of the Charter were implicit in the draft. The New Zealand amendment was put to the vote and rejected. The draft resolution itself was adopted and became Resolution 3417A (XXX).

In conclusion, it may be observed that the General Assembly developed a chaotic system of recruitment guidelines which are often contradictory (for example, in the varying emphasis on region in relation to individual states, or the degree of development in relation to nationality) and which, to a large extent, fall outside the intent of the Charter. The Secretary-General, who was given by the Charter the power to appoint officials to the Secretariat, is thus in the unenviable position of having to weigh and reconcile constantly changing and often contradictory guidelines. The contradictions and the chaotic nature of the system tend at times to hamper the exercise of administrative discretion; in other cases they may give the administration too great a latitude in choosing between the various guidelines. It is clear that despite the ritualistic reaffirmation, from time to time, of the principle of merit, that principle which according to the Charter was to be paramount has been relegated to a secondary position. Moreover, as we shall see in Chapter 10, the system did not prevent gross overrepresentation of some countries.[41]

---

[39] A/C.5/SR.1756, at 12–13.
[40] *Ibid.*, at 15.
[41] See e.g., A/10184, Annex, Table 8.

3

National Attitudes: Rhetoric and Practice

Hammarskjöld–Khrushchev Controversy

In his Oxford speech, Dag Hammarskjöld recalled the statement made by Chairman Khrushchev in his interview with Walter Lippmann that, while there are neutral countries, there are no neutral men, and Lippmann's conclusion that, in this deeply divided world,[1] there can be no such thing as an impartial civil servant. Hammarskjöld himself took, as is well known, an extremely serious view of this attitude, which he regarded as challenging the basic tenets of the philosophy of both the League of Nations and the United Nations. He insisted that, according to this attitude, we would be thrown back to 1919, and regress from the use, on the international arena, of permanent organs, assisted by a neutral civil service carrying out executive functions on behalf of all members of the Organization, to traditional conference diplomacy.[2] In his view, neutrality, understood to mean that the international civil servant must remain wholly uninfluenced by national or group interests or ideologies when involved in talks with political implications, was basic to the Charter concept of the international civil service. Although no man was neutral in the sense that he was without opinions or ideals, it was nevertheless possible to have a neutral Secretariat and anyone of integrity, not subjected to undue pressures, could, regardless of his own views, readily act in an exclusively international spirit.

The basic clash between the Hammarskjöldian conception of the international civil service and that of the Soviet Union, although unresolved, has become muted. On the one hand, the Secretaries-General who succeeded Hammarskjöld have taken a more cautious view regarding the notion of the executive authority of the Organization. As regards the Soviet position, its articulation, though not necessarily its dogmatic substance, has considerably softened through the years.

---

[1] THE INTERNATIONAL CIVIL SERVANT IN LAW AND IN FACT (Clarendon Press, 1961), at 3. See also *ibid.*, at 14. 5 PUBLIC PAPERS OF THE SECRETARIES-GENERAL OF THE UNITED NATIONS 471 (CORDIER & FOOTE, Eds., 1975. COLUMBIA U. PRESS, 1975).

[2] For a classical exposition of Hammarskjöld's views, see INTRODUCTION TO THE ANNUAL REPORT OF THE SECRETARY-GENERAL ON THE WORK OF THE ORGANIZATION, 16 GAOR, Supp. No. 1A (A/4800/Add.1) (1961).

The Soviet Union

At the height of the confrontation, in 1961, representatives of the Soviet Union in the General Assembly argued that the term "geographical" in Article 101(3) had been used by the authors of the Charter mainly in its political sense and that the existence of three main groups of nations and the alignment of forces they represented must be recognized and reflected in the composition and the personality of the Secretariat, if that organ was to have the confidence of all Member States. Moreover, it rested with a Member State to decide whether or not a given person was one of its nationals and whether or not he or she was qualified to represent it in the Secretariat. Therefore, it was the duty of the Secretary-General to consult the Member State concerned before taking any action affecting its national quota in the Secretariat.[3] Similarly, the Soviet expert on the Georges-Picot Committee, A. A. Fomin, claimed that in setting quotas of Secretariat posts for Member States, it was necessary to proceed from the fact that the United Nations consisted of three basic groups of states, which must be represented in the Secretariat on the basis of equality.[4] The concept of a "permanent civil service" was not justified as regards staff falling under geographical distribution and was a cover for recruiting staff on a one-sided basis, in the interests of Western military alliances. He argued that persons filling posts subject to geographical distribution should be granted only temporary contracts. Only such a method would ensure the necessary influx of new strength and the constant contact and interplay between the Secretariat and the Member States with varying political tendencies and social systems.[5] Among the steps proposed by Fomin was the putting of an immediate end to the practice of granting permanent contracts to all members of the staff. As regards existing permanent contracts, those granted to directors and higher grades should be eliminated entirely, while the number of such contracts for persons serving in lower grades should be reduced to no more than certain percentages (30–40). Recruitment of nationals of countries adequately represented should be stopped.[6]

Platon D. Morozov, the Soviet member of the 1968 Committee on the Reorganization of the Secretariat, although making no reference to the equal representation in the Secretariat of three main groups of states, insisted that permanent contracts should no longer be issued and that the existing ones should be replaced with fixed-term contracts for a period of not more than 10 years. Such a change was explained by Morozov as de-

---

[3] A/5063, 16 GAOR, Annexes, Agenda Item 64, at 20.

[4] A/4776, 16 GAOR, Annexes, Agenda Item 61, at 11.

[5] *Ibid.*, at 8.

[6] *Ibid.*, at 13.

signed to increase the efficiency of the Secretariat. Moreover, Morozov did not exclude the possibility of the Secretary-General's extending contracts in individual cases, where there were good practical reasons for doing so.[7]

In 1975, E. N. Makeyev, the Soviet delegate to the Fifth Committee, expressed the view that the members of the staff were not citizens of the world, but nationals of Member States who carried with them their national qualities and peculiarities.[8] General Assembly resolutions required that recruitment should not be restricted to one group of countries, as had been the case for a long time. The Secretariat must be freed from the political and cultural domination which that group of countries had secured through preferential recruitment. He noted with satisfaction that the representation of Soviet nationals in the Secretariat (desirable range: 189–271. Number of staff on 30 June 1975: 154 including 1 under-secretary-general, 10 D–2 and 10 D–1) had improved recently and that the power of the Western countries was now a thing of the past. The Soviet Union had very many qualified persons capable of filling any position whatever in the Secretariat. He praised the positive action taken by the Secretary-General and his aides with regard to these matters. Restating the traditional Soviet attitudes, Makeyev maintained that an end should be put to appointments benefitting the overrepresented countries and that staff should be appointed only for fixed terms. He justified this demand by the need for the Secretariat to adapt itself to changing attitudes and ways of thinking, by frequent renewal of its staff. He did not, however, reiterate the demands for the termination of all existing permanent appointments.[9] On the question of ensuring an equitable balance between men and women in the Secretariat, he objected to the view that a real breakthrough would not be possible as long as the recruitment of women would remain subjected to the guidelines concerning the geographical distribution. Obviously suspicious that a departure from the principle of equitable geographical distribution would favour the overrepresented countries, he insisted that the procedure used in the recruitment of women be compatible with the principle of geographical distribution and be applied within the desirable range established for each state.

Such views coming from a country that has suffered from a chronic underrepresentation in the Secretariat can easily be understood. Indeed, it may be recalled that, for exactly the same reasons, the Soviet Union was instrumental in prevailing on the World Conference of the Interna-

[7] A/7359, at 63–65.

[8] A/C.5/SR.1753, at 9.

[9] In rather stronger terms than the Soviet Union, the delegate of the Ukrainian SSR argued in 1975 that permanent appointments should be eliminated altogether. He objected strongly to the legitimation of the practice of awarding permanent contracts, since it violated the Charter [sic!]. A/C.5/SR.1754, at 15.

tional Women's Year, held in Mexico in 1975, to have the emphasis of the resolution on the situation of women in the employ of the United Nations and the specialized agencies shifted from women alone to a recommendation that efforts be made to bridge the gap in the recruitment of staff, including women, between the overrepresented and the underrepresented countries, "in accordance with the principle of equitable geographical distribution contained in the Charter of the United Nations."[10] Although the motive for the Soviet Union's insistence on the constant and rigid implementation of the principle of equitable geographical distribution and on the fulfillment of the desirable ranges is clear, it is a fact that the Soviet Union—despite some recent progress—could have been more forthcoming in presenting candidatures of women for recruitment. The Soviet Union is reluctant to send single women abroad and, if they are married, it may be difficult to arrange jobs for both the husband and wife in the Secretariat (in posts requiring special language qualifications, some exemptions under Staff Rule 104.10 have been granted). Given the Soviet Union's belief that Soviet nationals in the Secretariat serve Soviet national interests and in light of the large supply of highly qualified women in the Soviet Union, that country could benefit from the current emphasis on the recruitment of women and thus fill more rapidly its desirable range. The recent equalization in the rights and privileges of women and men staff members, whereby the travel to the duty station of the husband of a woman staff member is being paid for even though he might not be technically a "dependent," should have positive effects.

The long years that have passed before the Soviet Union took any real interest in staffing, while Western nationals were moving into career positions, may be one reason for Soviet underrepresentation. By now, chronic underrepresentation is, however, largely a result of the Soviet policy of objecting to the grant of permanent contracts to Soviet nationals and of consenting only to the recruitment of Soviet nationals to the Secretariat on fixed-term contracts and on the basis of secondment.[11] The large turnover which follows and the time which elapses until other Soviet nationals are appointed are a major factor in this regard. On 30 June 1974, the three Soviet Republics had 181 staff members in the Secretariat, in posts subject to the geographical distribution. Between that date and 30 June 1975, 34 Soviet staff members were separated from the service. Thus, much recruitment effort and expense has had to go into just keeping up with the constant turnover.

Improvements in this situation may come about as a result of several factors. In the first place, the Soviet Union and the UN administration have reached a high degree of cooperation in recruitment. Indeed, there is

[10] E/5725, at 75–76.
[11] At the moment, one Soviet member of the Secretariat serves on a permanent contract. See A/10184, Annex, Table 9.

reason to believe that Kurt Waldheim gave the Soviet Union a commitment to bring that country's representation in the Secretariat up to the lower limit of its desirable range within three years of his appointment as Secretary-General. Every year, the Permanent Representatives of the Soviet Union, the Ukrainian SSR, and the Byelorussian SSR submit to the Secretary-General lists of persons proposed for recruitment to posts specified in the lists. The lists also mention members of the staff who, in light of the information available to the Soviet Union, should be promoted [sic!]. On the basis of these lists, Secretariat recruitment missions are sent—as they have been for many years—to the Soviet capitals of Moscow, Kiev, and Minsk. In the course of 1975, the Soviet Union expressed interest in 45 vacancy announcements of posts subject to the geographical distribution. The Soviet Union submitted names of about 160 candidates and the Secretariat recruitment mission interviewed 142 candidates. In addition to the Secretariat recruitment missions, the Technical Assistance Recruitment Service (TARS) also sends recruitment missions to the Soviet Union. It should be observed that the Moscow Academy of Foreign Trade has a special faculty for training personnel for service with international organizations. In the past, the Secretariat made it known to the Soviet Union that it expected from her more than one candidate for each post. Some officials of the Secretariat view the present practice, whereby more candidates are submitted by the Soviet Union and interviewed by the representatives of the Secretariat than the number of vacancies, as implying acceptance by the Soviet Union of the principle of multiple candidatures. It may well be that the quality of the candidates and their linguistic skills have also improved. Another factor of importance is the increasing Soviet flexibility on the question of the duration of the fixed-term contracts that may be accorded to Soviet members of the staff. It appears that an understanding has recently been reached between the Soviet Union and the Secretariat whereby Soviet nationals would be able to serve in the Secretariat for periods of up to eight years, instead of the five-year ceiling generally applied at present. This would reduce losses due to staff turnover and result in lowering underrepresentation. Beyond and above that, such a development would tend to increase the influence of Soviet officials in the Secretariat. Moreover, some Soviet nationals who have served in the Secretariat in the past are sent back for additional periods of service after spending some years in the Soviet Union. Such persons return to the Secretariat with considerable expertise. So far the Soviet Union has maintained its traditional reluctance in allowing Soviet nationals to stay abroad for longer periods of time.[12] As a result of the Soviet

---

[12] Given the fact that Soviet nationals are not allowed to make their entire careers in the Secretariat, some of them may be interested in returning to the Soviet Union after relatively short periods of time in the Secretariat, in order to resume their careers and to reintegrate in their own national life.

Union's insistence that its nationals serve in the Secretariat only for relatively short periods of time and never on permanent appointments, the influence and power as well as the efficiency of Soviet nationals in key policymaking posts have been adversely affected. The Soviet Union probably realizes now that its interests in the Secretariat would be better served by Soviet nationals who would stay for longer periods of time and build up individual expertise and organizational influence and power.

The Soviet Union has recently been active in energetic recruitment not only of staff for posts subject to the geographical distribution but also for posts with special language requirements. The language training programme conducted by the Moscow Pedagogical Institute for Foreign Languages trains translators and interpreters with potential to be employed by the United Nations. The programme is subsidized by the United Nations, which appropriated $275,000 for the biennium 1976–77, as its share for the training of 40–50 translators, interpreters, and editors.[13]

The establishment of the Russian language training programme in Moscow has a rather interesting background. For many years, the Soviet Union has been objecting to the employment in the United Nations of non-Soviet interpreters into the Russian language. This opposition was related to the fact that many of the interpreters were expatriate "white Russians" or their descendants. It appears that one of the understandings reached between the United Nations and the Soviet Union pertaining to the establishment of the Moscow programme was that in the future the United Nations would not recruit Russian interpreters (and translators) except from the Soviet Union. Thus, an exception was established to the salutary policy of the United Nations whereby language staff (which is not subject to the principle of geographical distribution) is recruited on the basis of competitive examinations open to all. There may, of course, be some substance in the Soviet contention that the Russian language has changed greatly since the Revolution and that expatriates are not familiar with recent language developments. But, if this is so, would the weakness of the expatriate interpreters not be demonstrated in the course of their examinations?

A question of particular interest is that of the Soviet attitude towards so-called national preserves within the Secretariat– a question to be discussed in greater detail in Chapter 5. We have already mentioned the principle, supported by the General Assembly, that geographical distribution applies to the Secretariat as a whole, and that no post may be considered as the exclusive preserve of any individual Member State or of any region. What is the situation in reality? The Soviet Union claims that all senior policymaking posts now manned by Soviet nationals should also con-

---

[13] PROPOSED PROGRAMME BUDGET FOR THE BIENNIUM 1976–1977, 30 GAOR, Supp. No. 6 (A/10006), para. 22.164; and Supp. No. 8 (A/10008), para. 22.69.

tinue to be manned by Soviet nationals in the future. An obvious example is the post of under-secretary-general in charge of the Department of Political and Security Council Affairs or, on a lower level, the post of the director of the Codification Division in the Office of Legal Affairs. In practice, the Soviet claims to such posts have been largely accepted by the Secretariat. But it would be wrong to single out, in respect to the more senior posts, the position of the Soviet Union from that of other great powers, except, perhaps, in the intensity of the Soviet claims. Where the attitude of the Soviet Union differs from the attitudes of other powers is in her claim that practically every post in the Secretariat, at whatever level, which is or has been manned by a Soviet national, should also be filled by a successor from the Soviet Union in the future. Indeed, the Permanent Mission of the Soviet Union is most active on the departmental level, and on all levels of the administration, including that of the Secretary-General, in insisting on the Soviet representation not only in the Secretariat as a whole, but also in the various departments of the Secretariat, and with respect to the manning of specific posts. In fact the Soviet Union often claims posts at the P–3 level as her "national preserves." Such a "Balkanization" of the Secretariat is of course in obvious conflict with the provisions of the Charter regarding the international character of the Secretariat. But here, too, the reasons why the Soviet Union has taken such an attitude may be related to its traditional underrepresentation. Given the short terms of service of Soviet nationals in the Secretariat, the administration has considerable and legitimate difficulty in maintaining the proportion of the Soviet staff members and, even more, in attempting to increase it. From the administrative point of view, the simplest thing to do is to appoint Soviet nationals to the posts vacated by Soviet nationals.

The administration may have been an accessory to Soviet occupation of otiose posts, having actually created a number of senior posts in order to satisfy Soviet demands. A post specifically created for the Soviet Union may sometimes have no other purpose. Moreover, other posts manned by fixed-term Soviet employees sometimes fail to be useful and may tend to lose their value. Rather than reintegrating a function that has fallen into desuetude, the administration may prefer to use it for the satisfaction of Soviet claims to better representation. It may well be that the Soviet Union would agree to other posts, presumably on the same level, if such posts were offered. Anxious to maintain its positions in the Secretariat, however, the Soviet Union prefers to play it safe, by insisting on the right to man the positions vacated by Soviet nationals. National preserves are thus created *de facto*. This, however, does not always result from Soviet insistence or pressure but from difficulties of planning on the part of the administration which, in turn, are caused by the insistence of the Soviet Union on the short periods of service of their nationals in the Secretariat. Insofar as the Soviet interests are concerned, the wisdom of insisting on such national preserves in all cases and on all levels is questionable. We have already indicated that the importance and influence of a post that has been occupied by Soviet nationals for many years often declines with time. In cases where a Soviet national served for a short period of time and did not perform effectively, he was in fact bypassed by both his subordinates and by his superiors. He often remained in solitary splendour, like a general without an army. With greater representation in the Secretariat, the Soviet Union may well become more flexible with respect to national preserves.

The Soviet Union insists that the recruitment of all its nationals can take place only through the auspices of its Foreign Ministry and, as already pointed out, it holds the view that all Soviet nationals must serve on fixed-term contracts on the basis of secondment. The attitude of the Soviet Union, although much more subtle and pragmatic than in the early sixties, still creates considerable difficulties in terms of the Charter concepts regarding the exclusively international character of the Secretariat and the exclusive authority of the Secretary-General to select and to appoint staff (Articles 100 and 101). Difficulties also arise in terms of the principle of the equality of states enunciated in Article 2(1) of the Charter. If the Soviet Union can insist on the exercise of control over the recruitment of its nationals to the Secretariat and over their terms of service, why cannot other states claim equal rights with disastrous consequences for the character and the future of the Secretariat? The Soviet Union's attitude that Soviet nationals in the Secretariat fulfill a function on behalf of the Soviet Union and serve her national interests does not appear to have changed, but it is no longer articulated publicly. There is every reason to believe that the Soviet Government continues to exercise strict control over its nationals in the Secretariat, including control over the duration of their stay abroad.

Although many countries exert pressures of various kinds on the Secretariat, the Soviet Union goes particularly far. Of all the big powers, it is the most active in pressing the claims of its nationals and sometimes even of nationals of other Eastern European states, to appointment—especially to key positions—and to promotion.

The United States

The United States (desirable range: 358–523. Number of staff on 30 June 1975: 485 including 1 under-secretary-general, 2 assistant-secretaries-general, 14 D–2 and 33 D–1) takes a strong position in favour of the merit principle and against politicization of appointment procedures. Let us first turn to statements of policy (rhetoric).

In 1974 the representative of the United States in the Fifth Committee complained that the shift of emphasis in the use of the desirable ranges from a flexible tool of management to a precise indicator of how many staff members of any particular nationality or region should be in the Secretariat at any given time[14] grossly distorts the intent of Article 101 of the Charter, according to which the principle of merit is to be paramount. The appointment, transfer, and promotion of staff must be based on the fundamental need to secure for each job individuals with the highest standards of efficiency, competence, and integrity, as required by the essential concept of a career international civil service. Members of the Secretariat must demonstrate discipline under Article 100 of the Charter and possess a genuine devotion to the ideals of the Organization and especially to the fundamental concepts embodied in an international civil service. In 1975, the representative of the United States complained that Member States press hard the claims of their nationals to employment and fair treatment in the Secretariat, straining to the utmost the capacity of the senior officials to make personnel decisions dispassionately with primary regard to efficiency. She strongly opposed the proposed change in the formula whereby the weight of the membership factor would be increased from one to six posts to two to eight posts. Moreover, the United States urged the Secretary-General to reexamine the need for the allocation of 200 posts to the population factor. The United States preferred to return to the previous population reserve of 100 posts.

On the question of national preserves, the United States expressed strong support for the principle that equitable geographical distribution should be applied to the Secretariat as a whole and that no particular post or element within the Secretariat should be considered as the exclusive holding of any one state or region. Assignments within the Secretariat must always be based on the essential principles of the Charter.[15]

It is, however, obvious that the United States is not willing to lose to other states, certainly not to the Soviet Union, positions of influence in the Secretariat. It has also come to realize that the trend towards emphasizing the principle of geographical distribution and giving greater weight to the membership factor in the formula for the calculation of desirable ranges cannot but weaken the representation of the United States nationals in the Secretariat. The United States appears ready to vigorously protect its position as a superpower and as the greatest single contributor to the budget of the United Nations.

[14] A/C.5/SR.1666, at 18–19.

[15] A/C.5/SR.1682, at 21.

The Government of the United States is concerned at the reversal of the order of merit and geography. It regards resolutions such as those giving priority to nationals of developing countries as eroding the existing formula. The Secretary-General feels duty-bound to apply some of the measures recommended in such resolutions, although he has some leeway, as a person entrusted with the interpretation of the Charter and with the interpretation of the guidelines laid down by the General Assembly.

In practice, during the last few years the United States Government has been more active than before in recruiting United States citizens to work for international organizations. Indeed, there has been some congressional pressure urging the Department of State to intensify American recruitment to international organizations.[16] A special unit in the Department of State (the United Nations Personnel Policy and Recruitment Staff, Bureau of International Organization Affairs) has been enlarged and coordinates the efforts of the United States Government to place more Americans with the United Nations and with the specialized agencies. The United States explains its vigorous recruitment role as based on its interest in the efficient management of the United Nations and of its limited financial resources. It wants citizens of the United States to serve the United Nations so as to reflect the United States national philosophy, culture, and efficiency. This does not mean that all United States nationals now apply for employment with the United Nations through the Department of State. Indeed, most United States citizens apply directly to the Secretariat but with respect to higher grades (D–1 and above) the percentage of those who apply and are recruited following the referral by the Department of State is, of course, much higher.

As regards candidates for important and sensitive jobs, the Department of State is likely to show great interest in recruitment of qualified candidates, but once they have been appointed the stated policy of the United States Government is to leave them alone to exercise their international functions without pressure or interference. In some quarters of the Secretariat, allegations have been made that, during the last few years, candidates for recruitment who have been supported by the Department of State have been, in some cases, disappointing. These allegations referred in particular to American candidates who have joined the Secretariat upon obtaining early retirement from the civil service of the United States, or after having been "selected out" from the Department of State. Although the United States does not always offer the best candidates it could find, the author has not, however, seen any persuasive evidence

---

[16] SENATE COMMITTEE ON FOREIGN RELATIONS, DEPARTMENT OF STATE AUTHORIZATION ACT OF 1973, REP. No. 93–176 on S. 1248, 93rd Cong., 1st Sess., at 18 (1973).

that its candidates are of a lower calibre than other (non-American) Secretariat officials.

In order to encourage civil servants to serve for a period of time with international organizations, the American administration may pay Federal Government employees transferred to international organizations so-called equalization payments, that is, amounts equal to the difference between the monetary benefits paid by the international organizations and the monetary benefits that would have been paid by the agency from which an employee had been detailed. Such equalization payments can only be paid after the employee's separation from an international organization, if and when he is exercising his reemployment rights.[17] It should be observed that equalization payments are a factor of importance in posts outside the United States.

It may be of further interest to observe that, although many United States civil servants serve on secondment with various specialized agencies, not many seconded officials serve in the United Nations Secretariat. Thus, in December, 1974, 18 (professional) persons served on secondment from the United States Government in the Secretariat of the United Nations.

Formally, the United States regards only one post in the Secretariat as its "national preserve," namely, that of the assistant-secretary-general in charge of the Office of General Services, on the grounds that this post, which involves contacts with American suppliers, contractors, and so forth, requires knowledge of the local New York scene. Even the post of under-secretary-general for Political and General Assembly Affairs is not formally claimed as an American preserve, but in fact it is clearly viewed as such. Since the United States expects a United States citizen to serve in a political (cabinet-level) post, the denial by the United States of her claim to this post as a national preserve has little practical significance. If, for example, the American director of the General Legal Division, were to retire, it could be expected that the United States would claim for another United States citizen that post, or an equally senior post in the Office of Legal Affairs. The United States does claim the post of the administrator of the United Nations Development Programme (UNDP is not formally subject to the principle of geographical distribution), on the ground that the programme is to a large extent financed by the voluntary contributions of the United States. The impression in the Secretariat is that, in practice, the United States exerts pressures to have its nationals appointed to key positions.

The Department of State and the Permanent Mission of the United States to the United Nations continuously identify important posts in the

---

[17] Regarding the legality of equalization payments, see *infra*, Chapter 4, note 66.

United Nations which they would like to have manned by United States nationals. The mission in New York and the substantive departments in Washington have a say in the decision whether an attempt should be made to have such a post filled by an American national. Thus, the United States has in effect "flagged out" posts of interest.

Even for senior posts, it continues to be the stated American policy to submit multiple candidatures for every post (in practice, this policy is not always followed and not only in the case of very senior candidatures, such as to the post of under-secretary-general) and to leave to the Secretary-General the selection of the best available candidate.

The United Kingdom

The United Kingdom continues to be an overrepresented country (for a desirable range of 81–112, it had, on 30 June 1975, 128 staff members including 1 under-secretary-general, 4 D-2, and 16 D-1).

Publicly, the United Kingdom articulates a strong pro-merit policy. It has been a strong supporter of the career service and of the strictly international character of the Secretariat. In 1975 the representative of the United Kingdom on the Fifth Committee complained that many countries imply that candidates for posts in the Secretariat can normally be regarded as candidates proposed or sponsored by governments and that, if a country is overrepresented, it appears that this is so because it has been greedy and able to manipulate the system towards its advantage.[18] He stressed that the interventions of the United Kingdom with the Office of Personnel have been extremely rare and that the overwhelming majority of United Kingdom nationals have taken the initiative in applying directly to the Secretariat. Although there have been occasional secondments from the civil service of Britain in the past, no United Kingdom officials were serving on secondment with the Secretariat (December, 1975). He took satisfaction from the fact that United Kingdom nationals were selected without outside political pressure being applied.

The British delegate further expressed emphatic belief in the concept of an independent career international civil service supported only to the minimum extent consistent with efficiency by officers on short-term contracts. In his view the widespread use of temporary seconded officers to fill senior posts must make it much harder to recruit top quality young career professional staff. As could be expected, the British delegate opposed the change in the minimum range of posts allocated to each state especially in view of the steadily increasing weight of the membership factor consequent to the admission of new members. He was also strongly

---

[18] A/C.5/SR.1754, at 16.

opposed to any move to make language staff subject to national quotas. Such a move would result in putting the United Kingdom so far over its maximum desirable range that it would have to consider ways of stopping any recruitment whatsoever of the United Kingdom nationals to areas, such as statistics and translations, where the United Kingdom was already strongly represented.

The facts of the situation are that the United Kingdom delegation, which in the past has been one of the very few delegations which refrained completely from exercising pressures on the Office of Personnel, has recently become somewhat more active, perhaps to counter influence by other states that would have jeopardized the chances of British nationals. The United Kingdom delegation has expressed interest in the recruitment of British nationals to some posts (it feels that the United Kingdom should be better represented in the political departments) and it may have also taken an interest in the promotion of British nationals in the Secretariat. In any event, some of the British members of the staff feel that the United Kingdom is not indifferent now to their careers and their chances of promotion. Nevertheless, the United Kingdom continues to be one of the countries which seldom approach the Secretariat with claims on behalf of their nationals.

The People's Republic of China

In posts subject to geographical distribution, the People's Republic of China is still clearly underrepresented (for a desirable range of 83–115, China had, on 30 June 1975, 47 members of the staff, including one under-secretary-general, 2 D–2, and 6 D–1). Given the great need for skilled personnel in China itself, China has not so far regarded recruitment to the United Nations as a matter of priority. Neither has it articulated, as yet, its general policy towards the staffing of the Secretariat and towards the international civil service. It is, therefore, difficult to ascertain the attitudes of China towards United Nations personnel policies. Insofar as conclusions can be drawn from practice, China does not appear to be opposed to the principle of career service or to permanent appointments. Except for a small number of senior staff members who joined the Secretariat on the basis of secondment, Chinese recruits, primarily junior professional officers and linguists, have joined the Secretariat during the last few years on probationary appointments leading to career appointments or on fixed-term appointments.[19] The first priority of the Secretariat was to urgently recruit new language staff from China, given the fact that Chinese, previously a little used official language, has also become a working

[19] See, e.g., A/10184, Annex, Table 9.

language of the Security Council and of the General Assembly. The Permanent Mission of China maintains correct relations with the administration and has refrained from exercising pressures for Chinese nationals. In one case, however, it expressed strong objections to an attempt to move a Chinese official from one post to another. The attempt was dropped.

When the People's Republic of China began, in 1972, to participate in the work of the United Nations, it faced a potential dilemma about the members of the staff from China. It appears that the Government of China has adopted a pragmatic, flexible, and humane attitude towards them. Both the Secretariat and China regard all Chinese members of the staff as simply nationals of China. The Chinese members of the staff have been permitted, if they so wished, to take up passports of the People's Republic of China and have been allowed to travel to China on home leave.

France

France (desirable range: 88–124. Number of staff on 30 June 1975: 132 including 1 under-secretary-general, 6 D–2, and 17 D–1) has in the past taken the lead in introducing the principle of linguistic balance in the staff of the Secretariat and in acting against any discrimination against French-speaking staff members. It advocates the principle of merit and in 1975 it supported the New Zealand amendment to the draft resolution pertaining to the representation of the developing countries in senior positions.[20] In practice, France does not appear to interfere with French nationals in the Secretariat and fully respects the international character of their functions. Where France shows considerable activity, however, including pressure on the Secretariat at times, is in manning key Secretariat positions. The Government of France carefully follows developments in the Secretariat and tries to obtain posts for French nationals. In Paris it maintains a special office in charge of recruitment of French nationals to international organizations. The post of under-secretary-general in charge of the Department of Economic and Social Affairs is now regarded as a French national preserve. For key posts on a somewhat lower level, especially in the political field, France has also made great efforts to maintain them in the hands of French nationals, not always with success.

Japan

Like other underrepresented countries Japan strongly objected, in 1975, to any shift in emphasis, suggested by the Gardner Group and supported

---

[20] A/C.5/SR.1756, at 17.

by the Secretary-General, from a national to a regional balance in the composition of the Secretariat. Japan (desirable range: 107–150. Number of staff on 30 June 1975: 65 including 1 assistant-secretary-general, 1 D–2, and 1 D–1) stressed that there are geographical regions in the world that are simply not homogeneous enough culturally, linguistically, and socially to make possible the equitable application of a regional balance. This, in its view, was true of the region of Asia and the Pacific.

Japan expressed support for the development of a competent, efficient, well-motivated, and impartial international civil service, which is truly representative of diverse nations and cultures. Talent and calibre were by no means the monopoly of any single state or group of states. As a major contributor, Japan expressed strong objections to reducing the factor of contributions in the formula for calculating the desirable range for each state. Japan could contribute to the United Nations not only financially, but also in terms of skilled human resources. Alluding to the language difficulties that may have been a barrier to greater recruitment from Japan, its delegate drew attention to the example of the World Bank, which selects people on the basis of their professional qualifications and gives them intensive language training after recruitment.

The Government of Japan shows considerable interest in the recruitment to the Secretariat of Japanese nationals. It has cooperated in arranging competitive examinations in Japan in 1975 and it maintains active contacts with the Secretariat in order to encourage recruitment of Japanese nationals.[21]

The Federal Republic of Germany

Another major contributor and underrepresented country, the Federal Republic of Germany (desirable range: 105–148. Number of staff on 30 June 1975: 47 including 1 assistant-secretary-general, 3 D–2, and 3 D–1), cautioned against attaching too much importance to the distribution of posts according to regions, as this tended to "dilute" the principle of equitable distribution. Regional representation should be viewed not as the standard rule but rather with mistrust, as an instrument to maintain privileged positions.

The German delegate to the Fifth Committee complained that, despite the joint efforts of the administration and of Germany, an equitable representation of German nationals in the Secretariat is still a long way off. In his view, obstacles were caused by both recruitment procedures, which were too slow, and by the fact that the various departments were often

[21] A/C.5/SR.1745, at 21.

guided in their decisions by considerations other than those set forth in Article 101(3).[22]

Germany appears to feel that it is underrepresented not only in the staff as a whole, but also in senior posts. Of course, late entry into the staffing race does take a long time to make up.

Italy

Similarly, Italy (desirable range: 56–76. Number of staff on 30 June 1975: 59 including 1 under-secretary-general, 1 D–2, and 2 D–1) stressed, in 1975, that the problem of the "underrepresented countries, such as Italy" could not be solved on the basis of the recommendations of the Gardner Group.[23]

Romania

Similar reservations were expressed by Romania. Although other Warsaw Pact countries do not normally express reservations about the regional emphasis in the distribution of posts, this does not hold true for Romania in light of her national policy of distinct identity and independence. Thus, the delegate of Romania complained in 1975 that it was one of the countries that had no nationals at the D–1 and higher levels in the Secretariat and insisted that a spirit of equity and equality should be reflected in the composition of the staff. He too expressed reservations as to the acceptability of the recommendations of the Gardner Group because they would not meet the concerns of states that wish to be better represented in the United Nations.[24] There is reason to believe that at times when the Secretariat allowed higher representation of well-qualified Romanians or Poles, on the ground that their region was underrepresented, the Soviet Union had expressed displeasure.

Scandinavian Countries

The Scandinavian countries, which in the past have not exerted much pressure on the Secretariat, have become somewhat more active not only

[22] A/C.5/SR.1750, at 13. Germany too has a special office for recruitment of German nationals to international organizations.

[23] A/C.5/SR.1750, at 17.

[24] A/C.5/SR.1751, at 6–7. The delegate from the German Democratic Republic, an orthodox supporter of the Soviet Union, complained of the underrepresentation of his country as part of the underrepresentation of the regional group of socialist states of Eastern Europe. A/C.5/SR.1751, at 5.

about recruitment, but also about the promotion of their nationals. Sweden and Finland have been relatively more active than the other Scandinavian countries. In general, Scandinavian countries stress the principle of merit.[25] Finland's neutrality in international affairs and her acceptability to the Soviet Union have proved to be extremely helpful factors in the appointment of Finns to a disproportionate number of senior positions.

Developing States

The developing countries realize that to compensate for their relative weakness as individual countries, in comparison to the superpowers and the developed countries, they must act in unity, present their positions jointly, and push through the General Assembly favourable recruitment guidelines by taking advantage of their voting majority. Despite the lack of homogeneity of the group, the developing countries are motivated by certain relatively well-defined objectives, including that of assuring the responsiveness of the United Nations administration to their social and developmental goals. Moreover, many developing countries—for instance the Arab or the African States—also have their own national and regional reasons (the former, the dispute with Israel, the latter, Southern African issues) for pressing for greater representation of their nationals in the Secretariat. It is erroneous, therefore, to attribute pressure for posts only to patronage.

The developing countries have felt that, unless they are fairly represented in the Secretariat as a whole, and on the policymaking level in particular, their interests as developing countries will not be adequately protected. This is of particular importance, of course, at a time when the bulk of the activities of the Secretariat is related to the advancement of developing countries. Thus, the representative of Kenya stated in 1975 that in requesting that the developing countries be given equal opportunity to participate in policymaking, they were not asking favours, but rather were seeking to protect their rights.[26]

It was in large measure because of the demands of the developing countries that the post of assistant-secretary-general in charge of the Office of Personnel Services was entrusted to a national of a developing country (Tunisia). There is reason to believe that it was decided, in advance, to "give" the post to Tunisia, a North-African Francophone country, and that several candidates from that country were considered for appointment!

---

[25] See, e.g., statement by Sweden (desirable range: 24–28. Number of staff on 30 June 1975: 31) in 1975. A/C.5/SR.1754, at 21.

[26] A/C.5/SR.1756, at 15.

In the preceding chapter we have already alluded—primarily in connection with the resolutions adopted during the thirtieth session of the General Assembly—to the powerful role of the group of developing countries. On several occasions, this group has pushed through guidelines that placed the emphasis on preference to be given to nationals of the developing countries. Delegates of many developing countries regard the principle of merit as an excuse put forward by the delegates of the developed countries in order to obstruct or to delay the satisfaction of legitimate claims of the developing countries to greater participation in the Secretariat as a whole and in senior positions in particular. The delegates of the developing countries have also been a force in favour of changing the existing formula for the calculation of the desirable ranges by increasing the weight of the membership factor. There is no doubt that sooner or later the developing countries will force a change of the formula, which will give increased weight to the principle of equality of states at the expense of the factor of contributions.

The representatives of the developing countries have also been active in pressing upon the Secretariat their claims for better and more senior representation of their nationals. Although a great many developing countries are indeed underrepresented and have just claims to more equitable representation of their nationals in the Secretariat, it should be pointed out that this is far from true for all of the developing countries. Indeed, some developing countries are grossly overrepresented. Some such countries, for example India or Egypt, however, may be assumed to be among the principal beneficiaries of the regional "population reserve." Not surprisingly, the overrepresented developing countries are relatively silent during the annual General Assembly debates on the composition of the Secretariat, and—when they do speak up—they emphasize the principle of merit, rather than that of geographical distribution.

A case in point is India, a heavily overrepresented developing country (desirable range: 22–26. Number of staff on 30 June 1975: 52 including 1 under-secretary-general, 3 D–2, and 15 D–1). As could be expected, India complained that the population factor played too little a part in the formula for fixing the desirable ranges.[27] Its delegate warned that in a multinational Secretariat political pressures might override the normal requirements for streamlining the administrative machinery, but that, in the promotion of staff, greater weight should be given to efficiency and experience than to political considerations. He warned of the demoralization of the Secretariat as a result of political considerations being given undue weight in appointments and promotions.[28]

---

[27] A/C.5/SR.1756, at 14.

[28] A/C.5/SR.1710, at 7.

The developing countries, as a group, have also been active in press-ing for special preference to be given to their nationals in "special inter-est" bodies, such as the United Nations Industrial Development Organi-zation (UNIDO), which were created to assist in the advancement of the developing countries. They have also provided a strong political base of support to their allies in the secretariats of such bodies. Although under General Assembly Resolution 2152 (XXI) (1966), UNIDO's Secretariat was to be appointed in accordance with Article 101 of the Charter, the group of the developing countries in the Industrial Development Board suggested, in 1974, the application of the following considerations in the filling of posts in the Secretariat of UNIDO: the UNIDO Secretariat should be regarded as separate from the Secretariat of the Unted Nations; since UNIDO was created essentially for the benefit of the developing countries, those countries should have a larger representation, particular-ly in the higher and policymaking levels of its Secretariat; their represen-tation at such levels should be on the same basis as their representation in the Industrial Development Board. As regards promotion, the developing countries complained that, of the seven D–2 posts, only one was filled by a national of a developing country; this situation should be quickly reme-died by the promotion to three posts of D–2 of nationals of the developing countries.[29] It is not easy to reconcile such demands either with the prin-ciples incorporated in Article 101(3) of the Charter or with the unity of the Secretariat, under the authority of the Secretary-General. For the Secre-tariat as a whole, pressure has recently increased from developing states (including overrepresented ones) to give preference to their nationals not only in recruitment but also in promotion to senior posts. In Chapter 4, pages 52–53, we shall allude to the implications of such pressures for the Charter.

Conclusions

Stating the obvious, the attitudes of the various countries towards the principles that should govern recruitment to the Secretariat and, in broader terms, the personnel policies of the Secretariat, when properly analyzed, are directly related to the state of their representation in the Secretariat. Although underrepresented countries—the have-nots—stress the importance of the principle of equitable geographical distribution, overrepresented countries stress the importance of the principle of merit. Overrepresented countries sometimes invoke the principle of regional

[29] UNIDO, REPORT OF THE INDUSTRIAL DEVELOPMENT BOARD ON THE WORK OF ITS EIGHTH SESSION, 29 GAOR, Supp. No. 16 (A/9616), at 40–41.

representation, but underrepresented countries are wary of any shift to a regional basis, which they regard as endangering their own chance to fill their own national desirable ranges.

The attitudes towards changing the formula for calculating the desirable ranges are also dictated by the situation of each individual state. The small contributors are in favour of giving greater weight to the factor of membership; the larger contributors insist on maintaining the overriding role of the factor of contributions. Populous countries stress the weight of the population factor. Most of the developed countries support the principle of merit, especially when they are overrepresented in the Secretariat. The developed countries that are underrepresented place greater emphasis on the principle of geographical distribution and oppose a shift towards a regional formula.

There is a great deal of hypocrisy in the public articulation of national attitudes. The stress on a particular principle enunciated in Article 101(3) of the Charter results not so much from a commitment to a particular interpretation of the Charter as from the need to justify national policy with regard to the staffing of the Secretariat and to obtain the most in terms of number of posts, and influential posts in particular. Practically all states regard the presence of their nationals in the Secretariat as serving their national interests and are active in pressing upon the Secretariat the claims of their nationals for appointment and promotion. But, although some states still continue to play the game according to the rules, others do not hesitate to act in violation of Articles 100 and 101 of the Charter.

4 Selected Legal Questions

The Principle of Merit and the Principle of Geographical Distribution

Recruitment

Following the admission to the United Nations of 16 new states in 1955, the Legal Counsel gave an opinion (1956) on the meaning of the principle of geographical distribution and on its application. Basing himself on the statement by the Secretary-General in 1948 that geographical distribution meant that the Secretariat should be enriched by the experience, culture, and philosophy of each nation,[1] the Legal Counsel expressed the view that geographical distribution, although requiring consideration of legal nationality, also called for an examination of the candidate's culture and of how far he represents his national culture and traditions and could contribute an understanding of them to the Secretariat.

The Legal Counsel pointed out that there was an obligation to consider the principle of geographical distribution in recruitment to posts subject to geographical distribution, but under both the Charter and Staff Regulation 4.2 the principle of geographical distribution is obviously subordinate to the necessity for securing the highest standards of efficiency, competence, and integrity.

As pointed out by the Legal Counsel, there is no question at all that the principle of merit should be paramount. But the Legal Counsel did not suggest what this in fact means. In simple terms the meaning of this principle is that, in the case of two candidates for recruitment who are different in quality, the superior candidate should be selected even though he might be a national of an overrepresented country and the other candidate might be a national of an underrepresented or unrepresented country. A

Parts of this chapter appeared in the October 1976 issue of the *American Journal of International Law*.

In the preparation of this chapter the writer has been greatly assisted by a number of unpublished opinions of the Legal Counsel of the United Nations and his staff. In accordance with the understanding reached with the Legal Counsel, names of countries and individuals involved in the various opinions may not be identified. These opinions have been provided to the writer but he himself has not examined the files, and thus is not familiar with the exact factual context in which each opinion was given.

[1] A/652, 3 GAOR, Plenary Meetings, at 157. See also General Assembly Resolution 153(II)/(1947). A/519, at 62.

strict implementation of this legal interpretation of the paramountcy of the principle of merit is of course extremely difficult to achieve in practice. Indeed this is an area where the legal principle comes into conflict with the political, social, and administrative realities of a multinational political organization. Experience indicates that the paramountcy of merit is not consistently upheld. This problem should not, however, be approached in simplistic terms. The United Nations Secretariat has not developed, as yet, a complete and sophisticated system of comparing various national university degrees, systems of education, types of practical and professional experience acquired in different states, and so on. An administration, constantly pressured to achieve a speedy improvement of the equitable geographical distribution, is thus given considerable latitude in deciding who is the "superior" candidate and in making the choice whom to recruit. Even in national administrations, such as that of the United States, the principle of merit sometimes has to give way to the need to seek adequate representation of members of minority groups, women, or even of regions. In view of the growing sophistication and complexity of many professions in great demand in the Secretariat, especially in the economic and technical fields, a clear and consistent application of the principle of merit would bring about a situation in which so many posts would be staffed by nationals of developed nations and by nationals of a small number of already heavily overrepresented developing nations (for example, India, Pakistan, Egypt) that the composition of the staff would be politically unacceptable to the great majority of Member States. As a result of claims by some states to certain senior posts as their own "national preserve," the emphasis on the fulfillment of national desirable ranges, and difficulties in developing competitive examinations, the choice of the "superior" candidate is often made not on a global basis as it should be, but from among candidates from one national group or from a few national groups.

Other circumstances, too, may prevent merit from being the sole criterion for appointment (and in certain circumstances for promotion). One is the fact that any part of the Secretariat performing tasks that may have political importance will not enjoy the confidence of all members if one nationality is disproportionately represented either in the staff of that unit as a whole, or in its upper echelons. Another is that in delicate political missions, including peacekeeping missions, the Secretary-General cannot use nationals of the states in conflict or of other states regarded as closely allied with them, since their mere nationality would be likely to destroy their effectiveness. To the extent that a Secretariat unit is involved in such delicate political tasks or expects to be called upon to supply staff to perform them, the nationality of a candidate may be a strong negative factor, regardless of his merit. This problem is also dealt with in Chapter 16.

There thus exist very considerable objective difficulties in the application of Article 101(3) of the Charter in accordance with its letter and spirit. Superimposed on these and other genuine difficulties are political preferences and phenomena of bias and nepotism.[2] Appointment procedures in the Secretariat also suffer from an inadequacy of safeguards, and from the absence of a system of counterbalances and due process. Such safeguards are particularly needed, for it is in recruitment (and promotion) that pressures by states, or groups of states, are strongly exerted on the Secretary-General and his senior aides. Only too often in the past the Secretary-General and his senior aides have given in to such pressures. Yet it is here that the Secretary-General should show great courage and leadership, setting an example to the Secretariat as a whole.

The Legal Counsel, in his above-mentioned opinion, pointed out that both the principle of merit and the principle of geographical distribution were to be administered entirely and exclusively by the Secretary-General, without any interference or pressure from governments of Member States.

The Legal Counsel was asked whether appointments of staff members could be terminated to create vacancies to be used for improving the geographical distribution through recruitment. None of the grounds enabling termination of permanent appointments under Staff Regulation 9.1(a) allowed termination for the improvement of geographical distribution. Nor was termination so motivated permissible under Staff Regulation 9.1(b) for staff members holding fixed-term appointments. The Secretary-General could, however, refrain from renewing fixed-term appointments (which, under Staff Rule 104.12[b] do not carry any expectancy of renewal or of conversion to any other type of appointment).[3]

In the view of the Legal Counsel, since the principle of geographical distribution is laid down in the Charter and in the staff regulations, a non-

---

[2] See in general, Finger & Mugno, *The Politics of Staffing the United Nations Secretariat*, 29 ORBIS 117 (1975).

[3] The Secretary-General has full discretion whether to extend fixed-term contracts and, in the absence of countervailing circumstances, nonrenewal does not give rise to any rights for the staff member. The United Nations Administrative Tribunal has, however, developed the legal expectancy principle, according to which the staff member has certain legal rights if in the circumstances of the case he could reasonably expect to remain in the service of the United Nations. Where legal expectancy of continued employment has been created, the claims of the staff member can be litigated by the Administrative Tribunal and, in some cases, compensation has been awarded. See *Bhattacharyya v. The Secretary-General of the United Nations*, Judgment No. 142; *Surina v. The Secretary-General of the United Nations*, Judgment No. 178; *Lawrence v. The Secretary-General of the United Nations*, Judgment No. 185. Compare *Fracyon v. The Secretary-General of the United Nations*, Judgment No. 199. No expectancy was found in the case of *Nath v. The Secretary-General of the United Nations*, Judgment No. 181. Regarding the election, by the General Assembly, of members of the Administrative Tribunal of the United Nations, see Article 3 of the tribunal's statute. Regarding the tribunal's jurisdiction, see Article 2 of the statute. AT/11/Rev. 4.

renewal for the purpose of improving its application should not be vitiated by the Administrative Tribunal on grounds of improper motive. The Legal Counsel concluded that, although temporary appointments of staff members could be terminated on the ground that "such action would be in the interest of the United Nations" (under Staff Regulation 9.1[c]), the Secretary-General's policy was not to do so for reasons of improving geographical distribution of the staff.

In the event of nonrenewal of a fixed-term appointment as to which there is a legal expectancy of renewal, one may well wonder whether the need to improve geographical distribution in the Secretariat—as distinguished from reasons pertaining to the individual staff member—would be considered by the Administrative Tribunal as proper motivation.

The Secretary-General has not so far justified nonrenewal of fixed-term contracts on this ground. In practice, of course, the improvement of geographical distribution must have been an important consideration in deciding whether to renew a fixed-term appointment. Where no legal expectancy of renewal has been created, this consideration appears to be proper and legitimate.[4]

Although the Legal Counsel stressed the "cultural" interpretation of the principle of geographical distribution, such an interpretation is not supported by the *travaux préparatoires*. Although the concept of requiring a candidate for recruitment to be representative of his country's culture and traditions is not unreasonable, it may be used by states to discredit nationals who are objectionable on political or other grounds. In practice cases have occurred of states claiming that a particular individual was not truly representative of his country. Similar arguments have been adduced by members of the staff who opposed the recruitment of particular individuals. Although a certain degree of connection and genuine link with the national state is a reasonable consideration, room is created for arbitrariness and bias once there is a departure from the relatively firm criterion of nationality.

To what extent is an Egyptian Copt representative of Egyptian culture or an expatriate Czech representative of the post-Dubcek Czechoslovakia? What is to be made of a Chilean who was an Allende supporter, or a Jew from an Arab country?

On occasion states have actually demanded that the Secretary-General terminate appointments of some of their nationals on such grounds as unfamiliarity with the new social, cultural, and political conditions prevailing in the country, or even with the new terminology of postrevolu-

---

[4] In the 1975 case of *El-Naggar v. The Secretary-General of the United Nations*, the applicant argued, *inter alia*, that the reason for not converting his fixed-term contract into a career one was related to difficulties in the geographical distribution of the staff (Egypt, of which El-Naggar was a national, is overrepresented). AT/PV.124, at 38; AT/DEC/205, at 13.

tionary regimes.[5] Moreover, there is a considerable artificiality in the "cultural" interpretation of the principle of geographical distribution. How does a statistician, a registry supervisor, or a computer programmer demonstrate in the discharge of his duties that he is truly representative of his national culture?

Promotion and Placement

If the geographical distribution is relevant to recruitment, is it also relevant to promotion of members of the staff? In one opinion (1956), the Legal Counsel expressed the view that there was no legal obligation to consider geographical distribution in transfers or promotions. This is certainly so, but the question arises whether geographical distribution *may* at all be considered in this context. In another opinion (1957), the Legal Counsel stressed that, under the first sentence of Article 101(3) of the Charter, the paramount principle of merit was relevant to the employment of the staff and to the determination of the conditions of service while under the second sentence the principle of geographical distribution was relevant to recruitment only. This difference, which was regarded by the Legal Counsel as fundamental, was clearly recognized by the General Assembly in Staff Regulation 4.2. Moreover, if the powers of the Secretary-General to evaluate the factors relevant to promotion were to be limited by the principle of geographical distribution, this would handicap him in the discharge of his responsibilities, as the chief administrative officer under Article 97 of the Charter.

Legally promotion must be based on merit and merit alone, including, of course, the observance of minimum periods of service in the grade, according to Staff Rule 104.14(f) (iii) (C). Could it not be argued that the principle of geographical distribution may be taken into account by the Secretary-General under Article 97 in relation to the organization of the Secretariat and therefore in relation to placement and transfers? For although the principle of geographical distribution is relevant to the recruitment of staff to the Secretariat as a whole, rather than to each individual department, it is obvious that the Secretary-General would have a legitimate interest in avoiding a situation in which particular units of the Secretariat would be staffed or dominated by persons of one particular nationality, or even one particular region or group of countries.[6] Placement and

[5] As already indicated in Chapter 3, it must be said to the credit of the People's Republic of China that it has not tried to oust from the Secretariat members of the staff appointed during Taiwan's representation in the United Nations. Rather, they have regarded all of them as "Chinese" and enabled those who wanted to do so to visit mainland China, take up passports of the People's Republic of China, and so on.

[6] Fifth Committee Report A/9980, para. 45(b) approved by the General Assembly at the

transfers are also subject to the limitation, already mentioned in the context of recruitment, that in delicate political missions the Secretary-General cannot use nationals of the states in conflict or nationals of their close allies.

Recently, promotion prospects for certain "pariah" nationalities have become extremely poor, especially to senior posts, regardless of merit.

Given the persistent feeling of the staff that geographical distribution has tended to become a coequal and sometimes even a factor prevailing over merit, Secretary-General U Thant felt compelled to refer in a speech to the staff to the sharpened sensitivity about the weight of merit in relation to the principle of geographical distribution, stating that, "in consonance with the letter and spirit of the Charter," it was his "intention to ensure that the principle of geographical distribution remains relevant only to staff recruitment. It cannot and will not play any role in the processes of promotion or placement."[7] U Thant's protestations obviously had little relevance to posts regarded as national preserves. Indeed, it can be said in general that constant pressures from individual states, and sometimes groups of states, have made it extremely difficult for the Secretary-General to adhere to the principle that promotion is based on merit and that nationality is an extraneous factor. In practice, representatives of interested states approach key members of the staff to urge the promotion of their nationals. Resolutions of the General Assembly insisting on a regional distribution of senior posts, providing for the election or the confirmation by the General Assembly of certain senior officials, or giving preference to nationals of developing countries in the filling of senior posts, although adopted in the context of recruitment, strengthened the pressures for a geographical distribution of senior posts in such a way as to adversely affect opportunities for promotion based on merit.

Sometimes groups of states make specific demands for the promotion of nationals of certain countries. Thus, a representative of the Group of Seventy-Seven, speaking in 1974 on behalf of the group (of developing countries), complained of the poor representation of developing countries in the higher and policymaking levels of the Secretariat of the United Nations Industrial Development Organization and called for a quick remedy "by the promotion to three posts of D-2 of nationals of the developing countries."[8] Although one may well sympathize with such claims, they

2324th plenary meeting. 29 GAOR, Supp. No. 31 (A/9631), at 139. One of the departments in which a cultural balance is necessary (between the common law and the civil law) is the Office of Legal Affairs.

[7] Text of Address by Secretary-General to Headquarters Staff of United Nations on Staff Day. Press Release SG/SM/1008 at 4, Sept. 20, 1968. See also El-Naggar v. The Secretary-General of the United Nations, AT/DEC/205, at 13.

[8] UNIDO, REPORT OF THE INDUSTRIAL DEVELOPMENT BOARD ON THE WORK OF ITS EIGHTH SESSION, 29 GAOR, Supp. No. 16 (A/9616), at 40–41.

adversely affect the legal principle of promotion by merit and the authority of the Secretary-General under the Charter.

Stateless Persons and Nationals of Non-Member States

Do stateless persons qualify for employment in the Secretariat? In an opinion given in 1961, the Legal Counsel pointed out that neither the Charter nor the resolutions of the General Assembly contained any legal prohibitions to the employment of stateless persons in the Secretariat. Staff Regulation 4.3 provides that selection of staff members shall be made, in accordance with the Charter, "without distinction as to race, sex, or religion," but no reference is made to distinction on grounds of nationality.

Various resolutions of the General Assembly on the geographical distribution of the staff provide that clear preference is to be given to the recruitment of nationals of Member States. Indeed, the system of desirable ranges of posts for each Member State leaves no allocation, or quota of posts, for persons who are not nationals of Member States. Therefore the recruitment of stateless persons should, according to the Legal Counsel, be exceptional. There is, of course, a broader latitude in the recruitment of stateless persons to posts that are not subject to geographical distribution, such as posts belonging to the general service category or posts requiring special language qualifications.

In 1954 the Secretary-General advised the Department of State that this subject should be of diminishing concern since, pursuant to the "requirements under the Charter with respect to geographic distribution of staff, and in accordance with the recognized interest of having nationals of Member States in the Secretariat," the recruitment policy was not in favour of hiring stateless persons.[9]

One should, however, distinguish between the employment in the Secretariat of stateless persons and the employment of nationals of non-Member States.[10] In practice, the Secretariat has recognized the special position of those states which, although not members of the United Nations, were members of such bodies as the United Nations Children's Fund, the Office of the United Nations High Commissioner for Refugees, UNCTAD, UNDP, or the regional economic commissions. According to internal instructions of the Secretariat, a national of a non-Member State who meets the required qualifications may be appointed as a staff member if

[9] 8 WHITEMAN, DIGEST OF INTERNATIONAL LAW 336(1967). On 30 June 1975, the Secretariat employed 28 stateless persons.

[10] See General Assembly Resolution 30(I).

the post for which he is proposed is directly related to the work of the subsidiary organ of which the state is a member or if his qualifications are of such a nature as to warrant his appointment. It was subsequently decided that the assessed contributions by a non-Member State to the relevant subsidiary organ would be taken as a basis for the determination of the number of posts to be filled by its nationals. No specific numbers have been set for non-Member States participating in the work of regional economic commissions.

Staff Members with Dual Nationality

The Legal Counsel advised (1952) that for purposes of recruitment persons having the nationality of two states can only be regarded as having one nationality, which should be determined by the Secretary-General rather than by the staff member concerned. This principle found a later expression in Staff Rule 104.8 according to which in the application of staff regulations and rules, a staff member's nationality shall be that of the state with which he is "in the opinion of the Secretary-General, most closely associated."

The nationality established at the time of recruitment[11] is, of course, also important for certain administrative purposes, and especially for the enjoyment of privileges accorded the internationally recruited staff members under Staff Rule 104.7, such as home leave, education grant, payment of travel expenses upon initial appointment and separation, and repatriation grant.

Permanent Residence Status in the United States

Following the adoption of the United States Immigration and Nationality Act of 1952, and the report of the Secretary-General[12] discussing the implications of this act for United Nations staff members with permanent residence status, the Fifth Committee considered the implications of this status for the staff of the United Nations. Support was expressed for the view that a decision by a staff member to remain in permanent residence status did not in any way represent a United Nations interest and was even undesirable in that it might weaken existing ties with the country of nationality.[13] Accordingly, international officials should be true represen-

---

[11] According to Staff Rule 104.4(c) a staff member who intends to change his nationality or permanent residence status must notify the Secretary-General of that intention before the change becomes final.

[12] A/2533, 8 GAOR, Annexes, Agenda Item 51, at 13.

[13] A/2581, 8 GAOR, Annexes, Agenda Item 51, at 25.

tatives of the culture and personality of the country of which they were nationals, and that those who elected to break their ties with that country could no longer claim to fulfill the conditions governing employment in the United Nations.[14] The Fifth Committee, having been informed that the Secretary-General would in the future refuse to recruit persons in permanent residence status for posts subject to international recruitment,[15] voted to approve a recommendation of the General Assembly's Advisory Committee on Administrative and Budgetary Questions that persons in permanent residence status (in the United States) should in the future be ineligible for appointment as internationally recruited staff members unless they were prepared to waive their residence status and change to a G–4 (or equivalent) visa status.

Some years later the question arose whether a staff member belonging to the general service category (which is not subject to geographical distribution) and who had acquired a permanent residence status in the United States had to waive that status as a condition for the implementation of a decision to promote him from the general service to the professional category (which is subject to geographical distribution). In an opinion given in 1971, the Legal Counsel answered this question in the negative. He pointed out that the commitment given by the Secretary-General to the Fifth Committee related only to the recruitment of persons for posts subject to international recruitment, and not to recruitment or promotion within the general service category. Moreover, in light of Article 101(3) the general understanding had been that questions of nationality were not relevant to promotions within the career service. Promotion should not be dependent on nationality, as it was extraneous to merit.

In 1975, the Secretary-General decided to grant staff members in the general service category with permanent resident status in the United States and who were about to be promoted to the professional category the option of either relinquishing their permanent resident status and accepting a G–4 visa, or maintaining their permanent resident status while losing certain entitlements.

Diplomats and Related Persons

On a number of occasions, members of national delegations to the General Assembly, or of permanent missions to the United Nations, have been recruited to the United Nations Secretariat. Upon joining the Secretariat, however, such persons lose all claim to diplomatic status and become subject to the legal regime applicable to the employees of the United Na-

---

[14] A/2615, 8 GAOR, Annexes, Agenda Item 51, at 45.
[15] *Ibid.*

tions Secretariat, that is, immunity from suit and legal process only in relation to acts performed in their official capacity.[16] Claims that members of the United Nations staff of Soviet nationality who had diplomatic titles while serving in the Soviet Ministry for Foreign Affairs or as members of the Soviet delegation to the General Assembly also benefitted from diplomatic immunities upon their joining the staff of the Secretariat have been denied. Thus, in *United States v. Egorov and Egorova*, the court held that "*[e]mployees* of the United Nations are separate and distinct from persons designated by foreign governments to serve *as their foreign representatives* in or to the United Nations."[17] This situation results both from the clear provisions of the legal regime applicable to the employees of the Secretariat (it should be noted that the Secretary-General and a number of his senior aides have additional privileges and immunities), and from Article 100 of the Charter. This article was invoked by the United States in *United States v. Coplon*, wherein the government stated "that by virtue of Article 100 of the United Nations Charter, one may not simultaneously be an employee of the United Nations and a member of one of the national delegations and defendant's acceptance of employment in the UN Secretariat terminated any membership he may have had in the Soviet Delegation."[18]

Proper Procedures: Some Problem Areas

In a highly politicized multinational organization, processes of recruitment and promotion can operate according to the principles and purposes of the Charter only if they are based on fair and impartial procedures and safeguards. Only if such procedures exist and are faithfully implemented can the principle of merit survive and coexist with the principle of geographical distribution. In the absence of such procedures, merit and morale suffer, while political-national considerations tend to become a runaway horse.

Given the natural suspicions that prevail between nationals of various countries, representing many different political, social, religious, and ra-

---

[16] Regarding the legal regime governing the privileges and immunities of members of the staff of the Secretariat, see the International Organizations Immunities Act, 22 U.S.C. §288 *et seq.*; the Convention on the Privileges and Immunities of the United Nations, done at New York Feb. 1, 1946, 2 UST 1418, TIAS 6900, 1 UNTS 16; the Agreement between the United Nations and the United States of America regarding the Headquarters of the United Nations signed at Lake Success, June 26, 1947, 61 Stat. 3416, TIAS 1676, 12 Bevans 956, 11 UNTS 11. See also *United States v. Melekh*, 190 F. Supp. 67 (S.D.N.Y., 1960).

[17] 222 F. Supp. 106, at 108 (E.D.N.Y., 1963).

[18] 84 F. Supp. 472, 476. (S.D.N.Y., 1949); see also *U.S. v. Coplon,* 88 F. Supp. 915 (S.D.N.Y., 1950).

cial backgrounds, and the fact that officials of the Secretariat often reflect, or are suspected of reflecting, the political attitudes of their countries, justice in personnel administration must not only be done, but must be seen to be done.

In recruitment, it is obvious that the principles established by Article 101(3) of the Charter, read together with the principle of sovereign equality of states expressed in Article 2(1) of the Charter, and with the prohibition imposed—under Article 8—upon placing of "restrictions on the eligibility of men and women to participate in any capacity and under conditions of equality" in the principal and subsidiary organs of the United Nations, have important consequences for the administration of the Secretariat. If these principles are to have any practical significance whatsoever, they must be translated into administrative arrangements that enable all candidates for recruitment to be considered for appointment under fair and equal conditions. Under Staff Regulation 4.3, "[s]o far as practicable, selection shall be made on a competitive basis." This clearly necessitates adequate knowledge of forthcoming vacancies in the Secretariat. Such knowledge can only become generally available if all vacancies and job descriptions are properly announced and circulated as they are in civil administrations of Member States. Yet, under the present arrangements—to which we shall return in greater detail in Chapter 10—the administration has a wide measure of discretion as to whether to circulate vacancy announcements at all. Thus, the administration is able to consider for recruitment handpicked candidates and to effectively exclude multiple candidatures. Under such procedures it is impossible to provide qualified candidates, especially but not exclusively those from adequately represented or overrepresented countries, with the minimum standards of fair consideration required by the Charter. The reluctance of the administration to commit itself to an all-embracing principle of circulation of vacancy announcements may easily be appreciated. The writer understands that, despite the progress that has already been made, about 30 percent of presentations of appointments (to posts subject to geographical distribution) made to the appointment and promotion bodies of candidatures to P–1—D–1 levels in the course of 1975 was not based on vacancy announcements. For vacancies to be filled by promotions, no vacancy announcements are circulated at all.

If imperative administrative or political needs (the United Nations is, after all, a political organization) require that vacancies of some posts (for example, of particular seniority) not be announced, the exceptions should be clearly defined and openly promulgated, preferably in the form of a staff rule. It should, however, be observed that, given the absence of a job classification system in the Secretariat, vacancy announcements can be tailored to fit a particular candidate. Vacancy announcements by themselves are therefore not a guarantee of a fair consideration and selection of candidates.

Obviously, the nonannouncement of forthcoming vacancies affects not only the fair opportunity of recruitment but also the promotion opportunities of the existing staff. For unless forthcoming vacancies in the Secretariat are brought to the notice of members of the staff, they cannot actively present their candidatures, especially with regard to *ad hoc* promotions, which will be discussed in Chapter 10. Staff Regulation 4.4, according to which, subject to Article 101(3) and without prejudice to the recruitment of fresh talent at all levels, "the fullest regard shall be had, in filling vacancies, to the requisite qualifications and experience of persons already in the service of the United Nations," may thus be rendered academic.

A second problem is publicizing vacancies that the administration has decided to announce. The administration has considerable discretion as to the distribution of the vacancy announcements. Restricted methods of distribution taken together with the administrative practices of filtering out candidates from overrepresented countries make it very difficult for qualified candidates from an overrepresented country and sometimes even from an adequately represented country to be considered for recruitment on a basis of equality with candidates from underrepresented countries. There may, of course, be entirely legitimate reasons for giving preference to persons from an underrepresented country, but all candidates must be given equal opportunity for the presentation and the consideration of their candidatures.

There does not seem to exist at present a suitable grievance procedure for the consideration of complaints related to the highly political questions of appointment and promotion. Thus, the Administrative Tribunal has recently confirmed the self-evident proposition that promotions are within the administrative discretion of the Secretary-General.[19] Indeed, no recourse whatsoever is available to people who have not been recruited and who are therefore not in a contractual relationship with the Organization. Even if this situation remains unchanged with regard to recruitment, an independent grievance procedure pertaining to promotion of staff members should be established, possibly by the appointment of a special ombudsperson for personnel, following the example set in 1973 by the United Nations Development Programme (UNDP),[20] who might have the authority to give publicity to his findings and recommendations pertaining to discriminatory practices. The present grievance procedures,

[19] *Nath v. The Secretary-General of the United Nations*, Judgment No. 181. Regarding arrangements for review of staff promotion, see ST/ADM/SER.A/1934(1976).

[20] See UNDP/ADM/PER/26, UNDP/ADM/PER/60, UNDP/ADM/PER/63.

discussed in Chapter 9, are weak in that "recourse" is to the same body that denied promotion in the first place, and is limited to new information.

Attention should be given to ways of insulating appointment and promotion processes from political pressures.

For recruitment, it might be desirable to have a group drawn from a panel of outside experts to advise the recruitment division and the appointment and promotion bodies on the professional qualifications of what one might hope would be multiple candidates. For promotion, the appointment and promotion bodies might establish subcommittees comprising persons of the same occupation or profession as that of the candidate.

All these suggestions are not without difficulties. Appointment and promotion bodies have legally only advisory functions. Although in most cases they can block an appointment (unless the Secretary-General decides to go against their advice), in matters of promotion or assignment they can advise, warn, or delay, but they cannot indefinitely reject the recommendations of a head of a department, for under the Charter all authority and responsibility are vested in the Secretary-General and are mostly delegated by him to officials who are responsible in their own fields. In the Secretariat, grades go with functions (posts), and the execution of the functions is within the authority and responsibility of the hierarchical superior. Letting politics outweigh competence, integrity, and efficiency in the choice of high officials is a sure road to demoralization and inefficiency. Neither the appointment of an ombudsperson, nor the reform of the appointment and promotion procedures, would cure all the ills of the system. Outside experts, if appointed on advice of delegations and on a political basis, might even further politicize the process. Committees drawn from one particular occupation may be more subject to pressure from senior officials in their field than the present appointment and promotion bodies. Despite all such doubts, given the politicization of the process of appointment and promotion, the development of a system of checks and balances is imperative especially since the appointment and promotion bodies do not always treat similar cases in the same way.

But such procedures would prove useful only if the Secretary-General and his aides would resist pressure for the appointment or promotion of particular individuals. The example must be set from above.

The Secretary-General is certainly in an unenviable position. Entrusted by the Charter with the power of appointment, subject only to general regulations set by the General Assembly, he may not accept instructions from states regarding particular appointments. But is it realistic to expect that a statesman interested in reappointment would steadfastly reject pressures in one of the few areas where it is in his power to grant favors?

Indeed, the narrower the power base of a Secretary-General, the greater his temptation to give in to pressure from influential states or groups of states. Of course, the Secretary-General needs the cooperation of states not only for reelection but also in various other areas, such as the implementation of programmes, political and budgetary support, and so forth. Given the fact that the nature of the duties of the Secretary-General requires him to constantly seek the support of governments on a wide variety of subjects, Jenks argued that the Secretary-General should be in a sufficiently strong position to resist political pressure and that there should be safeguards independent of the strength of character of any one individual. In the view of this author, a possible, although imperfect, safeguard against such vulnerability, might be a new practice whereby future Secretaries-General would not be reelected for a further term. Although the Charter neither contains nor authorizes a restriction upon the freedom of choice of the Security Council or the General Assembly, there would be nothing improper in a new gentlemen's agreement pertaining to the nonreelection of Secretaries-General. Since Article 97 of the Charter left this question open, the Preparatory Commission of the United Nations and General Assembly Resolution 11 (I) recommended that the appointment of the first Secretary-General would be open to renewal at the end of the first period for a further term, but suggested that the General Assembly and the Security Council were free to modify the term of office of future Secretaries-General in the light of experience.[21] Given the need to satisfy the various regional groups, a one-term Secretary-General is likely, in any event, to become the rule rather than the exception. There is no reason why such Secretaries-General should be regarded as political lame ducks. The limitation of the term of office for future Secretaries-General to one term only, although not a panacea for all the ills, would have a salutary effect on the quality, the morale, and the independence of the international civil service.

Sources of Law

It goes without saying that members of the staff have the right to know fully all the provisions pertaining to their rights and obligations, so as to be able to act accordingly, and to invoke such legal provisions whenever necessary. Yet, although the Charter, staff regulations, and staff rules are

[21] PC/20, at 87. That change with respect to the term of office of Secretaries-General is possible, is indicated by the flexibility shown by the Security Council (Resolution 227) and the General Assembly (Resolution 2147 (XXI)) (1966) in the case of the reappointment of U Thant. Jenks, *infra* note 67, at 139.

easily available and generally known, upon these principal sources there has been superimposed a labyrinthic structure of additional provisions that govern the lives of members of the Secretariat. Yet these provisions are so dispersed that few persons, even those on the staff of the Personnel Department, master them fully and easily. Moreover, some provisions have never been circulated to members of the Secretariat at large, and are contained in various internal memoranda, which have been made available only to officials directly concerned.[22]

The several types of letter of appointment currently in use (for a temporary appointment, for a fixed-term appointment, and for a permanent appointment) contain a provision whereby the appointment offered is in accordance with the terms and conditions specified in the letter of appointment and subject to the provisions of the staff regulations and staff rules, together with such amendments as may from time to time be made to such staff regulations and such staff rules. These letters of appointment do not refer specifically to any directives of the Secretary-General. It has been argued that such directives may therefore not be adduced against members of the staff, since the staff member's contract is only governed by the terms of the letter of appointment and by the staff regulations and the staff rules, and any directives not incorporated in the letter of appointment itself or in the staff regulations and the staff rules may not be treated as part of the staff member's conditions of employment. This view has been rejected by the Legal Counsel as early as in 1950 when he wrote that it was immaterial whether or not the various directives issued by the Secretary-General were specifically referred to in the letter of appointment, because they were solely designed to implement the staff rules. Since the letter of appointment is always subject to the staff rules, it naturally follows that it must be subject to any provisions designed to implement the staff rules and that therefore any directives of the Secretary-General issued in pursuance to the staff rules may quite properly be made to apply to the letter of appointment.

It is obvious that unless members of the staff are advised of all the provisions that govern their rights and obligations, basic principles of law and due process may be adversely affected. What are the various sources of law which are actually involved? It is relevant to mention the source material involved in a personnel manual, now under preparation in the Secretariat, which includes three categories: material of a legislative character (I), United Nations administrative instructions (II), and material evolved by the coordinating machinery existing between the United Nations and the specialized agencies (III).

---

[22] Such internal material includes many of the instructions issued by the Secretary-General to the Appointment and Promotion Board and its subsidiary bodies.

I. United Nations Staff Regulations

United Nations Staff Rules

Official Records of the General Assembly:

Resolutions

Summary Records and documents of the Fifth Committee (which contain "decisions" of the Fifth Committee)

Reports of the Advisory Committee on Administrative and Budgetary Questions, established under General Assembly Resolution 14 (I) (A)

Repertory of Practice of UN Organs

Judgments of the Administrative Tribunal

Regulations and Administrative Manual of the United Nations Joint Staff Pension Fund

II. Secretary-General's Bulletins

Administrative Instructions (which concern various benefits, entitlements, and so on)

Information Circulars (pertaining to working hours, language examinations, and so on)

Personnel Directives (directives of the Director of Personnel concerning the application of staff rules)

Summary of Rulings (rulings and interpretations by personnel officers which concern detailed applications of the staff rules)

Field Administrative Handbook (which applies to information centers and to field service only)

Minutes of Personnel Officers' meetings (where common problems are discussed and decisions are made which guide the administrative staff concerning matters such as the interpretation of various entitlements)

Minutes of the Joint Advisory Committee (the JAC established under Staff Regulation 8.2 comprises representatives of the staff and of the Secretary-General and formulates recommendations which are submitted to the Secretary-General)

Reports of the Joint Disciplinary Committee (under Staff Regulation 10.2 and Staff Rule 110.1) and the Joint Appeals Board (under Staff Regulation 11.1 and Staff Rule 111.1) and related decisions of the Secretary-General concerning interpretation of rights and duties

Registry files on any individual case

Legal opinion files

The files of the Section on the Rules and Personnel Manual

III. Documents and reports of the Consultative Committee on Administrative Questions (interagency material) and of the Administrative Committee on Coordination, which is a standing committee consisting of the UN Secretary-General, as chairman, and the executive heads of the specialized agencies

Reports of the International Civil Service Advisory Board

Reports and Decisions of the International Civil Service Commission

Documents and reports of the Special Committee for the Review of the United Nations Salary System (under General Assembly Resolution 2743 [XXV] [1970])

Even a cursory examination of these sources will show that they comprise material of a highly differing character and varying legal value. There are staff regulations, adopted by General Assembly resolutions; staff rules, which are promulgated by the Secretary-General and which have, of course, to be consistent with the regulations; administrative instructions, which elaborate on the staff rules; personnel directives, which are more limited in scope and often concern procedural aspects of the application of the staff rules and of administrative instructions; interpretations and rulings, which, although made in individual cases, may have much broader practical implications.

The interorganization material is not a primary source at all. It has to be incorporated or adopted in an appropriate rule or other valid provision before it can be given application in the Secretariat. The only exception to this relates to the new International Civil Service Commission which, in certain matters, has been endowed with decision-making powers going beyond a mere advisory role.[23]

The establishment of a proper hierarchical order between the various provisions is therefore a delicate and important task. Care must be exercised lest provisions of no legal value be incorporated in the manual in such a way as to make their identification difficult.[24]

It is unfortunate that serious work on such a manual is being carried out as late as 30 years after the birth of the United Nations (an earlier manual has not been put into use).

The problems discussed above are not merely academic. On a number of occasions the Administrative Tribunal of the United Nations (UNAT)

---

[23] See the statute of the commission approved by General Assembly Resolution 3357 (XXIX) (1974). As regards the authority of the International Civil Service Commission to make decisions with regard to the specialized agencies, it should be pointed out that FAO, ILO, UPU, ICAO, IMCO, WMO, ITU, UNESCO, WHO, and WIPO have already accepted, through decisions taken by their competent organs, the statute of the International Civil Service Commission. See, in general, Meron, *Administrative and Budgetary Coordination by the General Assembly* in UN ADMINISTRATION OF ECONOMIC AND SOCIAL PROGRAMS 37 (MANGONE, Ed., COLUMBIA U. PRESS, 1966).

[24] A report of the Staff Council recommended that the Secretary-General should assure that all personnel policies be incorporated in a revised manual, which should be the sole official document on personnel administration. Such a document should be available to all the staff members. 23/SC/WP/32 (1974).

regarded some of the "sources" mentioned above as creative of legal rights and obligations for members of the staff and the Secretary-General, depending on the content, intent, and form of the "source" in question.[25] In other words, the tribunal applied not only the Charter of the United Nations,[26] but also the staff regulations and rules, fundamental principles of law, especially of the law of contracts,[27] and resolutions of the General Assembly,[28] to mention just a few. UNAT held that the contractual relationship between the Secretary-General and the staff is governed not only by the staff regulations and staff rules, but also by any directives lawfully issued in pursuance thereto by the Secretary-General. The tribunal concluded that the then existing Administrative Manual, which was to be the official medium for the issuance of administrative policies, instructions, and procedures designed to implement the staff rules was binding upon the administration and the staff and was a document which the tribunal must apply under the terms of its statute.[29]

But the Field Administration Handbook which was designed to assist United Nations Field Offices in the application of staff regulations and rules and financial regulations and rules, and to provide brief explanations of administrative policies, procedures, and practices, was in the nature of a guide to the field offices and did not create or give rise to any contractual obligations between the administration and the staff.[30]

In another judgment UNAT dealt with the legal significance of a circular that contained principles to be followed by the review board established in conformity with Staff Rule 104.13. The tribunal noted that, in view of its importance to the staff, the circular was distributed to each staff member and that consequently each staff member was entitled to expect a correct application of that circular.[31] On one occasion, the Administrative Tribunal held that a circular of ICAO, which was addressed to all the relevant staff members, had—given its form and content—the character of a general circular and that each of the staff members in question was entitled to expect that his individual legal status would be determined on

---

[25] See in general, SZASZ, THE LAW AND PRACTICES OF THE INTERNATIONAL ATOMIC ENERGY AGENCY, 733 (1970), INTERNATIONAL ATOMIC ENERGY AGENCY LEGAL SERIES No. 7; AKEHURST, THE LAW GOVERNING EMPLOYMENT IN INTERNATIONAL ORGANIZATIONS (1967).

[26] See *Mullan v. The Secretary-General of the United Nations*, Judgment No. 162.

[27] *Ibid.*

[28] *Harris and Others v. The Secretary-General of the United Nations,* Judgment No. 67.

[29] *Robinson v. The Secretary-General of the United Nations*, Judgment No. 15. It should be observed, however, that the letters of appointment in use at the time of this judgment contained a clause whereby the appointment was also subject to "any directives lawfully issued in pursuance" to staff regulations and staff rules.

[30] *De Bonel v. The Secretary-General of the United Nations,* Judgment No. 145.

[31] *Ball v. The Secretary-General of the United Nations*, Judgment No. 60.

the basis of the interpretation given in that circular.[32] On another occasion, the tribunal held that an information circular concerning participation in the United Nations Joint Staff Pension Fund only paraphrased the relevant article of the regulations of the pension fund and that, in any event, the circular could not override the clear text of an article of the regulations.[33]

In one case, the tribunal held that the Secretary-General's bulletin, laying down rules relating to the retention in status of staff members holding temporary-indefinite appointments, although of a temporary nature, had the legal force of a provision of the staff rules and regulations, nonobservance of which could be invoked before the tribunal.[34]

UNAT went somewhat further holding that even a confidential memorandum (setting out policy decisions for the guidance of country representatives) could be legally binding upon the administration, depending on its content.[35]

The tribunal also ruled that a confidential document, which enunciated a new employment policy, created rights for the relevant staff members even though they might not have been aware of the existence of the document or of the rights that it created.[36]

The practice of circulating confidential documents that affect the contractual rights of staff members without bringing them to the notice of staff members is undesirable.

In another case, the tribunal held that the Secretary-General could rely on a decision of the Fifth Committee incorporated in its report to the plenary and designed as guidance for the Secretary-General in giving effect to certain policies, even in the absence of a formal resolution passed by the General Assembly.[37] The tribunal noted in particular that the Secretary-General had informed the staff in a circular of the decisions taken by the Fifth Committee and of the manner in which he intended to implement those decisions.

In another case pertaining to classification of posts under Staff Regulation 2.1, the tribunal found that understanding among the administrations of international organizations cannot limit the rights that Secretariat staff has under the staff regulations, unless the understandings are in a legal

---

[32] *Young v. The Secretary-General of the International Civil Aviation Organization*, Judgment No. 89. See also *Ashton v. The Secretary-General of the International Civil Aviation Organization*, Judgment No. 109.

[33] *Osman v. The Secretary-General of the United Nations*, Judgment No. 180.

[34] *Russell-Cobb v. The Secretary-General of the United Nations*, Judgment No. 55.

[35] *Hilpern v. United Nations Relief and Works Agency for Palestine Refugees in the Near East*, Judgment No. 65.

[36] *Sood v. The Secretary-General of the United Nations*, Judgment No. 195.

[37] *Khavkine v. The Secretary-General of the United Nations*, Judgment No. 66.

form binding on such staff. Mere requests by the administrative services of other international organizations could not have the effect of limiting the rights of United Nations staff members under the staff regulations.[38]

The jurisprudence of UNAT has thus clearly established that various circulars and directives of the Secretary-General may be creative of legal rights and obligations.[39] Although the tribunal has made a significant contribution to the establishment of the rule of law in the conditions of employment in the Secretariat,[40] and has introduced—to the displeasure of the administration—United States concepts of due process even to staff serving away from Headquarters, what is needed is the consolidation of the various sources of law, bringing them to the knowledge of all the members of the staff. The possibility of preparing a wholly revised and updated edition of the staff rules, which would incorporate most of the provisions now contained in the various circulars and directives, should be considered. This was not done in the 1976 edition of the staff rules (ST/SGB/Staff Rules/1/Rev. 3). Although a new personnel manual would resolve the problem of making the law open and accessible to the staff, it would leave unclear the status and validity of the various "sources" that it would contain. The problem is a difficult one. The more an administration provides its staff with information, the more it needs protection against costly rulings of the Administrative Tribunal viewing enlightenment as legislation. Although any new rights created through various circulars should be excerpted and codified in the staff rules, there must also be a level of advice or instruction that is in the nature of guidance and implementation, rather than legal conferment.

States and the International Civil Service

"Clearance"

The 1952 opinion of the Commission of Jurists expressed the view that "[t]he independence of the Secretary-General and his sole responsibility to the General Assembly of the United Nations for the selection and retention of staff should be recognized by all Member Nations and if necessary asserted, should it ever be challenged."[41] It goes without saying that

---

[38] *Champoury v. The Secretary-General of the United Nations*, Judgment No. 76.

[39] See Article 2 of the Statute of the Administrative Tribunal, AT/11/Rev. 4.

[40] See, in general, Bastid, *Le Tribunal Administratif des Nations Unies*, 22 ETUDES ET DOCUMENTS 17 (1970).

[41] 7 GAOR, Annexes, Agenda Item 75, at 27. In practical terms, however, the commission suggested that, in exercising his responsibility for the selection and retention of staff, the Secretary-General should regard it as of first importance to refrain from engaging or to re-

it is desirable and important for the members of the Secretariat to enjoy the confidence of governments. Nevertheless, the subjection of the recruitment of staff members to the consent or "clearance" of the governments of which they are nationals is clearly contrary to both the letter and the spirit of Articles 100 and 101 of the Charter.

What is the actual practice in this matter? When candidates for recruitment who are not citizens of the United States are considered for appointment to the staff of the Secretariat, governments are neither informed nor consulted in advance. The Secretariat follows this practice in view of the legal principle that prior consultation of the candidate's government would impinge on the exclusive powers of the Secretary-General under the Charter concerning the appointment of the staff. The assumption is that the checking of the personal references by the Secretariat (with previous employers, academic institutions, and so on) should suffice to reveal any derogatory information. It is, of course, normal and proper to consult a government for reference, when the government is or was the candidate's employer.

Formally, the Secretariat advises the government of the candidate for recruitment of its decision to hire him on the same date on which an offer of appointment is sent to the candidate. This is done by a *note verbale* addressed to the permanent mission concerned, whereby the government is informed that "the Organization has today offered" a particular type of appointment to a national of the state concerned. No comments or reaction are solicited. A different practice is followed for civil servants. In such cases the government is requested to release them for service with the United Nations, whether on secondment, or otherwise (thus, an official might resign from his national civil service in order to join the Secretariat). In order not to compete with governments and not to encourage a brain drain, government approval is also sought for students who have studied abroad on government scholarships. Normally, except in cases of secondment, the Secretariat communicates with the candidate's government only once, at the time of the initial recruitment. The government is not approached when a fixed-term contract of its national is extended for another period, or when the original appointment is converted to another type of appointment (for example, from fixed-term to probationary).

Since a contract of employment is formed by an offer of appointment and its acceptance, the fact that the Secretariat advises the government concerned of the issuance of an offer of appointment only on the date on which such an offer is sent to the candidate for recruitment may result in the Organization's involvement in legal liability towards the candidate if it withdraws the offer because of derogatory information about the candi-

move from the staff any person whom he has reasonable grounds for believing to be engaged, to have been engaged, or to be likely to be engaged in any subversive activities against the host country. *Ibid*. See also *infra*, notes 45 and 48.

date, which may be subsequently received from the government, or for other reasons.[42]

The above description of the practice of the Secretariat suffers, however, from considerable artificiality. It should be observed in the first place that written communications are sometimes sent to governments that go further.[43] And although individual candidates may and, except for nationals of Eastern European States, do apply directly to the Secretariat offering their services, a growing number of candidates are recruited on the basis of secondment from governments and on the basis of referral by governments.[44] Obviously, governments would not agree to the secondment, or even to the referral of candidates, to whose employment in the Secretariat they may be opposed for various reasons. National recruitment offices that routinely advise the Technical Assistance Recruitment Service of the Secretariat about the qualifications of technical assistance experts presumably often exercise the function of "clearance" for such candidates. The sovereign decision on the part of the government whether to agree to secondment or to submit—refer a candidature to the Secretariat—is, thus, a lawful substitute for a government "clearance." Moreover, permanent missions to the United Nations are, of course, in frequent informal oral contacts with the Secretariat pertaining to recruitment and have many opportunities of learning about candidates from among their nationals who are being considered for appointment. It is not at all infrequent for the permanent missions to express reservations or even objections to the recruitment of some individuals. Yet, despite the clear legal principle involved, it has become rare for the Secretariat to appoint an individual to whose recruitment his government is strongly and persistently opposed. States that exert pressure of this character and the Secretary-General who yields to such pressures may be reproached for violating Articles 100 and 101 of the Charter.

The Secretariat follows a wholly different practice when the candidate for recruitment is a national of the United States, on the basis of a long-standing understanding[45] between the Secretariat and the Government of the United States in pursuance of the Executive Order No. 10422 of January 9, 1953, concerning Loyalty Procedures for Employees, as amended.[46] If the United Nations is seriously interested in a particular candi-

---

[42] *Camargo v. The Secretary-General of the United Nations*, Judgment No. 96; *Witmer v. The Secretary-General of the United Nations*, Judgment No. 194. See, however, *Kimpton v. The Secretary-General of the United Nations,* Judgment No. 115.

[43] See *infra*, note 56. See also the letter of 3 September 1968 quoted in AT/DEC/192, at 3.

[44] See *infra*, note 62.

[45] 7 GAOR, Annexes, Agenda Item 75, at 12.

[46] 22 U.S.C. § 287. See also 7 GAOR, Annexes, Agenda Item 75, at 37 (1952). Executive Order No. 10422 was amended by Executive Order No. 11890 of December 10, 1975, which simplified some of the procedures and eliminated in certain cases the need to conduct a full

date, it asks him to fill appropriate forms. Such forms are, upon completion, transmitted by the United Nations to the United States Civil Service Commission, which conducts an investigation.

According to the executive order, derogatory determinations are transmitted "as advisory opinions, together with the reasons therefor stated in as much detail as the [International Organizations Employees Loyalty] Board determines that security considerations permit, to the Secretary of State for transmission to the Secretary-General of the United Nations for his use in exercising his rights and duties in respect to the personnel of the United Nations as set out in the Charter and in regulations and decisions of the competent organs of the United Nations." The standard to be used by the board in making advisory determinations is whether or not there is, on all the evidence, a reasonable doubt as to the loyalty of a candidate to the United States.

In the past, information about a candidate was transmitted orally by a representative of the Permanent Mission of the United States to the United Nations to a designated officer in the Secretariat (at the present the director of the Division of Recruitment). Formally, the derogatory information was regarded by both the United States Government and the Secretary-General of the United Nations as only advisory, but it is not clear in how many cases and in what circumstances has the Secretary-General actually appointed to the Secretariat United States nationals about whom derogatory information has been received from the government. Were the Secretary-General to follow the receipt of derogatory determinations by a consistent practice of not appointing the persons concerned, this might suggest that the advisory determinations were in fact decisive, which would amount to infringement of Articles 100 and 101 of the Charter (except, of course, in case that all the derogatory determinations were based on convincing findings of facts, which also demonstrated unsuitability under the Charter standards for appointments). Derogatory determinations pertaining to loyalty have become very rare and, in fact, according to the Department of State, no such determination has been forwarded to the Secretariat since 1966.

Another question arises as to the scope of the derogatory information that might be transmitted to the Secretariat. Under the order, the standard is strictly one of loyalty to the United States. Should any derogatory information be transmitted that is not relevant to "loyalty," this would amount to an arbitrary abuse of the executive order. It is understood that no such information is at present furnished to the Secretariat. It appears, however, that in the context of the reference checks of candidates for recruitment who have asked for assistance of the Department of State (UN

---

field investigation. 40 Fed. Reg. 240 (1975). The new executive order provides that the investigation to be conducted must be consistent with the Privacy Act of 1974, 5 U.S.C. § 552a.

Personnel Policy and Recruitment Staff), information pertaining to their qualifications or lack thereof and their suitability or unsuitability for United Nations employment sometimes has been transmitted informally to the Secretariat.[47]

The Legal Counsel of the United Nations pointed out (in 1970) that in the letter addressed to the permanent representative of the United States on 14 January 1953,[48] the Secretary-General made no reference to the extent to which the selection and retention of United Nations staff of United States nationality would be subject to the standards of loyalty set forth in the executive order. The Legal Counsel acknowledged that a Charter question would arise if receipt by the Secretary-General of a favourable determination from the United States Government was, in its practical effect, a condition for United Nations employment, and if therefore a delay in an advisory determination that there was no reasonable doubt pertaining to the candidate's loyalty would result, as a matter of course, in suspending further consideration of a candidate, without any independent evaluation of the relevance of the derogatory information to suitability for work in the United Nations. This—in the view of the Legal Counsel—would be different from providing the necessary identifying data to the authorities of the United States and requesting information about suitability of a particular recruit, which would be similar to requests for employer references.

One may well wonder whether the executive order serves a meaningful and necessary purpose, or is it a mere anachronism and an invasion of privacy that survived the McCarthy period, in which it originated.

Demands by states that their nationals be "cleared" by them for service in the Secretariat have not been infrequent. In one case, a government proposed to the Secretariat the establishment of procedures for handling applications of its nationals, whereby offers of appointment would not, in the first instance, be made to the individuals concerned, but to the foreign ministry. The Secretariat replied that such procedures would enable the government to exercise control, to the point of a veto, over the employment of their nationals in the Secretariat and would thus be clearly contrary to the Charter principles governing recruitment. The Legal Counsel expressed the opinion (1964) that this reply correctly reflected the legal principles involved. The government then agreed that, at least as

---

[47] Information received from the Department of State. The Privacy Act of 1974, 88 Stat. 1896, 5 U.S.C. § 552a and the Freedom of Information Act of 1974, 88 Stat. 1561, 5 U.S.C. § 552, may exercise a salutary restraining influence on the scope of information which is transmitted.

[48] See *supra* note 45. In the same opinion, the Legal Counsel expressed his view that the Secretary-General should avoid any reliance on the 1952 Report of the Commission of Jurists, pointing out, *inter alia*, that some of the conclusions and recommendations of the commission were invalidated by the Administrative Tribunal.

far as persons who were not in its civil service were concerned, the Secretary-General should feel free to make or not make appointments, but that it would be of value to the Secretary-General to have the government's comments on questions of the candidate's suitability. In addition, at least as a matter of courtesy, the government should be informed when an offer of appointment was made to one of its nationals. With regard to this revised request, the Legal Counsel expressed the view that, although governments might not exercise a veto over the employment by the United Nations of candidates of their nationality, this did not preclude them from submitting information on such candidates, provided that it was clearly understood that it was left to the Secretary-General to assess the weight to be attached to such information and to arrive at an independent decision whether or not to appoint the candidate concerned. The Secretary-General was under no legal obligation to seek information on candidates and it was a matter of policy for him to determine when such information should be requested. The Legal Counsel advised therefore that the Secretariat could inform the government when an offer of appointment was made to one of its nationals.

In another case, the Legal Counsel was asked by his counterpart in another international organization for his reaction to a *note verbale* from a certain government that proposed that employment contracts offered to nationals of the country concerned should receive prior endorsement of the government. The Legal Counsel replied (1969) that, from the point of view of the United Nations, the proposal ran counter to the Secretary-General's authority and duties under Articles 100 and 101 of the Charter concerning the appointment of staff and to the government's obligation to recognize the exclusively international character of the Secretary-General's responsibility with respect to recruitment. He went on to suggest that consultations with the government about appointments were not precluded. The United Nations had, in the past, recognized the need, particularly of developing countries, to retain within their country or in their government services scarce technical and professional personnel. The Secretary-General could, consistently with the Charter, consider such interests as well as information from governments relating to the suitability of candidates, which might assist him in securing the standards established in Article 101(3).

In view of the delicate and political character of the problem of "clearance," it is not surprising that it has never been dealt with in any written rule or directive. The only public statement on the subject was made in 1974 by the counsel for the Secretary-General in the *Levcik* case before the Administrative Tribunal as follows:

It is however clear that if he [the Secretary General] is to make informed decisions on the subject . . . then he has to receive the maximum amount of information on applicants to the Secretariat. The source of such information of course frequently is the latter's Government...

Now some Governments—and this is well known—have informed the Secretary-General that they expect to be routinely consulted about the employment of any staff members or certain categories of staff members, so that they might supply to the Secretary-General whatever information they may have ... When Governments have so indicated, special procedures have been worked out to accommodate those requests and to permit them to communicate whatever information they wished to.

The best known of such procedures, of course, are those that apply to United States citizens. ...

With respect to the nationals of some States, [most Eastern European] their applications are almost always received from the national Missions of their Governments ...

Whether a Government has made standing arrangements with the Secretariat, or whether it supplies information about particular candidates on an *ad hoc* basis, it has always been made clear that information so supplied is treated merely as one basis for the Secretary-General to make his decision about appointing a candidate to the staff of the Organization.... However, in no case has the Secretary-General undertaken not to appoint staff members merely because of the expression of unspecified objections by his Government.[49]

This statement confirms the legal principle that it is up to the Secretary-General to make the decision whether to appoint a particular candidate. But the statement is vague. What about the procedures that have been worked out to accommodate requests of governments for routine consultations pertaining to appointments? And although the Secretary-General has not undertaken not to appoint staff members merely because of the expression of unspecified objections by the governments concerned, what is the actual practice of the Secretary-General? The test of a legal principle is not in its reaffirmation, important as this may be, but in its consistent application, in face of persistent political pressures. Another question is whether the practice of Eastern European countries requiring that all candidatures of their nationals be submitted through governmental channels is not in violation of the Charter. And if it is a violation, should the Secretary-General (who in practical terms can, of course, do little about this) pass over it in silence, as he does?

The question of the "clearance" with the candidate's government of his appointment to the Secretariat should, however, be clearly distinguished from the question of whether the agreement of a state receiving United Nations assistance is necessary in order for an expert to be assigned to work in that state. It should be pointed out that, according to technical assistance agreements between the United Nations and recipient states, experts who are to render advice and assistance to or through the Government shall be selected by the Organization in consultation with

---

[49] AT/PV.119, at 29–30 (24 Sept. 1974).

the Government.[50] In practice the notion of "consultation" appears to have been interpreted as tantamount to a formal approval of the expert's nomination by the recipient government.[51] The United Nations should not be reproached for this practice.

Unless a technical assistance expert enjoys the confidence of a government on whose territory he functions, and with whom he must closely work and consult, his task would become impossible. Subject to all the relevant agreements and circumstances, similar considerations requiring consultation with, and even consent of, the recipient government would seem to arise with regard to the "clearance" with the host government of other United Nations "emissaries," whose performance of functions requires its confidence and cooperation, as well as appointment to peace-keeping forces.[52]

The international character of the Secretariat would, however, be impaired if the receiving state could demand the right to clear the assignment to its territory of any staff member, such as interpreters to a United Nations conference. A reasonable criterion would therefore be whether the United Nations officer needs, for the performance of his functions in the host country, a close cooperation with and confidence of that state.

Indeed, the Legal Counsel was of the view that a request of a government to have UNICEF provide it with the names and personal histories of UNICEF staff members for clearance prior to their being posted to the country concerned should not be complied with, as contrary to Articles 100 and 101 of the Charter (1974). The Legal Counsel felt that to grant governments the right to accept or reject individuals proposed for assignment within a given country would be contrary to the independence and international character of the staff and to the Secretary-General's responsibility for the selection and the assignment of staff. Although consultations with host governments could be held, governments should not—in the view of the Legal Counsel—play a determinative role in the assignment of international staff within their borders. The only exception had been made for technical assistance experts.

A similar position was taken by the Legal Counsel (1970–1971) with respect to locally recruited United Nations Development Programme staff

---

[50] See, e.g., the Revised Standard Agreement between the United Nations... and the Government of ... in INTERNATIONAL ORGANIZATION AND INTEGRATION 313 at 314 (1968).

[51] See, e.g., *Mirza v. The Secretary-General of the International Civil Aviation Organization*, Judgment No. 149. The tribunal agreed that an expert cannot be retained against the wishes of an assisted government. Legal liability towards the expert can, of course, arise as a result of the termination of a fixed-term appointment following a request by the assisted government, see *Coll v. The Secretary-General of the International Civil Aviation Organization*, Judgment No. 113.

[52] Obviously, heads of bodies, such as UNEF, UNDOF, UNTSO, UNMOGIP, or even UNRWA must be acceptable to the states concerned.

in a particular country, where the government requested the Secretary-General to replace all local employees not possessing the nationality of the host state with individuals possessing such a nationality and to appoint only the nationals of that state for service with the Organization on its territory. The Legal Counsel was of the view that locally employed personnel had the same status as the internationally recruited staff of the United Nations. A unilateral determination by a Member State that only its citizens may be appointed by the Secretary-General for service within its territory was in direct conflict with Articles 100 and 101 of the Charter, for such a determination impinged on the constitutional responsibility of the Secretary-General for the appointment and retention of staff, and conflicted with the principle that the Secretariat should be international in character.[53]

Termination of Appointments and Types of Appointment

Experience indicates that states have exerted pressures on the Secretary-General to have the appointment of certain of their nationals terminated. Pressure has also been directed against the extension of a fixed-term appointment of a certain individual or against the conversion of an appointment of a certain individual from fixed-term to probationary-permanent. Moreover, certain states have insisted that the Secretary-General should employ their nationals on fixed-term appointments only.

It would be appropriate to recall the cases of termination of (permanent) appointments of United States nationals for reasons related to their having invoked the Fifth Amendment. Such terminations were considered by the Administrative Tribunal[54] to have been in violation of the staff regulations and belong now to the realm of history.

Pressures exerted by states against the continued employment in the Secretariat of certain individuals from among their nationals are often related to the staff member's having lost the confidence or goodwill of his

---

[53] In several opinions (1959, 1961, 1965) the Legal Counsel expressed the view that host governments should not be allowed to regulate and enforce conditions of service of their nationals, locally recruited by the United Nations, in a manner that would be incompatible with the Charter and staff rules and regulations. Elsewhere, the Legal Counsel rejected (1960) demands for prior confirmation of locally employed UNEF personnel by the host government.

[54] See the Report of the Commission of Jurists of 29 November 1952, 7GAOR, Agenda Item 75, at 23, and the Report of the Secretary-General of 30 January 1953, *ibid.*, at 3. See also Administrative Tribunal of the United Nations Judgments Nos. 29–37 and the Advisory Opinion of the International Court of Justice on the *Effect of Awards of Compensation made by the United Nations Administrative Tribunal*, [1954]ICJ REP. 47. See, in general, Bastid, *Le Tribunal Administratif des Nations Unies*, 22 ETUDES ET DOCUMENTS 17 (1970).

government following a change of government or other social and political changes that have occurred in his home country subsequent to his initial appointment to the United Nations.

In 1955, following pressures from a certain government, the Legal Counsel of the United Nations was asked for his opinion about, first, the nationality status and, second, the geographical distribution status of certain staff members who has had ceased to be *personae gratae* with their government. Regarding the first question, the Legal Counsel expressed the view that, since nationality was a legal question governed by the applicable national law, unless the Secretariat was satisfied that a nationality had been lost, the presumption would be that it had been retained. No account should be taken for the purpose of listing a staff member's nationality on the staff lists of the fact that he may have ceased to enjoy his government's protection through the withdrawal or nonrenewal of a passport. As regards the second question, the Legal Counsel expressed the view, given the "cultural" interpretation of the principle of geographical distribution, that, although the fact that a person is not *persona grata* with his government is not relevant *per se* to geographical distribution, some of that fact's possible consequences may sometimes be relevant. Thus, if a person has long been absent from his country, especially if rapid and profound changes have taken place in the whole national outlook, if his higher education has been acquired in a foreign country, or if his exile has meant a loss of understanding of his native land, it might not be appropriate for the Secretary-General to consider that the principle of geographical distribution is fully implemented by the presence of such a person in the Secretariat. This was a matter of delicate judgment case by case and no general rules could be laid down. Having made these comments with respect to someone who already was a staff member, the Legal Counsel went on ritualistically to clarify that the principle of geographical distribution was relevant only to recruitment.

The practical implications of this opinion of the Legal Counsel are not clear. The writer has already had occasion to draw attention to some of the dangers inherent in the "cultural" interpretation of the principle of geographical distribution. Was the opinion intended to clear the way for an increase of the number of new recruits from the country concerned so as to "compensate" it for the fact that persons unacceptable to it occupied posts subject to the geographical distribution? Or was it suggesting that such persons should not be listed under their own nationality for purposes of geographical distribution? If the individual concerned was serving on a fixed-term contract, were his chances of having his appointment extended adversely affected?

In one case, a state requested the United Nations to refrain from extending the fixed-term appointment of a staff member possessing its nationality or from offering him any other form of contract. The government also requested that the staff member concerned return to his country. The Legal Counsel pointed out (1963) that the United Nations had entered into no understanding or agreement with the government concerned with regard to the staff member in question. He had not been in government service and had not been seconded to the United Nations. The Organization could therefore reach a decision on the staff member's future employment on the same basis as with regard to any other staff member serving on a fixed-term appointment. The staff member himself had, however, signed, after entering the service of the United Nations, an undertaking to return to his country but claimed that the undertaking had been signed under some pressure. The Legal Counsel expressed the view that, since the signing of that undertaking, there had occurred a revolutionary change of government in the staff member's country, and the staff member felt that, were he to return home, his life would be in jeopardy. In view of the changed circumstances, the undertaking should not be given any particular weight in determining the staff member's future contract status. He concluded that there was no legal objection to renewing the appointment, if it should be considered in the best interests of the United Nations to do so.

The reference by the Legal Counsel to the best interests of the United Nations is interesting. Would the best interests of the United Nations be interpreted to include good relations with the government pressing for the return of its national or only questions relevant to the performance of a certain job?

In another case (1963), a state requested that one of its nationals serving on a probationary appointment be immediately released from the Secretariat. It also appears to have objected to the fact that the person concerned had been given a probationary, rather than a fixed-term, appointment. The Legal Counsel expressed the view that the form of contract to be offered was to be determined by the Secretary-General and not by governments. According to a reply that he suggested, the government should be advised that a probationary appointment could only be terminated for specific reasons contained in the staff regulations. A request by a government for the release of one of its nationals was not one of those reasons.

In one case, the Legal Counsel was asked by his counterpart in another international organization for his reaction to a *note verbale* from a certain government proposing that employment contracts offered to the nationals of the country concerned be on a temporary basis only. The Legal Counsel replied (1969) that, from the point of view of the United Nations, the proposal ran counter to the Secretary-General's authority and duties under Articles 100 and 101 of the Charter concerning the appointment of staff and to the government's obligation to recognize the exclusively international character of the Secretary-General's responsibilities. The Secretary-General could not agree to such a demand, which would exclude the nationals of the country concerned, as a group, from other types of appointments, including career appointments, provided in the staff regulations and rules.

This opinion of the Legal Counsel is certainly sound. There is no dodging the qualitative difference in the Secretary-General's relationship with an Eastern European state resulting from the quantitative effect of all its nationals serving on secondment and on fixed-term contracts. The Charter and the staff regulations and rules are based on the principles of equal rights, equal conditions of employment, and on the exclusive right of the Secretary-General to appoint members of the staff and to decide what type of contract should be offered to each of them. But should not the law that is applied to a small country, as it was in this case, be equally applied to great powers? One may well ask, therefore, whether the Secretary-General should have agreed to limit the appointments of *all* the nationals of the Soviet Union, and indeed of other Eastern European countries, except Yugoslavia, to fixed-term appointments, on the basis of secondment.[55] It is one thing to appoint to the Secretariat some nationals of a certain country on a fixed-term or secondment basis; it is quite a different thing to preclude entire national groups from accepting permanent appointments in the Secretariat. Indeed, the practice of both the governments concerned and of the Secretary-General in this regard would appear to be questionable in light of the Charter.[56] The technical consistency of the Secretary-General (in that a seconded official from another country is treated in a similar way to a Soviet official, for example) is not a sufficient justification for his failure to dispute the Soviet Union's insistence that all its nationals can only be seconded to the Secretariat through governmental channels.

Whatever its social system may be, a state cannot evade the Charter requirements concerning appointment and service in the Secretariat by declaring that all of its nationals are government employees who can only

[55] One Soviet national serves on a permanent appointment. Some recent recruits from the People's Republic of China have joined the Secretariat on career appointments.

[56] The Administrative Tribunal drew attention in the *Levcik* case—where the Secretariat decided to extend Levcik's appointment for a few months despite the objections of his government (Czechoslovakia)—to a letter from the Director of Personnel to the Permanent Representative of Czechoslovakia according to which the "action" taken was of an "exceptional nature" and "did not in any sense reflect a desire. . .to change the policy of close consultation with the Czechoslovak authorities, which, as in the past, continues to be our rule." See *infra* note 57, at 16. The practice of the Secretariat appears to be not to give serious consideration to the candidatures of Eastern European nationals (who live abroad) that are not submitted through government channels.

be seconded to the Secretariat for fixed terms. Obviously, the technique of secondment gives the seconding state a veto power over the continued employment of its nationals in the Secretariat.

The issues here under discussion were illustrated in the *Levcik* case.[57] Levcik, a distinguished economist, was one of the very few Czechoslovak nationals who, during the upheavals related to the Dubcek regime, applied directly to the Secretariat and was recruited. He was at that time in Geneva on leave of absence without pay from the Czechoslovak Academy of Sciences and temporarily employed by the International Labour Organization. In September, 1968, he applied for employment with the Economic Commission for Europe (ECE) which, after obtaining the agreement of the Czechoslovak Government to Levcik's "recruitment on the temporary basis," offered him an appointment for an 11-month period, which he accepted. In March, 1969, the Permanent Mission of Czechoslovakia in New York agreed to the "extension of . . . secondment by two years," and, following a recommendation of the Appointment and Promotion Board, the Secretary-General approved the appointment of Levcik "on a fixed-term secondment basis for a period of two years." Although in the course of the discussions with the Permanent Representative of Czechoslovakia, however, officials of the Office of Personnel accepted the Czechoslovak premise that Levcik was serving on the basis of secondment, the fixed-term two-year appointment offered Levcik in April, 1969, and accepted by him, made no mention of secondment. In August, 1969, Levcik was advised by the Czechoslovak Academy of Sciences that his leave of absence would end at the originally approved term, that is, 31 December 1971. In November, 1970, the executive secretary of ECE recommended an extension of Levcik's fixed-term appointment for a further period of not less than three years, and the director of personnel in New York asked the Permanent Representative of Czechoslovakia for his government's consent for the extension of the "secondment" until 31 March 1974. The government persistently refused, and, after a few short extensions, Levcik was separated from the service on 31 March 1972.

The unusual feature of this case is that Levcik, having been recruited, was able to seize the Administrative Tribunal of some of the political issues relating to clearance and to secondment. Obviously, if Levcik did not serve on the basis of secondment, the Secretary-General should not have insisted on the consent of the government to the extension of the appointment (the tribunal viewed the initial contacts with the Czechoslovak Government as merely designed to ensure that Levcik's prolonged absence from his country was in order from the point of view of the

---

[57] *Levcik v. The Secretary-General of the United Nations,* Judgement No. 192.

Czechoslovak Government). The tribunal, following the *Higgins* case[58] (which pertained to secondment of members of staff from one international organization to another), held that in a secondment, the situation of the official in question must be defined in writing and must be brought to his knowledge and that his consent must be obtained. Any subsequent change in the terms of the secondment, including its extension, required the agreement of each of the three parties—the government, the Organization, and the official. Since these requirements had not been met with regard to Levcik (the agreement reached in New York between the Secretariat and the Czechoslovak Mission was not brought to Levcik's knowledge, and his consent was not obtained), his situation was not one of secondment.

In the absence of a secondment agreed to by all the parties, the Secretary-General could not, in view of Article 100 of the Charter, "legally invoke a decision of a Government to justify his own action with regard to the employment of a staff member." Only in a situation of secondment could the Secretary-General's reliance on the government's refusal to approve an extension of the appointment have any legal validity.

The tribunal's reference to the Secretary-General's own action with regard to the "employment" of a staff member obviously embraces both the initial recruitment and the subsequent extension of an appointment. Having decided that the situation was not one of secondment, the tribunal could either determine that the Secretary-General had violated Article 100 or that the premise of secondment was based on "an error of law." Despite the considerable pressure which the Czechoslovak Government exerted in this instance on the highest echelons of the Secretariat, the tribunal chose the latter alternative.[59] Since a legal expectancy of renewal had been created, the tribunal ruled that Levcik was entitled to compensation for the decision not to extend his appointment.

It is important to observe that in order rapidly to improve the geographical distribution of the staff and for other reasons, including doubts in some quarters about the need for a career service, the recruitment

---

[58] According to *Higgins v. The Secretary-General of the Inter-Governmental Maritime Consultative Organization*, there are "three parties to the arrangement, namely, the releasing organization, the receiving organization, and the staff member concerned." Judgment No. 92 at 50. According to Staff Rule 104.12(b), fixed-term appointments may also be granted for periods not exceeding five years to persons "temporarily seconded by national Governments or institutions for service with the United Nations."

[59] Nevertheless, it is quite possible that in March, 1969, officials of the Office of Personnel acted *bona fide* in assuming that Levcik (like all other Eastern European nationals) must have been appointed on the basis of secondment. It is not clear at what stage the Office of the Legal Counsel became involved in the case. In any event, in the later stages, the Legal Counsel could not but buttress the position of the Secretary-General as best he could.

trends show a clear preference for fixed-term rather than career (probationary-permanent) appointments. For many years the view of the administration of the United Nations was that employees on fixed-term appointments should comprise about 25 percent of the staff. As of 30 June 1975, out of 2,469 members of the staff in posts subject to geographical distribution, 948 or 38.4 percent held fixed-term appointments.[60] But, in light of the composition of the staff by age and the fact that within a few years most of the veterans serving on permanent appointments will be separated from the service, what is of particular significance is that, out of 298 appointments to posts subject to geographical distribution made in the period 1 July 1974 to 30 June 1975, as many as 254 were noncareer, fixed-term appointments.[61] It should be pointed out that, although some fixed-term appointments are imposed by governments, others are decided upon by the Secretariat, for example, in cases of overrepresentation of a particular nationality, which would be worsened by a career appointment. Exact figures on how many of the fixed-term appointees serve on the basis of secondment are not available, but the numbers are clearly considerable. During the calendar year 1974, out of 288 presentations of candidates to appointment and promotion bodies for fixed-term appointments, about 95 were presented as secondments.[62]

The question of the ratio of fixed-term staff to career staff is usually discussed in terms of the administrative and budgetary problems of staff turnover and in terms of greater or lesser efficiency (efficiency is, of course, mentioned in Article 101 as one of the standards to be secured in the recruitment of the staff). Obviously, in terms of efficiency there are pros and cons in fixed-term appointments. Although some positions require considerable experience and continuity of service, some technological fields are in constant and rapid change. It may be wise not to retain experts in such fields beyond relatively short terms as their expertise quickly becomes obsolete when, in the Secretariat, they lose contact with the mainstream of their profession. It is also true that tenure sometimes encourages loss of drive and interest on the part of some staff members. The composition of the staff by the type of appointment is, of course, related to the goals of the Organization. As the United Nations becomes more development-oriented, it needs fewer bureaucrats and more experts.

---

[60] A/10184, Annex, Table 9.

[61] *Ibid*., Table 11. Some fixed-term appointments are subsequently converted to career appointments or extended for additional periods of time. In the period 1958 to 1975, about one out of every five fixed-term appointments was subsequently converted to a career (probationary) appointment.

[62] Data received from the Secretariat. In these cases, presentations explicitly mentioned secondments. The number of actual secondments appears to be higher. The Secretariat does not maintain statistics on private individuals recruited to the Secretariat following referral by governments, but their number appears to be considerable.

The steadily increasing percentage of staff on fixed-term appointments (including secondment) should, however, be discussed primarily in the context of its inevitable impact on the independence and the international character of the Secretariat. The Charter provided not only for a staff recruited on a wide geographical basis but for a staff that would also be completely independent from governments and have an exclusively international character. It is to be feared that the percentage of staff on fixed-term appointments (particularly including persons serving on secondment) may reach a "critical mass," a point where the Secretariat will have been transformed from an international to a quasi-intergovernmental one, thus negating the principal values set out by the Charter for the staff of the Organization. Staff members on fixed-term appointments are likely to show a far greater consideration for the views and the interests of their governments, whose goodwill they might need either for the possible extension of their fixed-term contracts with the Secretariat or upon return home. It is not necessary to elaborate on the dependence of seconded officials on their governments. Members of staff serving on permanent appointments are considerably less vulnerable to pressure.

Maurice Bertrand of the Joint Inspection Unit went as far as to suggest a system of alternating secondments that would permit staff with permanent appointments to serve alternately with the Organization and with the civil services of the Member States of which such staff were nationals. Thus, in addition to secondment from national services to the Secretariat, secondment in reverse would be instituted.[63] Fortunately, the Secretary-General turned this suggestion down for a number of reasons, including the possible effect that it would have "on the international character of the Secretariat which he has an obligation to safeguard in a manner consistent with the intent and purpose of Article 100 of the Charter."[64]

Some of the dangers for the independence of the staff inherent in the concept of secondment of national civil servants to the Secretariat are reflected in the claim made by the Federation of International Civil Servants' Associations (FICSA) that governments have resorted to the practice of supplementing the salaries paid to civil servants seconded to international organizations, in conflict with the Charter.[65] Indeed, there is reason to believe that a growing number of governments give various material advantages to their nationals on secondment to the Secretariat, presumably in order to encourage them to agree to serve with the Organization and thus further the interests of these states. This may range from the provision of cars to a number of senior officials to social benefits above and beyond those granted by the Organization. Obviously, such material advantages

---

[63] A/8454, Part I, at 29–32; Part II, at 323.
[64] A/C.5/1601, at 9.
[65] 2 REPORT OF THE SPECIAL COMMITTEE FOR THE REVIEW OF THE UNITED NATIONS SALARY SYSTEM, 27 GAOR, Supp. No.28 (A/8728), at 153–54.

are in violation not only of the Charter, but also of Staff Regulation 1.6 prohibiting staff members from accepting from any government any favour, gift, or remuneration.[66]

In his famous Oxford speech, Dag Hammarskjöld warned that a risk of national pressure on the international official may be introduced by the terms and duration of his appointment. A national official seconded by his government was in a different position psychologically and politically from the permanent international civil servants who did not contemplate a subsequent career with the national government. A notion that the civil service should be developed as an "intergovernmental" Secretariat ran squarely against the principles of Articles 100 and 101. Should the Secretariat have a large porportion (he mentioned one-third) in the seconded category, this would be likely to impose serious strains on the ability of the Secretariat to function as a body dedicated exclusively to international responsibilities.[67]

Conclusions

The essential legal principles governing the staff of the Secretariat according to the Charter were that the staff was to be an international, independent, and continuing body, recruited primarily on the basis of merit, but on as wide a geographical basis as possible. The Secretary-General was to decide independently of governments on the selection and recruitment of the staff. National pressures were strictly prohibited. The Secretariat was

---

[66] The equalization allowance that the United States Government may pay an employee of the federal government transferred to an international organization, with respect to the difference between the monetary benefits paid by the international organization and the monetary benefits that would have been paid by the agency from which he had been detailed to serve with an international organization, at least has the redeeming feature that it can be paid only after the employee's separation from the international organization and if and when he exercises his reemployment rights in the government. See 5 U.S.C. § 3581–84; § 3343. Regarding equalization payments, see section 352.310 of the Civil Service Commission's Regulations on Detail and Transfer of Federal Employees to International Organizations, Attachment to FPM Ltr. 352–3, under Executive Order 11522 of 24 August, 1970. In December, 1974 only 18 United States nationals served in the Secretariat on secondment. Critics of equalization payments argue that the concurrent accumulation of governmental monetary entitlement should not be allowed under Article 100(2) of the Charter and that such benefits might undermine the official's independence of his government.

[67] The International Civil Servant in Law and in Fact 15–19 (Clarendon Press, 1961). Reprinted in PUBLIC PAPERS OF THE SECRETARIES-GENERAL OF THE UNITED NATIONS 471 at 480–83 (CORDIER & FOOTE, Eds.,COLUMBIA U. PRESS, 1975). Oscar Schachter prepared the draft of this speech. See id., at 470. Jenks, Some Problems of an International Civil Service, 2 REPORT OF THE SPECIAL COMMITTEE FOR THE REVIEW OF THE UNITED NATIONS SALARY SYSTEM, 27 GAOR, Supp. No. 28 (A/8728), at 132.

[68] See RUSSELL & MUTHER, A HISTORY OF THE UNITED NATIONS CHARTER 369–70 (1958). Hammarskjöld, supra note 67.

to be international in the sense of being staffed by appointees of the Organization, paid exclusively by the Organization, and responsible solely to it. The Secretariat was to be the very opposite of an intergovernmental body that is staffed by nationals temporarily seconded from national governments and serving in a quasi-representative capacity.[68] The purpose of these Charter requirements was to assure not only that the Secretariat would be an efficient and competent organ, but also that it would be independent and neutral and "wholly uninfluenced by national or group interests or ideologies."[69]

These fundamental concepts appear to have been increasingly challenged. The process of recruitment and promotion has become highly politicized. Considerations of nationality often prevail over considerations of merit. Governments have an increasing say in the selection of their nationals for service in the Secretariat and, in general, regard them as assisting or serving the national interests, however they may be conceived. Although some states wish their nationals to work actively to promote such interests, under guidance from the permanent missions, others believe that their nationals should merely reflect the national outlook, philosophy, and concepts. The increasing role of government referral of candidates to the Secretariat and of secondment of national officials, together with the trends in favour of fixed-term appointments, increase the dependence of members of the staff on their governments and endanger the concept of a career and independent civil service.

It should be pointed out that recently there appears to have occurred a marked decline in the number of requests for legal opinions from the Secretary-General and from various departments of the Secretariat, including the Office of Personnel Services. This may be another indication of the politicization of the Secretariat, of the diminishing role of law in the Organization, and of the increasing power of the various departments that want to be free to establish policy without submitting themselves to legal opinions. Indeed, it may well be that many salutary opinions of the Legal Counsel on questions such as clearance are rapidly becoming anachronistic.

Despite the emphasis on the factor of nationality in recruitment and, to a degree, also in promotion, this writer believes that the Secretariat as a whole performs its functions with a fair degree of efficiency. Some members of the staff have great ability and commitment but they support a great many parasitic "deadwood" employees and employees serving primarily the political interests of their governments. The sections whose members are selected strictly on the basis of merit as determined by competitive examinations (the language service) are of very high quality. The principle of merit can in the long run be protected only by fair and objec-

---

[69] Hammarskjöld, *supra* note 67, at 14.

tive procedures and safeguards, which are subject to law and to effective grievance procedures. But efficiency is not the only goal. It is necessary to assess the current trends in terms of the type of Secretariat that we might have in the future, should the present trends continue. Such a Secretariat might or might not be technically effective, but it would be much closer to a multilateral, even an intergovernmental, body. The staff would probably be suspected of lacking neutrality and might lose the confidence of some Member States. The result might be paralysis of the Secretariat, which would be unable to play an effective role in situations of crisis.

It may well be that the majority of states regard the Charter concepts as an anachronism and desire that the pendulum should swing even faster from an international to an intergovernmental Secretariat. But it is our duty to analyze the trends, according to the law of the Charter, and to focus on the probable consequences.

5

Erosion of the Powers of the Secretary-General: The New Barons and National Preserves

It has already been pointed out that the Founding Fathers intended that the Secretary-General should be free to appoint all the officials of the Organization, including his most senior aides, without the need to submit such appointments for confirmation to the General Assembly. And, under Article 97 of the Charter, the Secretary-General was to be the chief administrative officer of the Organization and thus free to organize the Secretariat and to assign or transfer the various members of the staff as necessary. The question is to what extent have these Charter prerogatives been eroded by the legislative bodies of the Organization, by customs and procedures, and, primarily, by the inroads made by governments and by the political pressures exerted by them on the United Nations Secretariat.

As early as 1946, Trygve Lie accepted an understanding among the Big Five regarding the distribution to their nationals of posts of assistant-secretaries-general thus paving the way for future erosion of the Charter powers of the Secretary-General.[1]

As regards the Secretary-General's authority to appoint even the most senior officials of the Organization, this authority has always been limited with respect to bodies financed from extrabudgetary funds or by voluntary contributions. But what about bodies whose staff (though not always operational activities) are financed under the regular budget and which form part and parcel of the main body of the United Nations Secretariat?

Appointment of Senior Officials and Autonomy of Major Organizations

In 1949 the General Assembly decided, by Resolution 319(IV), that the High Commissioner for Refugees (administrative expenditures relating to the high commissioner's office are borne on the regular budget of the United Nations) should be elected by the General Assembly, on the nomination of the Secretary-General.

In 1964, the General Assembly decided by Resolution 1995(XIX) to establish the United Nations Conference on Trade and Development (UNCTAD) as an organ of the General Assembly. Arrangements were to be made, "in accordance with Article 101 of the Charter, for the immediate

---

[1] TRYGVE LIE, IN THE CAUSE OF PEACE 45 *et seq.* (MACMILLAN, 1954).

establishment of an adequate, permanent and full-time secretariat within the United Nations Secretariat.'' The UNCTAD secretariat was to be headed by a secretary-general, who was to be appointed by the Secretary-General of the United Nations and confirmed by the General Assembly. The expenses of UNCTAD, including those of its secretariat, were to be borne by the regular budget of the United Nations.

In 1972, the General Assembly decided, by Resolution 2997 (XXVII) to establish the United Nations Environment Programme (UNEP). The first Executive Director of UNEP, Maurice Strong of Canada, was a dynamic and powerful individual who pressed for a maximum delegation of powers to UNEP's secretariat, especially with respect to personnel. The arrangements eventually worked out represented a compromise between the demands of Strong for more autonomy and the resistance of the Secretary-General and of the central administration to such demands. A ''small'' secretariat was to be established to serve as a focal point for environmental action and coordination. The environment secretariat was to be headed by the Executive Director of UNEP, who was to be elected by the General Assembly on the nomination of the Secretary-General. The costs of providing the ''small'' secretariat were to be borne by the regular budget of the United Nations, while operational programme costs were to be financed from a special environment fund. Administrative costs of the fund were also to be borne by the fund.

In 1973, the Secretary-General referred to the General Assembly the administrative arrangements that he proposed to apply to the employment of the staff paid from the resources of the environment fund. According to the arrangements suggested by the Secretary-General, staff regulations and staff rules were to apply to staff paid from the resources of the fund in the same manner in which they applied to the rest of the Secretariat. He delegated to the Executive Director of UNEP, however, the direct responsibility of administering, in the name of the Secretary-General, the staff regulations and staff rules in respect of staff paid from the fund. The Secretary-General, in consultation with the Executive Director, established an appointment and promotion board whose composition, functions, and procedures would be generally comparable to those of the Headquarters Appointment and Promotion Board, to advise the Executive Director as regards staff members paid from the fund. Staff members would, however, be recruited specifically for service with UNEP rather than with the Secretariat as a whole and their movement between UNEP and other parts of the Secretariat would be subject to the same conditions and arrangements as those applicable to staff serving with voluntary programmes of the United Nations. Thus, staff members appointed for the fund were limited to employment with the fund, and could not automatically qualify for posts financed under the regular budget of the United Nations. The principle of recruitment on as wide a geographical basis as possible would govern the staff paid from the fund in accordance with the guidelines approved for the voluntary programmes.[2]

Tendencies to erode the central appointment authority of the Secretary-General were even more apparent in the case of the United Nations Industrial Development Organization (UNIDO), owing to persistent pressures exerted by the powerful group of the developing countries for greater and greater autonomy. These centrifugal tendencies have culminated in the decision to transform UNIDO into a specialized agency, completely independent of the United Nations.

It may be recalled that UNIDO was established in 1966 by General Assembly Resolution 2152(XXI) as an organ of the General Assembly, which was to function as an autonomous organization within the United Nations. Under the constitutive resolution that established it, UNIDO was to have an adequate permanent, and full-time secretariat whose staff was to be appointed in accordance with Article 101 of the Charter and was to avail itself of the other appropriate facilities of the Secretariat of the United Nations. The secretariat of UNIDO would be headed by an executive director to be appointed by the Secretary-General of the United Nations. This appointment was to be confirmed by the General Assembly. Expenses for administrative and research activities of UNIDO—but not for operational activities—were to be borne by the regular budget of the United Nations.

In 1971, the General Assembly, in Resolution 2823(XXVI), expressed the view that it was desirable that UNIDO should have greater autonomy in administrative matters, including recruitment of personnel.

In 1973, the Industrial Development Board, by Resolution II (VII), requested the General Assembly to examine the question of the transfer to UNIDO of full powers for the allocation of resources, including the appointment and promotion of all its staff members, as well as experts.[3] The General Assembly was also requested to consider the establishment of a United Nations industrial development fund, based on voluntary contributions. In 1974, the group of the developing countries on the Industrial Development Board claimed in a policy statement that UNIDO's Secretariat should be regarded as separate from the United Nations Secretariat

---

[2] A/C.5/1505/Rev. 1, paras. 8–11. The General Assembly, at its twenty-eighth session, approved these arrangements. Report of the Fifth Committee, A/9450, para. 120(c); A/PV.2206. As regards the staff of the Secretariat of UNEP, which is financed under the regular budget, they are regarded as part and parcel of the United Nations Secretariat and no special arrangements regarding their recruitment have been made. Regarding the delegation to the Executive Director of UNEP of various powers of the Secretary-General under staff rules and regulations, see ST/AI/234, Annex V(1976).

[3] UNIDO, REPORT OF THE INDUSTRIAL DEVELOPMENT BOARD ON THE WORK OF ITS SEVENTH SESSION, 28 GAOR, Supp. No. 16 (A/9016), at 74.

and that the representation of the developing countries at higher and policymaking levels in its Secretariat should be on the same basis as their representation on the Industrial Development Board.[4] In a report submitted in 1974[5] the Secretary-General expressed strong opposition to the proposal of the Industrial Development Board with respect to the administrative autonomy of UNIDO and especially to the 1973 proposal of the board to transfer to UNIDO full powers pertaining to the appointment and promotion of all its staff members as well as experts. The Secretary-General pointed out that, according to the General Assembly resolutions pertaining to UNIDO, it was intended that the new organ should have the autonomy it would require to carry out its activities and programmes, but it was not contemplated that UNIDO would carry out its activities outside the established framework of the United Nations Secretariat. The powers and responsibilities, with regard to the appointment and management of the staff, are vested in the Secretary-General by virtue of Articles 97 and 101 of the Charter and the Secretary-General could not be divested of such powers and responsibilities, except by an amendment of the Charter itself. The Secretary-General has therefore interpreted the General Assembly resolutions to mean that he continued to be responsible for the recruitment and management of UNIDO's staff, but that the maximum amount of delegation of authority should be extended to UNIDO, consistent with the requirement to maintain intact, at least so far as the regular United Nations budget is concerned, the concept of a single unified secretariat.[6] The Secretary-General warned that to give in to the demand of the Industrial Development Board would create irresistible pressures for similar autonomy for other organizational units. He further warned that, carried too far, the autonomy of the various units comprising the Secretariat could lead to such a degree of fragmentation as to lead to the loss of effective control at the centre. It was the duty of the Secretary-General under the Charter and under the financial and staff regulations to safeguard the concept of a single unified United Nations Secretariat.[7]

The transfer to UNIDO of full powers over the appointment and promotion of all its staff members as well as experts could not be reconciled with the Secretary-General's role as chief administrative officer of the Organization under the Charter responsible for the Secretariat. Were the Secretary-General to be relieved totally of his responsibilities for the appointment and promotion of UNIDO personnel, that personnel would

[4] UNIDO, REPORT OF THE INDUSTRIAL DEVELOPMENT BOARD ON THE WORK OF ITS EIGHTH SESSION, 29 GAOR, Supp. No. 16 (A/9616), at 41.
[5] A/C.5/1616.
[6] *Ibid.*, at 4.
[7] *Ibid.*, at 7.

cease to be an integral part of the United Nations Secretariat.[8] The Secretary-General enumerated the many powers of appointment and promotion that he had already delegated to the Executive Director of UNIDO. He reserved to himself the authority to appoint, however, for a period of one year or longer, all professional and higher category staff of the Secretariat regardless of the organ or office to which they were assigned. This reservation of power arose out of the concept of the Secretariat as an integrated unit. The existence of the central appointment and promotion board ensured the application of the same suitability criteria throughout the Secretariat and made possible the interchangeability of the staff between any of the activities and offices of the United Nations. The only units that were excluded from the purview of the appointment and promotion board were subsidiary organs financed wholly or largely from voluntary funds.

In addition to safeguarding the unity of the Secretariat, the Secretary-General was obliged to carry out the directives of the General Assembly concerning the geographical distribution of the staff. He also was making efforts to achieve a reasonable measure of regional and geographical balance within the individual organizational units such as UNIDO or UNCTAD, although no General Assembly resolution laid down such requirements. The staffing of each unit had, of course, an effect on the overall geographical balance of staff within the Secretariat. If full powers over recruitment and promotion were to be transferred to individual organizational units, the Secretary-General would have no means of achieving the overall balance for the Secretariat as a whole, as contemplated in Article 101. The Secretary-General concluded that as long as UNIDO remained a part of the United Nations Organization, its Secretariat should remain an integral part of the United Nations Secretariat, subject to the same general policies and directives, under the authority and control of the Secretary-General, as other organizational units. The Secretary-General proposed, however, with regard to the contemplated establishment of an industrial development fund comprising voluntary contributions to UNIDO, to authorize the Executive Director of UNIDO, to appoint and promote the staff that would be financed from that fund, under procedures comparable to those granted to the Executive Director of UNEP with respect to the staff of the environment fund.[9]

In 1975, the second general conference of UNIDO held in Lima, decided to recommend to the General Assembly that UNIDO be converted into a specialized agency. It was further decided, with regard to the secretariat of UNIDO as a specialized agency, that the number of officials from developing countries at professional and higher levels should be increased

[8] *Ibid.*, at 12.
[9] *Ibid.*, at 15.

"within the desirable range of equitable geographical distribution to be established by the Industrial Development Board, with due regard to the need for ensuring the highest standards of efficiency, competence, and integrity."[10]

The above formula regarding the composition of the secretariat reverses the order of the principles of merit and geography, in comparison to Article 101(3) of the Charter, and allows the Industrial Development Board to determine what was meant by the desirable range of equitable geographical distribution to be applied to the future secretariat of UNIDO.

In the draft constitution of a specialized agency for industrial development, prepared by the Secretary-General, the provisions of Article 9—pertaining to the secretariat—are based on Articles 100 and 101 of the Charter of the United Nations. As regards the appointment of the staff, the Secretary-General reinstated the order of principles (merit and geography) as spelled out in Article 101(3).[11]

Meanwhile, the Secretary-General is discussing with UNIDO interim arrangements to be made regarding greater autonomy for that body. It is expected that an appointment and promotion committee would be established in Vienna, with respect to appointments at levels P–1 to P–4. These arrangements do not, however, represent concessions of a special character. Indeed, it is planned to establish appointment and promotion committees in other organizations away from the headquarters (United Nations Office in Geneva, UNEP, and regional economic commissions). To ensure the application of uniform standards, and to safeguard the authority of the Secretary-General, the recommendations of the committee would be subject to a confirmation by the Appointment and Promotion Board at United Nations Headquarters.

Given the misgivings of some major contributors, and particularly of the United States, the implementation of the decision to convert UNIDO into a specialized agency has been delayed and is still being negotiated.

The proposed conversion of UNIDO into a specialized agency would, at least, represent an entirely legal and constitutional method of granting that organization complete autonomy without violating the powers of the Secretary-General under the Charter and the principle of the unity of the Secretariat.

The growing practice of having the chief executive officers of various organizations appointed or confirmed by their respective legislative bodies, rather than by the Secretary-General alone, is not a mere formality. Obviously, a wise Secretary-General would not proceed to the appointment of the chief officer of one of the subsidiary organizations of the Unit-

[10] A/10112, at 61.

[11] A/10202, at 8–9.

ed Nations without carrying out, prior to the appointment, extensive consultations within the Secretariat and with representatives of influential countries and groups of countries, thus ensuring that his chief aides enjoy the confidence of the Member States. The principal significance of these methods of appointing heads of various organizations is in that it confirms that they are to enjoy a measure of independence from the central authority of the Organization, from the Secretary-General. Moreover, these methods symbolize the existence of independent power bases for the heads of the various organizations, for example, the group of the developing countries as a power base of the Executive Director of UNIDO. They may also affect the right of the Secretary-General to terminate appointments of such officials.

Power of the New Barons

Experience indicates that the powers of senior officials have grown, as the central powers of the Secretary-General have been eroded. A senior official who is supported by either a great power or an influential group of countries, such as the group of developing countries, enjoys very considerable authority. Customs, procedures, and political factors have limited in practice the ability of the Secretary-General to impose his will on a recalcitrant senior official. Indeed, he is often compelled to negotiate with senior officials proposed changes of jurisdiction, or proposed transfers. He cannot, by simple command, force down their throats changes that are not to their liking. Parenthetically, it should be observed that the present method of budgeting (programme budget), too, imposes serious restrictions on the freedom of the Secretary-General to make changes in the Secretariat.[12] But quite apart from this factor, there have been indications of the growing power of the senior officials of the Secretariat, of the new barons.

This can be illustrated by reference to the implementation of the recommendations of the Administrative Management Service (AMS), a unit within the Secretariat concerned with the utilization of the Secretariat manpower.[13] Rather than order the implementation of certain proposals of the AMS designed to prevent duplication of effort and ensure more ef-

---

[12] Transfer of posts is only possible within the same section of the budget.

[13] Regarding AMS, see A/7476, 23 GAOR, Annexes, Agenda Item 74, at 124. See also ST/ADM/SER.A/1336. It should be pointed out that the Secretary-General has adhered to the view that he may carry out proposals made by AMS without the approval of the relevant legislative bodies. Experience indicates that the legislative bodies consider that changes proposed by AMS should be submitted to them first for examination and approval. In this connection, the proposals of AMS with respect to the restructuring of the Department of Economic and Social Affairs are significant. See A/C.5/1380(1971) and A/C.5/1506 (1973).

fective and economical utilization of personnel, the Secretary-General has been forced to bargain with and persuade senior officials of the Secretariat, hoping that, in due course, his views might be accepted. Indeed, it has become practically impossible for the Secretary-General, in the exercise of his powers under Articles 97 and 101 of the Charter, to reorganize the Secretariat or to reassign or to change the areas of responsibility of senior officials without their consent.

In 1971, the AMS proposed to reorganize the Department of Political and Security Council Affairs. According to the proposals of the AMS, the department was to comprise three divisions rather than four. The functions and responsibilities of the various divisions were to be rearranged. In particular, the Disarmament Division was to be eliminated as such and its functions were to be transferred to other units. The under-secretary-general in charge of that department claimed that the proposals ignored the political significance and importance of the Disarmament Division. In view of his strong opposition, the Secretary-General did not even endorse the recommendations of AMS. It was obvious that, given the strong opposition of the under-secretary-general, no changes were possible.

Another case in point is the organization of African affairs in the Secretariat. For many years now, African affairs have been dealt with both by units in the Department of Political Affairs, Trusteeship and Decolonization, and units in the Department of Political and Security Council Affairs. This has caused duplication of effort and wasteful use of both staff and financial resources.[14] In the Department of Political Affairs, Trusteeship and Decolonization there is an Africa Division that has two sections.[15] The Department of Political and Security Council Affairs also had a section on African questions. Recently, following the adoption of the General Assembly Resolution 3411F (XXX), this section has been reorganized and renamed the Centre Against Apartheid. Given the fact that the Department of Political and Security Council Affairs is under a Soviet under-secretary-general and that the Department of Political Affairs, Trusteeship and Decolonization is now under a Chinese under-secretary-general, these departments have become "untouchable" and immune to changes that would not be acceptable to their heads. Given the antagonism that prevails between China and the Soviet Union, nothing at all could be done to reorganize the handling of African affairs in the Secretariat, despite the fact that AMS had repeatedly complained of the overlap-

---

[14] The General Assembly's Advisory Committee on Administrative and Budgetary Questions drew attention to this matter in connection with the United Nations Council for Namibia in its report on the proposed programme budget for the biennium 1974–75. 28 GAOR, Supp. No. 8 (A/9008), at 118–20.

[15] Regarding the responsibilities of the Africa Division, see ST/SGB/Org., Section J, at 4 (Jan. 1974).

ping and the duplication between the units responsible for the handling of African affairs in the Secretariat.

National Preserves

One area where the erosion of the powers of the Secretary-General has been particularly apparent and where governments have made particularly great inroads into the Secretariat is that of the so-called national preserves.[16] We have already observed that the General Assembly has gone on record in declaring that no posts, units, or departments in the Secretariat should be considered the exclusive preserve of any country or any region. Formally, most countries, including the great powers with the possible exception of the Soviet Union, deny that they claim particular posts in the Secretariat as "belonging" to them. But what is the actual practice? More specifically, is it normal for senior posts to change hands between different nationalities and different regions when a vacancy occurs?

Highest Echelons

Let us look first, briefly, at the highest echelons of the Secretariat. Tables 5–1 and 5–2 which follow (unpublished), have been prepared by the Secretariat.

It should be pointed out, in the first place, that the five permanent members of the Security Council are all represented at the top of the Secretariat, at the level of under-secretary-general. The three superpowers, the United States, the Soviet Union, and the People's Republic of China each has a national with the rank of under-secretary-general for "Political Affairs" (and other affairs): the Soviet under-secretary-general heads the Department of Political and Security Council Affairs, a national of the United States is under-secretary-general in charge of the Office for Political and General Assembly Affairs and a national of the People's Republic of China heads the Department of Political Affairs, Trusteeship and Decolonization. There is no question at all that the post of the under-secretary-general in charge of the Department of Political and Security Council Affairs is regarded as an exclusive preserve of the Soviet Union. It is too early to speak of the post of the under-secretary-general in charge of the

---

[16] It may be recalled that the Preparatory Commission observed in its report that "paragraph 2 of Article 101 of the Charter is interpreted to mean that the Secretary-General has full authority to move staff at his discretion within the Secretariat but must always provide the Economic and Social Council, the Trusteeship Council, and other organs with adequate permanent specialized staffs forming part of the Secretariat." PC/20, at 88 (1945).

Table 5–1
Under-Secretaries-General as at 31 December 1975, 31 August 1970, and 31 August 1965

Functional Title	Dept.	1975 Name	Nationality	1970 Name	Nationality	1965 Name	Nationality
Under-Secretary-General	SG SPA(a)	Guyer	Argentina	Bunche	USA	Bunche	USA
Under-Secretary-General	SG SPA	Urquhart	United Kingdom	Rolz-Bennett	Guatemala	Rolz-Bennett	Guatemala
Under-Secretary-General	SGP GAA	Morse	USA	(Stavropoulos)	(Greece)	–	–
Under-Secretary-General	SGIAAC	Narasimhan	India	Hill	United Kingdom	–	–
Special Representative S-G	SG CLS	Zuleta	Colombia	–	–	–	–
Under-Secretary-General, Legal Counsel	LEGAL	Suy	Belgium	Stavropoulos	Greece	Stavropoulos	Greece
Under-Secretary-General	PSCA	Shevchenko	USSR	Kutakov	USSR	Nesterenko	USSR
Under-Secretary-General	PATD	Tang	China	Djermakoye	Niger	Amachree	Nigeria
Under-Secretary-General	ESA	Van Laethem	France	De Seynes	France	De Seynes	France
Commissioner Technical Co-operation	ESAOTC	Djermakoye	Niger	Hoo	China	Hoo	China
Under-Secretary-General	A+M	Davidson	Canada	Stark	United Kingdom	–	–
Under-Secretary-General	CS	Lewandowski	Poland	Nosek	Czechoslovakia	Nosek	Czechoslovakia
Under-Secretary-General, Director-General	UNOG	Winspeare-Guicciardi	Italy	Winspeare-Guicciardi	Italy	Spinelli	Italy
Disaster Relief Co-ordinator	UNDRO	Berkol	Turkey	–	–	–	–
Secretary-General of the Conference	UNCTAD	Corea	Sri Lanka	Perez-Guerrero	Venezuela	Prebisch	Argentina
Executive Director	UNIDO	Khane	Algeria	Abdel-Rahman	UAR	Abdel-Rahman	UAR
Executive Director	UNEP	Tolba	Egypt	–	–	–	–

a) See Table of Principal Abbreviations

Table 5-2

Assistant-Secretaries-General as at 31 December 1975, 31 August 1970, and 31 August 1965

Assistant-Secretaries-General

Functional Title	Dept.	1975		1970		1965	
		Name	*Nationality*	*Name*	*Nationality*	*Name*	*Nationality*
Executive Assistant to S-G	SGEOSG(a)	Ahmed	Pakistan	Narasimhan(b)	India	Narasimhan	India
Assistant-Secretary-General	SG SPQ	Farah	Somalia	–	–	–	–
Assistant-Secretary-General	ESADHA	Sipila	Finland	–	–	–	–
Executive Director	ESAWFC	Hannah	USA	–	–	–	–
Assistant-Secretary-General Controller	OFS	Debatin	Germany, FR of	Turner	New Zealand	Turner	New Zealand
Assistant-Secretary-General	OPS	Gherab	Tunisia	Gherab	Tunisia	Macfarquhar	United Kingdom
Assistant-Secretary-General	OGS	Ryan	USA	Vaughan	USA	Vaughan	USA
Assistant-Secretary-General	OPI	Akatani	Japan	Hamid	Pakistan	(Rolz-Bennett	Guatemala)
Special Representative S-G	GE COD	Hyvarinen	Finland	–	–	–	–
Executive Secretary	ECE	Stanovnik	Yugoslavia	Stanovnik	Yugoslavia	Velebit	Yugoslavia
Executive Secretary	ESCAP	Maramis	Indonesia	U Nyun	Burma	U Nyun	Burma
Executive Secretary	ECLA	Iglesias	Uruguay	Quintana	Mexico	Mayobre	Venezuela
Executive Secretary	ECA	Adedeji	Nigeria	Gardiner	Ghana	Gardiner	Ghana
Executive Secretary	ECWA	Al-Attar	Yemen	–	–	–	–
Secretary-General of the Conference	HABITAT	Peñalosa	Colombia	–	–	–	–
Assistant Executive Director	UNEP	Frosch	USA	–	–	–	–

a) See Table of Principal Abbreviations
b) Under-Secretary-General

Department of Political Affairs, Trusteeship and Decolonization as being a Chinese preserve, but it is possible that in due time it will become exactly that. To distinguish from the Soviet and the Chinese under-secretaries-general, the American under-secretary-general (since January, 1976, Mr. William Buffum) does not head a large department. Indeed, the important political, diplomatic, and troubleshooting functions previously fulfilled by American Under-Secretary-General Bunche (and shared to a certain extent with Jose Rolz-Bennett of Guatemala) have been divided between two non-American under-secretaries-general: Guyer of Argentina and Urquhart of the United Kingdom. Brian E. Urquhart is a rare case of an under-secretary-general who was a career official rising from junior ranks. The post of the American under-secretary-general does not, despite its title, have as much political content as previously. Nor does it entail management of a large constituent body of the Secretariat. Since the United States may not be entirely satisfied with that particular post, it should not necessarily be regarded as an exclusive American preserve. The United States expects, however, to be represented at the level of under-secretary-general.

The United Kingdom used to have a national preserve in the post of the head of the Department of Administration and Management. Unfortunately, that country nominated to that post career diplomats rather than management experts. One of the best appointments made by Secretary-General Kurt Waldheim was that of George F. Davidson of Canada, a person of great talent and managerial experience, to the post of under-secretary-general in charge of that department.

The post of the under-secretary-general in charge of the Department of Economic and Social Affairs should be regarded as a French national preserve *par excellence*. Indeed, when the present incumbent of that post leaves, it appears most doubtful whether the Secretary-General could replace him with a person of different nationality. At the very least, he would have to approach the French Government to negotiate a trade-off. In other words, with regard to some posts in the Secretariat, the Secretary-General has now a negotiating, or bargaining, role rather than a decisive and executive role.

It may be observed that it is entirely legitimate for the great powers, and indeed for the principal regions and groups of countries, to be represented at the senior echelon of under-secretary-general and assistant-secretary-general. Indeed, it might be better to regard such posts as primarily political and be quite open about that, especially if this would be linked with a depoliticization of D-2 and D-1 posts. What is, however, far more questionable is the emerging Balkanization of the Secretariat as a result of the parcelling out of senior executive posts, commanding areas of influence, to various countries or regions on a more or less permanent basis. In this context, the fact should be mentioned that the Eastern European region has in fact been given, as an exclusive preserve, the post of the under-secretary-general in charge of the Department of Conference Services. The post of under-secretary-general, director-general, in charge of the European Office appears to "belong" to Italy (while his deputy usually happens to be French).

The posts of the Secretary-General of UNCTAD and of the Executive Director of UNIDO appear to "belong" to nationals of developing countries. The post of the under-secretary-general in charge of administration and management appears to "belong" to a developed country, while that of the assistant-secretary-general in charge of the Office of Personnel Services is likely to remain in the hands of a national of one of the developing countries. The post of the assistant secretary-general-controller appears to rotate between nationals of developed countries (New Zealand–Federal Republic of Germany), while that of the deputy controller is held by successive nationals of the United States. The post of the assistant-secretary-general in charge of the Office of General Services appears to "belong" to a national of the United States (we have already alluded to the reasons why the United States regards this post as a *sui generis* one). While the posts of the executive secretaries of the various economic commissions usually rotate between nationals of the relevant region (and quite appropriately so), the post of the executive secretary of the Economic Commission for Europe has changed hands between two nationals of Yugoslavia. The post of the under-secretary-general, Legal Counsel, which has in the past been coveted by the Soviet Union, appears now to "belong" to the Western European region.

It should be observed that various senior officials often regard their departments and posts as vehicles for the advancement of the national interests of their countries. One particular phenomenon is of considerable interest. Several under-secretaries-general have special assistants of their own nationality. Thus, the under-secretary-general in charge of the Department of Political and Security Council Affairs has a Soviet special assistant; the under-secretary-general in charge of the Department of Political Affairs, Trusteeship and Decolonization has a Chinese special assistant; the under-secretary-general in charge of the Department of Economic and Social Affairs has a French special assistant; the under-secretary-general in charge of the Department of Conference Services has a Polish assistant. The Secretary-General himself has an Austrian assistant.

There may be some justification for the growing practice of enabling each under-secretary-general to have a special assistant of his own nationality on the grounds of ensuring the necessary confidence between the two and facilitating communication in their mother tongue. But such considerations are more than offset by the undesirable political significance of creating in the Secretariat national "cells" and thus strengthening the potential of the barons for the advancement of the national interests of their countries. Moreover, it is difficult to reconcile such practices with the international character of the Secretariat.

Posts at the D–2 Level

What is the position with regard to posts at the D–2 level, which formally at least are not political and which represent the highest echelon of the civil service? The calculations made by the author on the basis of data supplied by the Secretariat included cases where a particular post was upgraded, during the period under examination, from a lower level to a D–2 level, or whose incumbent was correspondingly promoted. The author has excluded from the calculations irrelevant posts, that is, posts that did not exist at all during one of the periods of time under consideration. Regions are taken to mean those used for the purposes of the geographical composition of the staff of the Secretariat, as given in the annual reports of the Secretary-General on this subject.[17] The author has not taken into account rotation of posts between nationals belonging to the same group (in the political or "electoral" sense) and especially the group of the developing countries (as distinguished from regions for the purposes of the geographical distribution). Such rotation has been regarded as representing mobility. In other words, the term mobility has been liberally interpreted.

Comparing the situation on 31 August 1965 and on 31 August 1970, 55 posts have been taken into account. From that number, 12 posts have been deducted in which the same persons served on both of these dates. As regards the remaining 43 posts, 15 posts or 34.9 percent changed hands between nationals of the same country; 4 posts, or 9.3 percent changed hands between persons from the same region; and in 24 cases, or 55.8 percent, there has been mobility, that is, the nationality of the occupants of these posts has changed not only from one nationality to another, but also from one geographical region to another.

For a comparison of the situation on 31 August 1970 and on 31 December 1975, 66 posts have been taken into account. From that number, 19 posts have been deducted in which the same persons served on both of these dates. As regards the remaining 47 posts, 17 posts or 36.2 percent have changed hands between nationals of the same country; 7 posts or 14.9 percent have changed hands between nationals of the same region; and for 23 posts or 48.9 percent there was mobility.

A comparison between the two relevant periods indicates a slight growth in the percentage of "national preserves," a more marked in-

[17] See, e.g., A/10184, Annex, Table 8.

crease in the percentage of "regional preserves," and a decrease in mobility of close to 7 percent. Thus, in less than one-half of the cases where posts have changed hands has there been mobility in the sense that the change was from persons from one region to persons from another region. In more than one-third of the cases, the change was between nationals of the same country. These figures are indicative even if some errors were made in the identification of posts, the functions of which may have changed between the years 1965, 1970, and 1975. In the cases where posts at the D–2 level changed hands between people of the same nationality, the following countries were involved: the USSR (15 cases), the United States (8 cases), France (3 cases), India (3 cases), China (1 case), United Kingdom (1 case), and Austria (1 case). (If during the period under consideration a post changed hands twice, both times between nationals of the same country, this was counted as two cases). This is significant because all Member States, with the possible exception of the Soviet Union, deny that they claim specific posts in "perpetuity." What is particularly obvious is that once a post of D–2 is held by a national of the Soviet Union, it appears to remain forever in the hands of successive nationals of the Soviet Union. On the other extreme appears to be the United Kingdom, which has not kept up with other important countries in maintaining D–2 posts in the hands of its nationals. As senior officials of British nationality leave the Secretariat, their posts are in most cases taken over by the nationals of other countries.

It should be emphasized that the director (D–2) posts are the most influential executive posts in the Secretariat as regards its daily operational functions. We have already noted that many such posts change hands only between nationals of the same country, the same region, and sometimes the same group of countries. This practice of establishing *de facto* national or regional preserves in the Secretariat cannot help but have a marked adverse impact on the international character of the Secretariat as well as on the powers of the Secretary-General as the executive head of the Organization, under Article 97 of the Charter and in respect to his theoretically exclusive power of appointment of staff under Article 101(3). If the Secretary-General must, in practice, appoint to a post that becomes vacant a national of a particular country or a particular region, it becomes clear that his powers under the Charter have been overridden by political claims. Moreover, this phenomenon must have an adverse effect on the opportunity for promotion of existing members of the staff. If a post is deemed to "belong" to a particular nation, it is not at all surprising that that nation will want to have a say, if not the decisive influence, regarding the choice of the individual who is to be appointed. On the other hand, an able member of the staff who would consider himself fit, on the basis of merit, for promotion to the relevant post, might not even be considered for it if he does not possess the "right" nationality. Thus it is obvious that the principle of geographical distribution is introduced through the back-door to the entire area of promotion (to distinguish from recruitment) in disregard of the Charter.

Posts at the D–1 Level

Let us now look at the situation as regards the D–1 posts. Here the examination has been with regard to two dates only: 31 August 1970 and 31 December 1975. The comments made with regard to the calculations made with respect to the D–2 posts apply, *mutatis mutandis*, to the analysis of D–1 posts.

From 173 relevant D–1 posts, 66 posts that continued to be held by the same persons have been deducted. As to the remaining 107 posts, 16 posts or 14.95 percent changed hands between nationals of the same countries; 28 posts or 26.2 percent changed hands between persons from the same region; and 63 posts or 58.9 percent changed hands between persons belonging to different regions.

The picture regarding mobility at the D–1 level is therefore considerably better than for the D–2 posts. Indeed, the higher the level of a post, the more difficult it is for the Secretary-General to maintain mobility.

The following countries appeared to have "national preserves" at the D–1 level: USSR (5 cases), USA (4 cases), France (4 cases), India (2 cases), and Argentina (1 case). As regards the USSR, it appears that only in one case has it "given up" a D–1 post held by one of its nationals (in favour of a national of India). Even in that case, however, the USSR national was given another post, previously held by an Indian national, so that these two changes cancelled each other. The success of France in maintaining in the hands of its officials senior positions is impressive.

It should be noted that the United States lost a number of D–1 posts to nationals of Middle-Eastern States (4 D–1 posts to nationals of Egypt, 2 posts to nationals of Jordan, and 1 post to a national of Lebanon). Indeed, in the last few years a decrease in the percentage of D–1 posts held by nationals of the United States has occurred (with, however, an increase in the percentage of D–2 posts held by them).

Conclusions

The author does not wish to suggest that in all cases the succession in posts between nationals of the same country was undesirable. Indeed, such a view would be tantamount to discrimination in reverse, on grounds of nationality. The present practice, however, raises serious questions not only because of its challenge to the international character of the Secretariat, but also because of discrimination in favour of certain states. Unless an end is put to the present tendency to allow the national preserves to survive and flourish, this practice will grow and gain full legitimacy. Despite the difficulties that such an initiative would encounter, the best thing to do would be for the Secretary-General to force a rotation of all senior officials, following a reexamination of the rationale underlying the present distribution of important portfolios. But this would give rise to political objections and administrative and budgetary difficulties and would require great personal courage on the part of the Secretary-General.

6

A Career in the International Civil Service?

The Charter itself did not specifically lay down any rules regarding the terms of appointment of members of the staff. Nevertheless, it can fairly be said that it was intended that the majority of the staff should serve on permanent contracts and should enjoy security of employment (tenure). Indeed, no other arrangement could ensure that members of the staff would be truly independent of their governments. Nor is it likely that young talented people would be interested in joining the Secretariat unless they could look forward to a long and satisfactory career. Thus, the notion of permanent appointments can be regarded as a necessary implication of Articles 100 and 101 of the Charter pertaining to the independence of the Secretariat and to the establishment of the necessary standards of efficiency, competence, and integrity.

Historical

As early as 1945, the various factors relevant to the ongoing argument of career *versus* fixed-term appointments were articulated by the Preparatory Commission—loyalty and international character, independence from national governments, the need to attract the best candidates, and the advantages of experience—as arguments in favor of career service. On the other hand, requirements of the geographical distribution of the staff, the need to bring in specialists in technical fields or persons with special political qualifications, the need to strengthen contacts between the Secretariat and national administrations, were given as arguments in favor of fixed-term appointments. From the very beginning, it was accepted that the most senior aides of the Secretary-General should serve on fixed-term appointments only.[1]

Broadly speaking, the General Assembly by Resolution 13 (I) accepted the guidelines laid down by the Preparatory Commission. Members of the staff who completed the period of probation were to be given contracts for an indeterminate duration subject only to review every five years on the basis of reports by their supervisors. Assistant-secretaries-general and other principal higher officers, as the Secretary-General

---

[1] PC/20 at 85, 92-93 (1945).

might determine, were, however, to be appointed under contracts not to exceed five years, subject to the possibility of renewal.

In 1955, Secretary-General Dag Hammarskjöld emphasized that the maintenance and the strengthening of a first-class Secretariat required that the majority of its staff be appointed on a career basis. At the same time, an adequate proportion of posts was to be filled by way of fixed-term appointments of staff made available from national services and other institutions. Hammarskjöld regarded such a policy as a condition for a gradual attainment of the objectives of Article 101(3) of the Charter. Fixed-term appointments would also give the Organization, according to Hammarskjöld, the advantages of a quicker turnover without sacrificing the elements of stability provided by a career service.[2]

In 1956, the merits of career *versus* fixed-term appointments were dealt with in the report of the Salary Review Committee, which was established under General Assembly Resolution 975 (X) (1955) and which comprised experts nominated by a number of governments.

The committee expressed support for the view that greater use should be made in the United Nations Secretariat of fixed-term staff obtained largely by secondment from government services, universities, and similar institutions. The advantages of such a policy lay in correcting an unbalanced geographical distribution of the staff and in ensuring the constant and substantial influx of new ideas and experience which were necessary if complacency and bureaucracy were to be avoided. The Salary Review Committee also drew attention to the advantages to be gained by having a body of people working in government services after having worked for a period of years in the international Secretariat. As regards the argument that noncareer staff could not have the same international loyalties or independence as career staff, the Salary Review Committee stated that the evidence did not support this view and that they were impressed by the assurances of the Secretary-General of the United Nations that seconded staff were in his experience extremely zealous in avoiding any tendency toward divided loyalties. Nevertheless, the Salary Review Committee emphasized that many of the posts in any international Secretariat were not suitable for filling on a secondment basis, but, of the posts that were suitable, the committee would see no objection if the proportion to be filled on a fixed-term basis, whether by secondment or otherwise, were to be brought up to, say, 20 percent.[3]

The Secretary-General was, however, of the view that it was not pos-

[2] A/3041, 10 GAOR, Annexes, Agenda Items 38 and 47, at 42.
[3] REPORT OF THE SALARY REVIEW COMMITTEE, UNITED NATIONS SALARY, ALLOWANCE AND BENEFITS SYSTEM, A/3209, 11 GAOR, Annexes, Agenda Item 51 (separate fascicle) at 14–15 (1956).

sible to differentiate posts suitable for filling on a secondment basis from other professional posts.[4]

In 1963, in a report presented to the General Assembly, Secretary-General U Thant explained that the steady rise in the proportion of fixed-term staff was due to the concentration of recruitment efforts in countries where candidates for career appointments were in short supply. Some fixed-term appointments were, however, converted subsequently to career appointments. The Secretary-General intended to continue with such conversion of contracts in order to bring within the career group an increasing number of staff from underrepresented regions. He expected to maintain the proportion of fixed-term staff at about 25 percent of the total.[5]

In a report presented to the General Assembly in 1965, the Secretary-General explained that the practice of maintaining the proportion of staff serving on career appointments to those serving on fixed-term appointments at about 3 to 1 was designed to balance considerations of efficiency of operation, in a Secretariat that increasingly demanded a high degree of experience in the job before the staff member could make his contribution felt, with the achievement of an equitable geographical distribution, and the use, for limited periods, of very specialized skills.[6]

The Secretary-General indicated his intention to continue with the conversion of fixed-term appointments to probationary appointments whenever this was deemed to be in the interest of a better geographical composition of the staff.[7]

During the twentieth session of the General Assembly (1965), the debate on the composition of the Secretariat in the Fifth Committee focused on the question of the desirable proportion of fixed-term staff. This debate took place against the background of the steadily rising proportion of fixed-term appointments (from 16.6 percent in 1959 to 28.1 percent in 1965).[8]

Advocates of career service argued that the considerations of efficiency, continuity, experience, and cost favoured holding the number of fixed-term appointments to a reasonable percentage. According to them, it was essential that the policy of fixed-term appointments should not weaken the concept of career service which stood as a vital cornerstone in the structure of the Secretariat. The use of fixed-term appointments was expensive because, in addition to costs arising from the more frequent

[4] A/C.5/724, 12 GAOR, Annexes, Agenda Item 51, at 20.

[5] A/C.5/987, 18 GAOR, Annexes, Agenda Item 66, at 5.

[6] A/5841, 20 GAOR, Annexes, Agenda Item 84, at 3.

[7] *Ibid.*, at 4.

[8] A/6215, 20 GAOR, Annexes, Agenda Item 84, at 37.

travel on appointment and separation, and so on, there was the cost of the time required for a new staff member to familiarize himself with the work of the United Nations. The greater the complexity of the assigned task, the longer the interval of time needed for "settling in." They argued further that there was a flaw to the argument that the developing countries, being short of specialists and experts, could release their nationals for only limited periods of service, because the loss of manpower to the country concerned was the same whether a person was appointed permanently to the United Nations or whether a succession of fixed-term appointments was involved.

On the other hand, the advocates of fixed-term appointments, led by the socialist countries of Eastern Europe, argued that, since the Western countries had monopolized most of the staff posts through the system of permanent appointments, an improvement in the geographical distribution could only be achieved if the organization reviewed all permanent appointments, set as a target their ultimate abolition, and gradually introduced a system of fixed-term appointments. Periodic injections of new blood into the Secretariat would not weaken its efficiency but rather raise the level of competence through the increase in new specialized knowledge in the political, economic, and technical fields.[9]

The Secretary-General himself stated that he would continue to adjust the geographical distribution of the staff by offering as many fixed-term appointments as were compatible with efficient administration. In his view, the Secretariat needed not only experienced staff but also the continued influx of temporary staff with fresh ideas and rare skills.[10]

The Secretary-General reported in 1966 that one development had begun to offset the wastage inherent in short-term service, namely, a progressive lengthening of the initial term of appointment and a greater acceptance of extensions for additional terms.[11] That year the General Assembly, by Resolution 2241A(XXI), recognized "the need for a large proportion of permanent contracts and fixed-term contracts of longer duration to ensure the stability and efficient operation of the Secretariat." The Secretary-General interpreted this resolution to mean that, although recourse to fixed-term appointments was desirable as a means of accelerated correction of imbalances in the composition of the staff by nationality, it need not have the effect of disturbing the desirable balance in the composition of the staff by type of appointment.[12]

In 1968, the Secretary-General indicated that the proportion of fixed-term staff had climbed to 31.8 percent. He justified this increase by point-

---

[9] *Ibid.*
[10] A/6077, 20 GAOR, Annexes, Agenda Item 84, at 19.
[11] A/6605, 21 GAOR, Annexes, Agenda Item 81, at 26.
[12] A/6860, 22 GAOR, Annexes, Agenda Item 82, at 7.

ing out that, in some areas, candidates were available only for fixed-term appointments. This was an obvious allusion to recruitment from Eastern Europe. As regards other areas, considerations of equitable geographical distribution often made it necessary to appoint staff on a temporary basis. This was an allusion to recruitment from overrepresented countries. Finally, there was the need to use fixed-term appointments in order to obtain the services of specialized personnel for work of a defined duration in various technical areas.[13]

This time the Secretary-General warned the General Assembly that the continuing decline of the proportion of staff holding career appointments—resulting from the policy of accelerated correction of geographical imbalances—had reached the stage where it could no longer be regarded as a development of limited significance. Since the influx of new talent into the Secretariat was chiefly of a temporary nature, it brought with it fewer replacements for experienced officials who would be retiring in the years ahead. Moreover, the higher proportion of temporary staff led to a less productive division of labor in the Secretariat.[14]

In 1969, the General Assembly, by Resolution 2539(XXIV), recognized once more that "long-term service is conducive to greater efficiency in certain posts entailing complex duties and responsibilities." In the following year, the General Assembly, by Resolution 2736 (XXV), approved, *inter alia*, the following guideline for the recruitment of staff: in considering candidates for posts "involving complex duties and responsibilities," preference should be given to those who were willing to accept a career appointment or a fixed-term appointment of not less than five years.

We have seen that the General Assembly has developed limited legislative guidelines regarding the relationship that should exist between staff serving on permanent appointments and staff serving on fixed-term appointments. While supporting the policy of the Secretary-General regarding the 3 to 1 ratio, it has refrained from laying down, on its own part, firm guidelines regarding a desirable ratio. The General Assembly did, however, consistently express the view that a large proportion of long-term contracts were needed to assure the stability and efficiency of the Secretariat and that long-term service was particularly important in posts involving complex duties and responsibilities. The policy with regard to the ratio has been developed by the Secretary-General in theory as a compromise between the needs of continuity and stability represented by the concept of the career service, on the one hand, and the need to recruit specialized talent for limited periods of time, on the other. It would appear, however, that the methods of appointment chosen in many cases resulted to a very

---

[13] A/7334, 23 GAOR, Annexes, Agenda Item 81, at 4.
[14] *Ibid.*, at 14–15.

large extent from the need to establish in the Secretariat an equitable geographical balance.

This consideration appears to apply not only to the initial recruitment but also to cases in which it was subsequently decided to convert a fixed-term contract into a permanent one. In other words, there is greater willingness to award permanent contracts to persons from underrepresented countries. Correspondingly, there is a lesser willingness to award permanent contracts to persons from overrepresented countries. On the other hand, the Secretary-General does not appear to have developed any systematic approach to the principle advocated by the General Assembly whereby the type of contract to be awarded should be related to the post to be filled, that is, in posts of greater complexity, long-term service would be desirable.

In 1971, Maurice Bertrand of the Joint Inspection Unit (JIU) referred to the question of the proportion between career officials and fixed-term appointees recognizing that the problem is difficult, that it has major political implications, and that the manner of solving it will go a long way towards defining the type of Secretariat that was desired.[15] While refraining from proposing a specific ratio, Bertrand suggested that cooperation between the United Nations Secretariat and the national civil services should be institutionalized. Interested governments should conclude agreements with the Secretary-General concerning the system of secondment of national civil servants to the Secretariat. The relevant staff rules should be amended to enable a number of staff members holding permanent appointments to suspend their service with the United Nations for periods of up to five years in order to resume employment in their national civil services. Such suspension would be permitted only after five consecutive years of service with the United Nations. Within the 75 percent of career posts proposed by the Secretary-General to the General Assembly in 1965, a proportion of about 15 percent might be reserved for the system of alternating secondments [16]

In 1974, the Secretary-General rejected the JIU proposed system of alternating secondments or secondments in reverse. The Secretary-General considered that, although there would be some advantages to such a proposal, there would also be disadvantages, especially in the interruption of the continuity of work in the Secretariat and in difficulties that would result for improved career development and promotional patterns.

[15] REPORT OF THE JOINT INSPECTION UNIT ON PERSONNEL PROBLEMS IN THE UNITED NATIONS, A/8454, at 30 (Part I). JIU was established in pursuance of the REPORT OF THE AD HOC COMMITTEE OF EXPERTS TO EXAMINE THE FINANCES OF THE UNITED NATIONS AND THE SPECIALIZED AGENCIES, A/6343, 21 GAOR, Agenda Item 80, at 72–73. See also General Assembly Resolution 2150 (XXI).

[16] Supra note 15, at 291 (Part II).

As regards the principle, the Secretary-General expressed concern as to the possible effect of such a system of secondments on the international character of the Secretariat which he had an obligation to safeguard in a manner consistent with the intent and purpose of Article 100.[17]

The Secretary-General may be commended for his clear rejection of the Bertrand recommendation pertaining to secondments in reverse. There is no doubt that such secondments would have had serious consequences regarding the international character of the Secretariat and the independence of the international civil service. What is surprising is that Bertrand, although recognizing that the question of the ratio between the career service and fixed-term appointments had clear political implications and affected the character of the Secretariat, should have made a proposal that, in the long run, could not but undermine the Secretariat's international character.

The Special Committee for the Review of the United Nations Salary System, composed of government experts from a number of countries, appointed in pursuance of General Assembly Resolution 2743(XXV), also expressed views—in its 1972 report—supporting exchanges of national and international officials. In its view, such exchanges would help the Member States and especially the developing countries to train their young graduates. This might take the form of exchanges of national and international officials for periods of not more than three to five years. The committee regarded such a system of exchanges as essentially an extension of the concept of fixed-term appointments. Strangely enough, the committee did not pause to consider whether this was a proper context for training programmes, nor whether such a scheme would accord with the Charter. The committee found that opinions varied on the central question of the relationship between the ratio of permanent staff and those on fixed-term contracts, and did not consider this question in detail.[18]

The members of the committee designated by the Governments of the USSR and of Poland went much further and proposed that the United Nations Secretariat should introduce a so-called "rotation contract." The rotation contract, unlike the permanent contract, would provide for the periodic rotation of staff between the secretariats of international organizations and national service. After working in the United Nations for five to seven years, the staff member would be given extended leave without pay and would return to his country. According to its proponents, the rotation contract would prevent the bureaucratization and the decline in staff members' efficiency, which—it was alleged—was observed in the case of permanent contracts. Such a system would ensure a constant flow

---

[17] A/C.5/1601, at 8–9.
[18] 1 REPORT OF THE SPECIAL COMMITTEE FOR THE REVIEW OF THE UNITED NATIONS SALARY SYSTEM, 27 GAOR, Supp. No. 28 (A/8728) at 26.

of new blood into the Secretariat. The international organization could decide whether to engage a staff member for a second or third period of service on the basis of an assessment of his previous work in the organization. Incompetent workers would thus not be able to return to the United Nations. The rotation contract would make it possible to place recruitment of United Nations staff on an organized basis in agreement with the governments of Member States. International organizations could not ensure lifetime careers for staff members.[19]

The views of the Polish and Soviet members of the committee reflect, of course, the continuing opposition of Eastern European countries to the concept of career in the Secretariat. Obviously, these proposals, which were not accepted, would have gone a long way towards converting the Secretariat into an intergovernmental one. It is of interest to observe that the Eastern European countries increasingly follow in their actual practice the principle that they advocated in their proposals for rotation contracts. More and more Eastern European nationals seconded to the Secretariat for a limited number of years are being sent back to the Secretariat for another period of time after an intervening period of service in their home country. This appears to be the Soviet answer to the need to increase the influence and authority, as well as the efficiency, of the Soviet staff members in the Secretariat while reconciling it with the official policy of not allowing Soviet nationals to stay permanently in the employment of the United Nations.

The United Nations Secretariat advised the interagency Consultative Committee on Administrative Questions (CCAQ) in January, 1976, that the needs of the Organization, particularly with respect to some UNCTAD, UNIDO, and UNEP programmes, require the constant hiring of staff with expertise in areas of their special concern who will return to their professional fields outside the Organization after a period of a few years to renew their professional skills and who will be replaced in the Secretariat by others who had been directly engaged in their professional fields during the same period. The Secretariat also drew attention to the growing interest of a number of Member States in seconding staff to serve with the United Nations for a few years only.

A Critique of Secretariat Policy

From such statements it might appear that the Secretariat has tried to identify posts that require the technical expertise that could best be provided by fixed-term staff or, conversely, the posts requiring continuity and Secretariat experience and—indeed—the assurance of impartiality which could best be filled by persons holding permanent appointments.

---

[19] *Ibid.*, at 37.

This question has, of course, obvious political implications in that it might become difficult for nationals of Eastern European countries, who serve on fixed-term appointments (secondment), to be assigned to certain posts. Perhaps, not surprisingly, none of this has in fact been done. The policy of the Secretariat has been allowed to drift. Pressures exerted by Eastern European countries against permanent appointments together with pressures of underrepresented states for a faster improvement of the geographical distribution, the difficulty some developing countries have in releasing skilled personnel for long periods of time, and the need to recruit highly specialized technical experts have resulted in a policy of awarding more and more fixed-term contracts and fewer and fewer permanent appointments. In allowing this drift, the Secretary-General does not appear to have singled out the posts whose political importance or sensitivity made it inadvisable that they should be manned by officials seconded from governments, or even by persons serving on fixed-term contracts. There is no evidence of concern lest such staffing practices compromise the ability of the Organization to find acceptance with all the parties in crisis situations. It has been the impression of the author that, if the post is a continuing one, if the person manning it or to be appointed to it has the required professional qualifications and the right nationality, that person may be awarded a permanent contract even if the post is of a highly technical nature. In other words, the administration itself does not appear to live up to its doctrine regarding the need to introduce new blood into posts of a technical nature.

The author has been told that, following the Yom Kippur war, a handful of veteran Secretariat officials, acting on the basis of their rich experience, laid down, within a day or so, the foundations for the 1973 UNEF, in circumstances where there was no time for historical research into precedents. A similar task could surely not have been carried out by temporary officials within such a short period of time. In size of operation and number of experienced personnel deployed, the quick capitalization in the Congo of people trained in UNEF in 1956 was even a better proof of the value of long service.

It appears that originally it had been envisaged that fixed-term contracts would be awarded to people with special talents who would come from academia, from industry, and from governments to work together with the permanent core of the Secretariat and enrich it. It is still possible to attract outstanding talent as special consultants on a temporary basis— if not to the career staff—but the Fifth Committee has traditionally discouraged wide-scale use of temporary consultants and experts. Moreover, recently demands have been made for a broader geographical basis of countries from which experts and consultants are appointed and for a larger number of experts and consultants from developing countries.[20]

---

[20] See, e.g., A/C.5/1681 (1975).

James pointed out that the posts most sought by member governments for their seconded officials are frequently the senior, sensitive political posts, where independence and continuity of experience are most valuable, but that successive Secretaries-General have nevertheless benefitted from the advice and presence of seconded officials. It was important to establish the correct balance. Although it was useful to have some seconded officials in the Department of Political Affairs, it would be "disastrous" if they were to dominate it. James suggested that continuity and experience should be the dominant consideration in political affairs, legal affairs, personnel administration, financial administration, conference services, and general services, where the balance should be in favour of career officials. Although agreeing with this list, the author would add to it the secretariats of the various organs and committees. He also agrees with James that in many economic and social fields the desirable balance might well be in favour of fixed-term appointees.[21] Persons on fixed-term contracts may also be suitable to serve as emissaries of the Secretary-General in various missions of a political character.

But, in reality, the fixed-term appointments have become just another method of recruitment, affected by the changing requirements of geographical distribution, rather than a way for enriching the Secretariat with special talent. To make a virtue of necessity some senior Secretariat administrators are now going overboard praising the increased efficiency that will result from an ever greater reliance on fixed-term contracts. Such persons question the "conventional wisdom" of permanent appointments and speak of various ways to make the fixed-term contracts the norm, and the permanent contracts the exception.

Thus, senior members of the Secretariat who participated in the Sixth Annual Stanley Foundation Conference on United Nations Procedures, in 1975, questioned the conventional notion that insulation from outside influences was necessarily assured by the security of tenure under a career appointment. They contended that dedication to the objectives of the Organization was evident both in staff members holding career appointments and those who held fixed-term appointments. There was no unity of view on the question of the correlation between efficiency and appointments policy. Although some were inclined to perceive a higher incidence of diminished efficiency among career staff over time, partly because of the difficulty of reassigning such staff to new areas of activity and to the protection afforded them against termination, other members stressed the inevitably slow process of settling in a new job and the lower efficiency inherent in a fixed-term appointment.[22]

---

[21] JAMES, STAFFING THE UNITED NATIONS SECRETARIAT 20–21 (ISIO MONOGRAPHS, SUSSEX, 1970).
[22] REPORT OF THE SIXTH ANNUAL STANLEY FOUNDATION CONFERENCE ON UNITED NATIONS PROCEDURES 11–12 (1975).

The dominant view in the upper echelons of the administration appears to be that the percentage of "deadwood" and incompetent people among members of the staff serving on permanent appointments is higher than amongst those serving on fixed-term contracts and that an increase in the percentage of people serving on fixed-term contracts would be a shortcut to achieving greater Secretariat efficiency.

In the view of the author, the argument that permanent appointments guarantee protection to deadwood personnel is exaggerated. Staff Regulation 9.1(a) and the related staff rules arm the administration, in spite of the Administrative Tribunal, against inefficient staff. Experience offers little evidence that the supervisor too weak to write adverse periodic reports and eventually initiate termination proceedings against an unproductive career official will be much tougher in refusing to extend a fixed-term appointment. Moreover, if the fixed-term appointment is a secondment, he will in addition hesitate to offend the seconding government. It would be worthwhile for the Organization getting rid of incompetent officials by compensating them generously.

Ideas circulate regarding the discontinuance of the granting of permanent (including probationary) appointments and their replacement by renewable fixed-term appointments. The first such appointment, for a two-year period, would, in fact, perform the function of the probationary appointment. Although acknowledging that many individuals would not be attracted to a service in which they could not gain tenure, some administrators claim that there is no discernible difference in terms of loyalty to the Organization between people serving on permanent appointments and people serving on fixed-term appointments. They further stress the advantages of greater mobility that would result.

Other administrators agree that there is a need for many fixed-term appointments in the highly technical areas (for example, environment) where specific qualifications are needed to perform a certain job. Modern administrations are, however, complex and efficiency, in many jobs, is largely a function of the time spent on the job. To maintain efficiency in the increasingly complex jobs that have to be performed, the core of the Secretariat must be permanent. In order to increase expertise, national administrations follow, for the greater part, the principle of permanent appointments. Another relevant factor is that to be fully effective in the Secretariat, one must have full command of English or of French. Those whose mother tongue is neither English nor French need a considerable time just to gain fluency in one of these languages. The opponents of the move towards fixed-term contracts also point out that the very talented young people are picked up very early upon graduating by various employers who offer them tempting career jobs with good prospects. Such young people would not want to join the United Nations if they could not expect tenure, or—in the absence of good prospects for reintegration in their own country—at least a substantial payment on termination. On the other hand, a person on a permanent contract has both protected employment with the United Nations (tenure) and protected retirement rights (pension rights).

Yet, no efficiency studies have been carried out to compare the performance of permanent or long-term staff in relation to fixed-term or short-term staff. In the same vein, some Secretariat officials, on the basis of their undocumented and unresearched impressions, reject the notion that temporary, or even seconded officials, are less loyal to the Organization than permanent or long-term staff. They argue that such assertions have not been proved. But can it really be doubted that seconded civil servants (especially from Eastern Europe and, indeed, from other countries) have a different relationship with their governments from that of other staff members? And can it truly be claimed that fixed-term officials are not far more vulnerable to the pressure of their governments than tenured officials are? Will they not need the goodwill of those very governments in the context of the possible extension of their contracts, especially if they occupy relatively senior positions, or, when they return to their home countries?

We have already mentioned the view of Dag Hammarskjöld that a risk of national pressure on the international official may be introduced by the terms and duration of his appointment. He emphasized the special psychological and political position of the seconded official.

The author had the impression that the confidence of the senior administrators in the loyalty and independence of noncareer staff is often not shared by other members of the Secretariat.

This is not to suggest that secondment or other types of fixed-term appointments should not be made at all, but rather that they should be made within measure, that it is important to identify the areas where such personnel should be increasingly used (for example, in highly technical posts), and where, conversely, they should be used very sparingly or not at all. The question is, of course, not a simple one. It has been pointed out that personnel policies must be tailored to suit different types of staff: (1) staff performing traditional Secretariat functions; (2) staff performing development functions; and (3) staff involved in special operations like relief.[23]

In fact, the situation is even more complicated and it is all the more regrettable that no attempt has been made to classify posts or at least areas of activity in relation to the types of contract. As the United Nations becomes increasingly development-oriented and as the role of economic activities becomes more important, the Organization is likely to need more

---

[23] GARDNER, THE FUTURE OF THE UNITED NATIONS SECRETARIAT, A REPORT, 26 (1972).

experts and fewer bureaucrats. The composition of the staff by type of appointment is, therefore, obviously related to the goals of the Organization.

What is, however, clear is that the discussion of the desirable mix of career and fixed-term staff members cannot be usefully held *in abstracto* or merely in terms of percentages of the total staff.

Conclusions can only be reached after a study of all posts and areas of activity in the Secretariat in terms of the desirable type of appointment. Such a study could be carried out in conjunction with the work begun on classification of posts. Unless something is done, the drift in favour of fixed-term contracts will continue without any differentiation between the various types of posts in the Secretariat, except for language posts and certain areas in conference services.

What should not be tolerated is the continuation of the drift, the lack of planning, and the ostrichlike habit of not wishing to see the direction in which the Secretariat is going.

The Federation of International Civil Servants' Associations (FICSA) frequently speaks out in favour of tenure and the maintenance of the career staff as the backbone of the civil service, capable of ensuring both professional excellence and an independent approach to international problems.[24]

Such statements do not appear, however, to have carried much weight in practice. Neither have warnings by Jenks,[25] and by scholars such as Goodrich[26] and Schermers,[27] regarding the greater dependence on their governments of seconded officials.

This writer would not like to suggest that some persons serving on secondment are not completely independent of their governments. Indeed, persons serving on secondment are often international civil servants of the highest qualifications both in terms of their technical expertise and their independence and commitment to the principle of the international character of the Secretariat. This is particularly so when the governments concerned are prepared to respect the independence and the international character of their seconded officials. An additional factor relates to the individual's qualifications. The wider the spectrum of his options and possibilities, the greater his independence tends to be. But, as a rule, there is no escaping from the assumption that secondments on a large scale are a threat to the international character of the Secretariat.

---

[24] E.g., *supra* note 18, Vol. 2, at 172.

[25] *Ibid.*, at 137–39.

[26] GOODRICH, THE UNITED NATIONS IN A CHANGING WORLD 102–04 (COLUMBIA U. PRESS, 1974). For arguments in favour of a large-scale use of secondment for achieving the aims of the Organization, see Kay, *Secondment in the United Nations Secretariat: An Alternative View*, 20 INT'L ORG. 63 (1966).

[27] 1 SCHERMERS, INTERNATIONAL INSTITUTIONAL LAW 210–11 (SIJTHOFF, 1972).

Obviously, there is some overlapping between the problem of fixed-term contracts and secondment, but the latter problem is potentially more delicate in terms of the international character of the Secretariat. Another problem relates to the quality of seconded officials. Although some of them are undoubtedly of a very high calibre, many are sent to the United Nations by their governments not on the basis of merit. Governments seldom second their best people to the United Nations. The average seconded official is markedly different from the bright people from academia and other fields who were supposed to join the Secretariat on fixed-term contracts and inspire the regular staff members. Indeed, it would be preferable by far if the Secretary-General were to recruit talented people from the universities or from the private or public sectors on fixed-term appointments rather than use this method of appointment for bringing in government officials of mediocre talent. It may also be observed that some governments use the technique of secondment in order to enable their officials to obtain expertise that may be of value in their future governmental service.

The fact that a person has been recruited on the basis of a fixed-term, rather than a permanent, contract is not necessarily conclusive. We have already alluded to the fact that many fixed-term appointments are subsequently converted into career appointments. It should, however, be borne in mind that the conversion of fixed-term appointments to career appointments is influenced by geography no less than by merit, just as the initial type of appointment is often a function of the need to correct the geographical balance in the Secretariat. If the Secretariat is unsuccessful in obtaining a candidate from an underrepresented country on a probationary appointment, it tends to appoint someone from an overrepresented country on a fixed-term contract with the advantage of freedom to get rid of him when the contract expires.

Persons serving on fixed-term appointments pose difficult questions in terms of promotion and career development. Many of them are not interested in either training for themselves or in supervising the training of others. Before the Staff Committee, Dag Hammarskjöld justified the increasing proportion of people on fixed-term appointments and their relatively higher grades at the time of recruitment on the ground that they were not subject to promotion. He argued that persons on fixed-term appointments are hired on a contractual basis at a certain grade that would remain the same until their separation from the service. Hammarskjöld's promises did not stand the test of time. The tendency for many years now has been to merge the career and fixed-term staff in terms of the jobs open to them and to enable persons on fixed-term appointments to be promoted during the life of their fixed-term contracts, if they fulfill the necessary requirements for promotion. Thus, persons on fixed-term appointments tend to get the best of two worlds: they join the Secretariat sometimes at relatively higher grades on the theory that their career at home is interrupted and that they are not given tenure; nevertheless, after a few years, they may be promoted to higher grades. At times they are even given career appointments. Promotion is also granted to persons serving on secondment. The impression is gained that staff members serving on fixed-term contracts are sometimes evaluated not according to standards and criteria normally applied to career civil servants, but by the more liberal standards of comparison with other staff members serving on fixed-term appointments.

Some administrators explain the higher ratio of people coming in on fixed-term appointments as being related to the fact that people are not sufficiently attracted to a career in the United Nations and that the best people do not want to join the Secretariat permanently, given the relative absence of proper career planning, mobility, and opportunities for promotion.

It appears that even strong opponents of permanent appointments in the Secretariat, including some officials from Eastern Europe, are not opposed to granting such appointments in certain areas requiring high technical efficiency such as personnel of the conference services and staff with special language requirements. They do emphasize, however, that top-notch technicians may turn into ineffective bureaucrats after some years of service in the Secretariat, during which they are away from the mainstream of their professions. They also stress that many permanent officials who joined the United Nations in the first rush after the establishment of the Organization became ineffective but could not be gotten rid of because of the system of tenure.

Some doubts about career service are, of course, legitimate. Persons become uprooted from their home environment, lose contact with the mainstream of their professions, may get out of touch with the reality of their countries and of the world outside Turtle Bay. Their children may encounter difficulties in their studies and often become expatriates. Some international civil servants lose, after many years in the Secretariat, the professional qualifications required for an outside job, for a change of career. They become boxed in, subservient to their superiors, dependent on the administration.

All this is true. But, nevertheless, there does not appear to be a viable alternative to a substantial core of the Secretariat serving on a career basis. James wisely observed that in some respects it would be easier to have a Secretariat entirely composed of seconded officials or of persons appointed for a short term, but that such a Secretariat would entirely alter the character and purposes of the Organization.[28]

[28] JAMES, *supra* note 21, at 22.

Statistical Analysis

Let us look at recent staff changes in posts subject to geographical distribution by type of appointment. In the period 1 July 1974 until 30 June 1975, 44 career appointments and 254 noncareer appointments were made. In other words, for every career appointment, there were 5.77 noncareer appointments.[29] As could be expected, there was a wide divergence between the various regions in respect of the type of appointment. Thus, as regards Eastern Europe, all the appointments made during this period were fixed-term. For the region of Asia and the Far East, for every career appointment there were 8 noncareer appointments. For the region of Africa, out of 35 appointments, only 1 was a career appointment. For the Latin American region, there were 4.2 fixed-term appointments for every career appointment. As to the North American-Caribbean region, for every career appointment, 4.66 noncareer appointments were made. As regards the regions of Western Europe and the Middle East, the ratio between career and noncareer appointments was somewhat better. In the Middle Eastern region, for every career appointment, 3.5 noncareer appointments were made. In the Western European region, for every career appointment there were only 2.68 noncareer appointments.

On 30 June 1975, out of 2,469 staff members subject to geographical distribution, 948 were serving on fixed-term appointments, that is, 38.4 percent.[30] Indeed, despite the marked preference for fixed-term recruitment, according to unpublished Secretariat data, the percentage of the entire professional staff—including staff not subject to geographical distribution—serving on fixed-term appointments has been climbing relatively slowly from 29.5 percent in 1966 to 34.4 percent on 20 January 1976. It should be observed, however, that in more technically-oriented organizations, the percentage of fixed-term appointments is considerably higher. Thus, in UNIDO, in January, 1976, 50 percent of the entire professional staff was serving on fixed-term appointments.

The slow rate of increase in the percentage of staff on fixed-term appointments can be attributed to several main factors. In the first place, there is the constant need for replacement of fixed-term appointees and a high number of fixed-term appointments is required to maintain the existing number of fixed-term staff. Second, a considerable percentage of fixed-term appointments are subsequently converted into probationary appointments. Thus, according to unpublished Secretariat data, in the period 1958 through 1975, 938 probationary appointments and 3,185 fixed-term appointments were made. During this period, however, 631 fixed-term appointments were converted to probationary appointments. Thus,

[29] A/10184, Annex, Table 11.
[30] A/10184, Annex, Table 9.

19.81 percent or about every fifth fixed-term appointment was subsequently converted to a career (probationary) appointment. But let us examine the developing trends.

In the five-year period 1958–1962, for every career appointment (that is, probationary appointments and conversions to probationary appointments combined), 2.05 fixed-term appointments were made. In the five-year period 1971–1975, for every career appointment there were close to 2.34 fixed-term appointments. The increase in the number of career appointments from 254 to 498 represented an increase of 96.06 percent. Fixed-term appointments, however, increased from 521 to 1,167, that is, by 123.99 percent. In conclusion, there is a steady—although not steep—increase in the fixed-term appointments over career appointments. Although the percentage of people in the Secretariat now serving on fixed-term appointments is not unreasonable, the developments must be watched carefully bearing in mind the age structure of the Secretariat and the increasing ratio of fixed-term appointments.

Thirdly, a considerable number of Secretariat officials are still in service from among those who joined the United Nations in its early years, most of whom served on the basis of permanent contracts. On 30 September 1975, there were 444 members of the staff who had served in the Secretariat 25 years or more, including 363 in posts subject to geographical distribution. But, when these members of the staff will have left the service, if the present trends continue without major changes, we will be witnessing a more drastic rise in the percentage of staff on fixed-term contracts.

It may be pointed out that nationals of several of the major contributors with a high percentage of career appointments are not far from retirement age. According to Table 6–1, which was prepared by the Secretariat (unpublished), 24.7 percent of United States nationals in posts subject to geographical distribution are over 55 years old (48.3 percent are over 50). For the United Kingdom the percentage is 27.1 (47.3); for France 17.6 (50.0); for Canada 20.4 (37.3).

Let us now examine the percentage of posts subject to geographical distribution occupied by staff on fixed-term appointment by geographical region over a period of time, according to Table 6–2, which was prepared by the Secretariat (unpublished).

In three regions, the percentage of staff on fixed-term appointments has been rather stable. As regards Africa, the percentage of staff on fixed-term appointments has levelled off at about 40 percent. As for Asia and the Far East, the percentage of staff on fixed-term appointments has levelled off at about 30 percent. The percentage of staff from Eastern European countries serving on fixed-term appointments has always been extremely high, has climbed slowly and steadily over the years, and has now reached 94 percent.

Table 6–1

Percentage of Staff of 10 Member States with Largest Contribution, in Posts Subject to Geographical Distribution by Age Group at 30 September 1975

	Canada	China	France	Germany Fed. Rep. of	Italy	Japan	Ukrainian SSR	USSR	UK	USA
Up to 24	1.7	–	–	–	1.7	–	–	2.5	–	–
25–29	3.4	6.0	2.2	4.1	20.7	7.7	8.7	1.9	4.7	4.0
30–34	10.2	2.0	7.4	16.3	17.2	18.5	21.7	7.5	4.7	9.9
35–39	8.5	14.0	15.4	18.4	19.0	13.8	26.1	23.0	14.7	9.7
40–44	25.4	14.0	7.4	30.6	10.3	26.2	8.7	28.0	12.4	12.1
45–49	13.6	10.0	17.6	18.4	17.2	15.4	34.8	26.1	16.3	16.0
50–54	16.9	14.0	32.4	4.1	3.4	7.7	–	6.8	20.2	23.6
55–59	15.3	30.0	15.4	6.1	8.6	10.8	–	3.7	20.2	19.6
60 and up	5.1	10.0	2.2	2.0	1.7	–	–	0.6	6.9	5.1
Total Staff	59	50	136	49	58	65	23	161	129	495
% 50 or over	37.3	54	50.0	12.2	13.8	18.5	–	11.2	47.3	48.3

Table 6–2

Percentage of Posts Subject to Geographical Distribution Occupied by Staff on Fixed-Term Appointments by Region, 1966–1975

Year Region	1966	1967	1968	1969	1970	1971	1972	1973	1974	1975
Africa	48.4	48.6	49.1	52.1	46.8	44.8	39.7	37.3	38.2	40.7
Asia and the Far East	25.9	26.4	27.4	29.0	31.9	30.9	30.5	31.5	30.9	30.7
Europe (Eastern)	89.1	89.1	90.6	91.9	91.3	90.1	89.8	91.3	93.9	94.0
Europe (Western)	17.2	16.5	19.4	21.8	22.5	22.4	22.8	24.2	28.6	28.9
Latin America	20.8	21.7	16.1	18.2	20.3	18.7	22.8	23.3	28.1	31.0
Middle East	19.4	20.5	21.2	29.5	32.4	29.9	30.1	31.5	29.8	36.6
N. America and the Caribbean	11.5	13.7	14.9	16.3	19.8	22.7	23.6	25.4	26.5	28.5
Others	24.2	27.3	58.3	42.1	50.0	50.0	50.8	53.2	29.3	24.4
Total	29.7	30.6	31.8	34.2	35.2	34.8	34.5	35.5	37.2	38.4

The percentage of Western European staff serving on fixed-term appointments has climbed steeply from about 17 percent in 1966 to nearly 29 percent in 1975. Regarding staff from Latin America, the percentage has climbed from about 21 percent in 1966 to 31 percent in 1975. The highest increase occurred with regard to staff from the Middle East where the percentage of fixed-term appointments went up from 19.4 percent to close to 37 percent and North America and the Caribbean (from about 11 percent in 1966 to about 28 percent in 1975).

These figures indicate that there is a close relationship between fixed-term appointments and geographical distribution. The percentage of staff serving on fixed-term appointments has increased more considerably for overrepresented regions than for underrepresented regions. This is not surprising given the fact that fixed-term appointments have always been used as a means to correct geographical imbalances. It is interesting to speculate what changes will occur in the policy governing the granting of fixed-term appointments now that a better geographical balance has been attained among the various regions.

Post Hoc Career

One particular problem to which attention should be drawn is that, although the international civil service has been traditionally conceived as a career service—and its conditions of service and remuneration are based upon this concept—a certain proportion of the staff in the higher categories has not enjoyed security of tenure in the form of a permanent appointment. Many have spent a considerable portion of their working lives in the international civil service but on a succession of fixed-term appointments without any *guarantee* of renewal. Unpublished Secretariat data indicate that (excluding project personnel and UNHCR) 21.46 percent of United Nations staff members serve on fixed-term contracts for more than five years. In some cases contracts have been renewed several times, cumulatively for many years. In a 1976 (unpublished) study, the Secretariat of the International Civil Service Commission observed that such a *post hoc* career, giving rise every three or five years to uncertainty as to whether one's appointment would be renewed, was psychologically and practically different from the security offered by a United Nations permanent contract.

ICSC, therefore, raised the question whether members of the staff for whom no career security is offered should not be given special compensation for the temporary interruption of a national career, entailing separation from one's national, cultural, and professional milieu.

The phenomenon of *post hoc* career has indeed certain important implications. Members of the staff serving for long periods of time on successive fixed-term contracts are likely to be vulnerable to pressure from their own governments. They become also more dependent on their supervisors, whose recommendations are instrumental in the renewal of their contracts. Moreover, the practice of awarding several successive fixed-term contracts to the same person appears to contradict the justification given by some states and some members of the Secretariat for fixed-term contracts as being the need to introduce to the Secretariat fresh talent.

Promotion Prospects

One of the disadvantages of a career in the United Nations Organization is that the prospects that the career official has of being promoted are much less favourable than they are in national civil services.[31] In a national civil service, an able and dedicated person can expect to advance steadily through the grades, according to his merit, subject to the availability of vacant posts at the higher grade. In national civil services, direct recruitment from the outside to higher grades is rare, except at the very high levels where appointments may be influenced by political considerations. In the United Nations, however, a person sometimes cannot be promoted unless his post has been reclassified (upgraded) to a more senior one (the more usual method of promotions through the promotion register will be discussed in Chapter 10) or he has been transferred to a more senior post, which is not frequent. Moreover, in the United Nations direct outside recruitment to posts at the level of P–5 and above is very frequent; the promotion prospects of serving officials are accordingly reduced. Indeed, significantly, the terms of reference of the 1975 Joint Advisory Committee (JAC) working group on appointment and promotion procedures included the examination of the effect of the expansion, diversification, and specialization of the activities of the Organization on the capacity of the Appointment and Promotion Board to ensure equity of grading between staff members recruited to fill posts of comparable duties and responsibilities, on the one hand, and between newly recruited staff members and those already in service, on the other. Because of the exigencies of the geographical distribution of the staff and political pressures, Staff Regulation 4.4, according to which, subject to Article 101(3) of the Charter, and without prejudice to the recruitment of fresh talent at all levels, the fullest regard shall be had, in filling vacancies, to the requisite qualifications and experience of persons already in the service of the United Nations, has often been ignored.

---

[31] See, in general, Bertrand's analysis, *supra* note 15, at 57–76 (Part I).

Certain circumstances that prevent merit from being the sole criterion for appointment and promotion should be mentioned. One is the fact that a part of the Secretariat performing tasks that may have political importance will not enjoy the confidence of all members if one nationality is disproportionately represented either in the staff of that unit as a whole, or in its upper echelons. Another is that in delicate political missions, including peacekeeping missions, the Secretary-General cannot use nationals of the states in conflict or of other states regarded as closely allied with them, since their mere nationality would be likely to destroy their effectiveness. To the extent that a Secretariat unit is involved in such delicate political tasks or expects to be called upon to supply staff to perform them, the nationality of a candidate may be a strong negative factor, regardless of his merit.

Staff Rule 104.14(f) (iii) (C) provides that "Minimum periods of service in the grade shall be established as a normal requirement for consideration for promotion." This provision is based upon the view that bright young people should not be promoted too quickly on the basis of conspicuous merit; if that happened, they would arrive too early at the top level they can attain (which in the Secretariat may well be no higher than P–5 or D–1, since geographical and political factors *do* have decisive importance in the selection of D–2's and, of course, of assistants and deputies to the Secretary-General) and would then remain at that level for many long years of increasing frustration and declining morale until they resign or retire. Though this view is debatable, it is nevertheless incorporated in the rules, and the consequence is that the promotion bodies, in considering recommendations for "accelerated" promotion (that is, promotion of persons with less than the minimum period of service in grade, which is two years from P–1 to P–2, three years from P–2 to P–3 and P–3 to P–4, and five years from P–4 to P–5 and P–5 to D–1), generally insist on a demonstration that the promotion is required by some interest of the United Nations, *apart* from the merit of the candidate. It should also be borne in mind that promotion prospects for certain "pariah" nationalities are very poor, especially but not only to the D–2 level, regardless of merit.

It is obvious that persons of proven ability hesitate to join the Secretariat unless they have reasonable prospects of attaining the highest positions in the service. Moreover, persons who have made their career in the United Nations are more likely to be imbued with proper international spirit and attitudes. Thus, career prospects are relevant both to the Charter requirement of acquiring the best qualified persons for service in the Secretariat and to the Charter requirements regarding the international character and the independence of the Secretariat. This question is directly related, of course, to the increasing influx to the Secretariat of persons recruited from the outside to the more senior positions on the basis of fixed-term contracts.

As already mentioned, in theory, the higher grade sometimes given to persons recruited on the basis of fixed-term contracts is supposed to compensate the recruit for the fact that he has been recruited only for a limited period, without any assurance that the appointment will be extended or converted into a career appointment, and for the dislocation caused to his career at home. But persons recruited on fixed-term contracts have their appointments often converted to probationary appointments (sometimes even at a still higher level) or have their fixed-term contracts extended for an additional period of time. They are also eligible for further promotions. Thus, they appear to have the best of two worlds.

Maurice Bertrand pointed out that political leaders who have themselves been appointed by political process (he referred to the election of the Secretary-General by the Member States) should be able to appoint the men of their choice and who enjoy their confidence to the top administrative posts. This could not be set aside by any legal or administrative rules. Although supporting the discretion and powers of the Secretary-General to appoint under-secretaries-general and assistant-secretaries-general, Bertrand recommended that for every appointment as such levels, the Secretary-General should approach at least two governments for candidates, each of the governments approached should submit at least three nominations and obtain the prior opinion of a panel of "wise men."[32] The Secretary-General, however, did not accept this suggestion. He argued that under-secretaries-general and assistant-secretaries-general occupied the most important and responsible posts. Such persons are in a sense his cabinet, his inner circle of advisers. In some cases, the important and sensitive nature of the appointment is such as to call for confirmation of the Secretary-General's appointee by the General Assembly. In choosing such candidates, the Secretary-General consults as widely as possible. It would be a mistake, in the view of the Secretary-General, to restrict his freedom of action by establishing more formal practices, requiring consultation in each instance with a prescribed number of governments and the solicitation and consideration of a prescribed number of candidatures.[33]

Maurice Bertrand also proposed that a fixed proportion, to be determined, of all D-1 and D-2 posts should be reserved for members of the Secretariat with at least 10 years' seniority in the international civil service. In his view, the proportion should be very high (for example, 70 percent) for the D-1 posts and about 60 percent for the D-2 posts.[34] This

[32] *Supra* note 15, at 157–58 (Part I).

[33] A/C.5/1601, at 7–8 (September, 1974).

[34] *Supra* note 15, at 158 (Part I) and 319 (Part II).

suggestion was also rejected by the Secretary-General. He argued that in accordance with Staff Regulation 4.4, it had been his practice to make appointments in such a way that 40 percent of posts at the D–2 level and 60 percent of posts at the D–1 level were filled by staff members who had served 10 years or more in the Organization. The Secretary-General went on to point out that 60 percent of posts at the D–2 level and 79 percent of posts at the D–1 level had been filled by promotion of staff who were already in the service of the Organization, even if such service was less than 10 years.[35] Since many of such staff members serve on fixed-term contracts, the Secretary-General's comments regarding percentages of persons promoted in relation to the proportion of persons recruited blurred the distinction between career service and fixed-term appointees.

What is the actual position? The unpublished Secretariat figures in Table 6–3 indicate considerable stability in the percentage of staff promoted to D–2 and D–1 posts. These figures are based on the distribution of staff in November, 1965, February, 1970, and January, 1975.

Let us now look at the trend in the last four years (1972–75), as it emerges from Table 6–4, prepared by the Secretariat (unpublished). As regards the D–2 level, it is of interest to observe that, although the balance is weighted in favour of recruitment from outside, there is a continuing stability in the percentage of staff appointed to D–2 posts. There is a growing feeling in the Secretariat that appointments to the D–2 level are increasingly regarded as political, and that political-geographical factors are decisive. Obviously, not only recruitment to the D–2 level, but also some promotions to this level are motivated by political considerations.

What could be of major significance is that appointments from outside to the D–1 level have sharply gone up from 28 percent in 1972 to 43 percent in 1975. This may be an indication that the D–1 level, too, which in the past had been regarded as a career level, is increasingly regarded as political.

Mobility

Another factor that contributes to making a career in the Secretariat rather unattractive relates to the notorious immobility of staff in the Organization. Many reports including the Report of the Special Committee for the Review of the United Nations Salary System, the Report of the Committee on the Reorganization of the Secretariat, and the [Gardner] Report on a New United Nations Structure for Global Economic Co-operation have drawn attention to the unsatisfactory situation with respect to career planning and absence of mobility of staff in the United Nations. The Commit-

[35] A/C.5/1601, at 8.

Table 6–3

Proportion of Staff Appointed at, and Promoted to, D–1 and D–2 Levels in 1965, 1970, and 1975

	1965	1970	1975
Director (D–2) Level			
Appointed at D–2	22 (40.7%)	24 (35.8%)	29 (36.7%)
Promoted to D–2	32 (59.3%)	43 (64.2%)	49 (63.3%)
	54	67	78
Principal Officer (D–1) Level			
Appointed at D–1	29 (25.7%)	29 (19.7%)	42 (20.8%)
Promoted to D–1	84 (74.3%)	118 (80.2%)	160 (79.2%)
	113	147	202

Table 6–4

Staff Appointed at, and Promoted to, D–2 and D–1 Levels during the Calendar Years 1972–1975

	1972		1973		1974		1975	
	No.	%	No.	%	No.	%	No.	%
D–2								
Appointments	9	56	7	41	11	65	7	58
Promotions	7	44	10	59	6	35	5	42
D–1								
Appointments	7	28	13	29	16	42	15	43
Promotions	18	72	32	71	22	58	20	57

tee on the Reorganization of the Secretariat recommended that senior officials (D–1 and above) should change assignments from time to time in order to maximize their usefulness and that, as a general rule, such officials should not remain for more than 10 years in the same post. With regard to lower grades, the committee also pointed out that a greater degree of transferability of the staff in the professional and higher categories would improve cohesion and restore a greater sense of unity between the various departments of the Secretariat. Such transferability would also open up opportunities for the staff for broadening their experience and competence.[36] Indeed, it would also make members of the staff more aware of the goals and objectives of the Organization as a whole.

Despite repeated statements in favour of a greater mobility of staff, no change has been apparent in the last 10 years. The situation in the Secre-

[36] A/7359, at 37–38.

tariat is such that in practice the agreement of at least four independent officials is required and the objections of any one of the four can prevent the transfer of an official from one department to another. The four "decision points" are as follows: (i) the releasing department, (ii) the receiving department, (iii) the Office of Personnel Services, and (iv) the staff member concerned. Staff Regulation 1.2 provides that staff members are subject to assignment by the Secretary-General to any of the activities or offices of the United Nations but the wishes and interests of the staff member are taken into account and his consent is usually required.[37] It is important that the Secretariat should clearly lay down procedures enabling the mobility of the staff to become a reality, according to predetermined standards and criteria, which would be applied even in the case of reluctance on the part of some of the "decision points." In terms of mobility and interchangeability of staff, the international civil service has never become a reality, not only as regards transfers between the United Nations and the specialized agencies, but even as regards UNOG and New York. The Secretary-General should be prepared to implement decisions to transfer members of the staff. It should be pointed out that a greater mobility would not only create greater opportunities for promotion and advancement but would also enhance the intellectual interest in a Secretariat career and create the possibility for eroding the various "national preserves" in the Secretariat.

Career Development

Career development and planning for members of the staff should have existed in the Secretariat, at least at the departmental level, for many years. Nevertheless, career development and planning remains still in the realm of theory and rather unclear plans for the future. It is unfortunate that as of now talented members of the staff, especially those who have been recruited pursuant to a competitive examination, have no way of an-

---

[37] An internal paper of the Secretariat prepared in April, 1974, points out as follows:

A number of factors militate against greater mobility. First the infrequency of movement makes staff wary of leaving one good post for another because of the risk of not being able to move again later if the new post is not fully satisfying or if it becomes unsatisfactory. Secondly, by moving and accepting a promotion which may be offered as an incentive by the receiving department, the staff member may create a further obstacle to his return to the releasing department. Thirdly, in order to safeguard the possibility of return to the releasing department the staff member may seek assignment for a fixed period and the releasing department may object because it would then have to block a post for the same period of perhaps several years pending the staff member's return. Fourthly, the tendency for separate secretariats to be established for subsidiary organs with their own governing bodies and other fragmentary tendencies encourage staff members to remain in one office. Staff outside such offices may be unwilling to join them for fear of limiting their career opportunities as a result. Further thought may bring other factors and possibly more important ones to light.

ticipating their promotional ladders, their future mobility, and assignments in the Secretariat, and so forth. Indeed, unless career development is effectively promoted, many of the newly recruited members of the staff may become frustrated and leave the Secretariat after a short period of service. Maurice Bertrand made an important contribution in proposing the systematic development of career planning in the Secretariat instituted along occupational lines.[38] Such a system would involve the creation of training and career planning committees, each specializing in a particular occupational group, which would replace the present Appointment and Promotion Committee. Such committees would also deal with the systematic planning of staff assignments. As early as 1974, the Secretary-General agreed with most of the proposals of JIU pertaining to career development and expressed readiness to test the proposed system in respect to selected occupational groups before deciding to institute the system throughout the Secretariat.[39] This general commitment of the Secretary-General has not yet been translated into reality. A working group under the auspices of the Joint Advisory Committee is to advise the Secretary-General on detailed procedures.[40]

The career planning committees, which will be further discussed in Chapter 10, would, apart from recommending appointments and promotions, make sure that departments and offices plan and decide on the type of training and experience that each member of the staff should have. Such committees should specify the techniques and substantive matters in which an official should, if possible, have experience in order to occupy higher posts. The committee should make recommendations concerning the assignment of particular tasks, missions, and overseas posts and on transfers and exchanges of staff. One problem that may arise is that of the authority of the career development committees *vis-à-vis* departmental managers. On the one hand it is the manager who is responsible to the Secretary-General for the performance of his unit. On the other, unless career planning committees are given some powers going beyond the hortatory ones, the proposed and much needed reform may well degenerate into an exercise in futility. It is possible that the work of the career planning committees will be further complicated by the cluttering of the manning tables with fixed-term staff.

---

[38] *Supra* note 15, at 171 *et seq.* (Part I).

[39] A/C.5/1601, at 10.

[40] There is now, in the Secretariat, a placement unit which deals with placement and transfers and which might be enlarged in the future so as to assist in career planning and which would operate in relation to occupational groups on a cross-departmental and cross-duty station basis.

Equal Pay for Equal Work?

Staff Regulation 2.1 provides that, in conformity with principles laid down by the General Assembly, the Secretary-General is to make appropriate provision for the classification of posts and staff according to the nature of the duties and responsibilities required. Nevertheless, 30 years after the founding of the United Nations, there is still no job classification system covering all posts in the Secretariat and ensuring a coherent and consistent relationship between the duties assigned to a post and the grade attached to it. This is not merely a technical question, for it involves a fundamental principle, namely that of equal pay for equal work. In the absence of a general classification system there are considerable differences between the grades attached to various posts that involve comparable responsibilities.[41] Such difference in grading results from past history, departmental, personal, or political pressures, and other factors. Moreover, a reclassification or an upgrading of a post sometimes originates in a desire to improve the promotion opportunities for the incumbent, *ad hominem* (and not infrequently for political considerations), rather than in a change in the level of qualifications and responsibilities attaching to the post. (We shall return to this question in Chapter 10.) In 1974, the Secretary-General agreed with and decided to give priority to the implementation of the AMS recommendations for a general job classification system.[42] In the beginning of 1976, work finally started on such a project, but it is still too early to anticipate its results.

The Intangibles

In any bureaucracy there are factors in operation that discourage and frustrate the talented and ambitious young person. In the United Nations Secretariat such factors are even more prominent than in many national administrations.

We have already discussed some of the relevant considerations such as unfavourable promotion prospects, lack of mobility, or career planning. Since many Secretariat officials spend their entire working life in the same posts and jobs, they suffer from an inevitable "cubicle orientation." They may understand and perform their own jobs satisfactorily, but they

---

[41] See, in general, Meron, *The United Nations "Common System" of Salary, Allowance, and Benefits: A Critical Appraisal of Coordination in Personnel Matters*, 21 INT'L ORG. 284 at 293 (1967).

[42] A/C.5/1601, at 3.

often have a highly inadequate grasp of the central aims and goals of the Organization, or even of the programmes with which they are associated. Few have a coherent conception of the whole.

Moreover, the work of many staff members has only a tenuous relationship with operational activities. Although officials of national administrations often have broad decision-making powers affecting the lives of many individuals, members of the staff feel far removed from the mainstream of decision-making. The limited size of the Secretariat and the limited scope of its activities in comparison to national civil services should also be taken into account. Some officials do important work in their professional fields. Others, especially those involved in the practical aspects of development or peacekeeping activities, may well have a justified feeling of having contributed to an important, useful, and practical operation; but a great many staff members spend their years in the Secretariat shuffling papers and preparing reports and studies that often are not acted upon. Such reports and studies are frequently of a compilatory, rather than analytical, nature, designed to offend as few as possible, for members of the Secretariat naturally prefer to tread on safe ground. In the course of the circulation of a draft from one official to another, each of them makes sure that the portions which he regards as objectionable are deleted. Soviet officials, in particular, have excelled in making certain that passages not favourable to the point of view of the Soviet Government disappear from the draft. The final product is often as unreadable as its contents are uninspiring.

An important factor that adversely affects the attraction of the United Nations as a career for an able individual is the large-scale recruitment from outside, especially to the more senior posts, and the politicization of the recruitment and promotion processes. Considerations of geographical distribution are preponderant in filling senior posts. The average Secretariat official views with distrust the reasons for the recruitment and sometimes for the promotion of various individuals, which he attributes, sometimes unjustly, to political considerations. In any event, there often is a lack of confidence in the objective qualifications of senior officials.

The decline in the political standing and reputation of the Organization in the media, at least in the United States, in academia, in the intellectual community, and in the public at large, as well as among many members of the Secretariat, following irresponsible positions taken by the legislative organs, also contributes to discourage potential worthwhile recruits to the Organization.

Another factor is related to the able individual's understandable need for recognition as a positive driving force. In the United Nations, the civil servant is compelled to adopt a low profile because of the requirements of team work, because of the international character of the Secretariat, and in order to protect members of the staff from pressure and complaints from national delegations. The Secretariat official is bound to adopt a bland, inoffensive style and labours under many self-imposed and Organization-imposed inhibitions and restrictions, both with regard to national delegations and intergovernmental bodies, as in the internal work of the Secretariat. Various documents and memoranda are often signed by more senior officials, without any acknowledgment of the role of the person who actually drafted and prepared the document in question.

Furthermore, although national civil servants tend to have an anonymous existence, anonymity is even more marked in an international organization. Indeed, strict limitations are imposed on the possibilities of a capable civil servant to gain recognition outside the Organization. Under Staff Regulation 1.6, staff members may not accept any honour or decoration from any source external to the Organization without obtaining the prior approval of the Secretary-General. More importantly, under Staff Rule 101.6(e), staff members may not, without the prior approval of the Secretary-General, perform acts such as accepting speaking engagements, or submitting articles, books, or other materials for publication, if such acts relate to the purposes, activities, or interests of the United Nations. In other words, the intellectual product of the member of the staff is cloaked in anonymity and he may not claim any credit or recognition for it outside the Organization. In this respect, the opportunities for personal recognition in national civil services are much greater. In the view of the author, it would be appropriate for the Secretary-General to relax the rules pertaining to anonymity and to consider as may be appropriate releasing in public the names of persons who have contributed to important studies, reports, or proposals. Such permission should not be granted in case of acutely controversial subjects.

In these circumstances it is not surprising that there is a growing cynicism about the motivation of applicants for service in the Secretariat. For many, the relatively high pay (in comparison to most national administrations) appears to be the dominant consideration. The author does not wish to suggest that some applicants are not motivated by lofty ideals, just as he does not suggest that some members of the staff are not dedicated international civil servants of the highest professional calibre and integrity. At the same time it would be wrong to ignore the fact that some sectors of the Secretariat have become intellectual slums.

It is not surprising, perhaps, that few luminaries in the various fields of intellectual endeavour are now joining the Secretariat. This, of course, creates a vicious circle as lesser stars, too, are discouraged by the demise of the glamour or prestige element in the Organization.

Oscar Schachter, in a brilliant but rhapsodic essay written in 1970 and probably influenced by Schachter's own positive experience as Director of the General Legal Division and particularly as a close collaborator of Dag Hammarskjöld, although pointing to bureaucratic inhibitions, wrote of the "excitement and stimulation in a multinational service made up of people diverse in interest, background, and values yet compelled to face up to common problems and to work together," especially in the operational field.[43] One may well wonder how many contemporary members of the Secretariat share this feeling. Or how many members of the Secretariat deal with meaningful action, closer to results, as a consequence of which the official's role "whatever his echelon—will seem concrete, less concerned with verbal resolutions, more with events."[44] Schachter spoke of a coherent doctrine that combines various goals which can attract different supporters, each group finding its own benefit in the totality and of a skillful leadership which can impart a sense of mission to staff and Member States alike. But the Organization today lacks such a coherent doctrine and suffers from weak leadership. One cannot help but feel that the vision, directive wisdom, and courage of which Schachter spoke so eloquently are rapidly being replaced by politicized, opportunistic officials who promote their own particular ends, often in the absence of a coherent and meaningful doctrine.

Why do people stay in such a system? Many, however superficially cynical they become, retain a core of idealism; some are fortunate enough to keep an abiding interest in their work. There is also the expatriation factor, which grows stronger as children are born and enter into the pattern of life in New York, and which is strongest when there is a great contrast between the way of life, including standard of living, in the home country and that in New York (or Geneva, for that matter). It is also true that practising a profession in the Secretariat is very unlike practising it outside, since the aims of the Secretariat are often not the same as those of a government service, a private business, or a university, and the difference in aims means a difference of approach and attitude. After a certain number of years of United Nations service, an official has largely lost his professional contacts at home, and he also shrinks from the thought of the change of attitude he would have to make if he went back there. Finally, the Secretariat offers a modicum of security in an insecure world, especially when so many countries suffer from violent economic fluctuations and political instability. Some staff members who left to accept glittering posts outside wound up in prison. They were no encouragement for others to leave. And it is well known that once a person leaves, it may be impossible to come back.

---

[43] *Some Reflections On International Officialdom*, INTERNATIONAL ORGANIZATION: LAW IN MOVEMENT 53 Fawcett and Higgins, Eds., OXFORD U. PRESS, 1973).
[44] *Ibid.*, at 59.

7 The View from Geneva

Although the United Nations has a considerable number of offices away from Headquarters, including a major office in Vienna (UNIDO), UNEP in Nairobi, and the various regional economic commissions, we shall consider only the United Nations Office at Geneva (UNOG), which is, in terms of importance and manpower, the principal United Nations office outside of New York.

Functions

It should be observed that historically UNOG developed as a conference center for UN meetings and as a facility for the provision of secretariat and conference services for UN meetings held in Europe, the Middle East, Africa, and certain other locations. In the course of time, however, UNOG became the abode for a number of substantive divisions and organs such as ECE, the Commission on Narcotic Drugs, the International Narcotics Control Board, the Office of the United Nations High Commissioner for Refugees, the UN Conference on Trade and Development, the UN Fund for Drug Abuse Control, the UN Research Institute for Social Development, the Office of the UN Disaster Relief Coordinator, and the Human Rights Division. In addition to these, UNOG comprises the Office of the Director-General and a number of divisions such as Conference and General Services, and Administrative and Financial Services. UNOG is headed by an under-secretary-general–director-general who, *inter alia*, represents the Secretary-General in relations with permanent missions to the United Nations and the specialized agencies located in Geneva, as well as the Swiss federal, cantonal, and municipal authorities, and exercises responsibilities devolving upon the Secretary-General under international narcotics treaties for the operation of the international narcotics control system.[1] He does not have a clearly defined authority over the heads of the various substantive divisions located in Geneva. Given the distance from New York, the fact that the substantive divisions in Geneva receive instructions from Headquarters in New York on matters pertaining to the areas within their responsibility, and the lack of authority of the

---

[1] ST/SGB/Org./Sec.S, at 1 (Feb. 1976).

Director-General, the baronial powers of heads of departments, which are so apparent even at Headquarters, are considerably greater when it comes to heads of departments located in Geneva. There appears to be a fragmentation of substantive responsibility and central guidance in Geneva and, often, a lack of clarity concerning the exact meaning and scope of the central policy laid down at United Nations Headquarters. In these circumstances the potential for lack of coordination and even friction between the Director-General of UNOC and the Geneva administration, on the one hand, and heads of the substantive departments in Geneva, on the other hand, appears considerable.

Personnel Policy

As regards personnel policy, certain matters were delegated by the Secretary-General to the authority of UNOG.[2] Basically, the situation is as follows: despite the large concentration of staff in Geneva, the appointment and promotion procedures for professional staff continue to be centrally controlled and administered in New York. In particular, professional appointments (except of short-term staff) have to be brought to the appointment and promotion bodies in New York through the Office of Personnel Services in New York.

The principle of geographical distribution is applied centrally from New York for the Organization as a whole, including UNOG. This does not mean that the administration in Geneva is completely divorced from the appointment process. In the first place it should be observed that the processing of recruitment for professional posts in Geneva, including the preparation of a short list of candidates and of a specific recommendation regarding the preferred candidate, is done by the chief of the Personnel Division in Geneva in respect of all parts of UNOG except for UNCTAD. The chief of the Personnel Division of UNOG normally presents—in person—recommendations for promotions of UNOG officials to the appointment and promotion bodies in New York. For recruitment, although the processing of applications is done by the Personnel Division in Geneva, the decision is one of the central administration and not of Geneva.

Of the various substantive departments in Geneva, only UNCTAD processes its own recruitment through its own personnel officer. Historically, the reason for this situation was the insistence of the first Secretary-General of UNCTAD, Raul Prebisch of Argentina (one of the great barons of the Organization, who excelled in obtaining the support and the pressure of the developing nations for most of the demands that he chose to make on the central administration), on his power to control at least the

[2] ST/AI/234 (7 Jan. 1976); ST/SGB/151 (7 Jan. 1976).

processing of recruitment and the making of recommendations for the appointment of a candidate. Prebisch's argument was that, if recruitment processing was done by UNCTAD, this assured not only the speeding up of the process, but also a better coordination between the personnel administration and the people familiar with the substantive problems and job requirements.

There has been strong pressure on the part of the representatives of the staff for the setting up of an appointment and promotion committee in Geneva. The obvious problem that would arise from the establishment of a permanent appointment and promotion committee in Geneva would be that in the present circumstances, when the central personnel policy is not always entirely clear or made clear to the officers away from Headquarters, it might be difficult to maintain such a central policy. Indeed, there might be a danger of parochial interests prevailing. The question would be how to apply the same yardsticks to the decisions to be made. Given the feeling of the staff that candidates of the departments in New York are presented more forcefully and enjoy the advantage of being actually known to important senior officials whereas members of the Geneva staff are only names in the files—one possibility which has been suggested is for the central appointment and promotion bodies to meet from time to time in Geneva. The composition of these bodies could be modified for the Geneva meetings in such a way as to give a greater representation to members of the staff serving in Geneva. It should be recalled in this connection that the representatives of the staff in Geneva have repeatedly complained that members of the general service category in Geneva, who are recommended for promotion to the professional category, have to be screened twice, rather than only once; in the first place, in Geneva by the Geneva Appointment and Promotion Panel, and second, at Headquarters by the Appointment and Promotion Committee.

Although the trend is in the direction of the establishment in Geneva of a local appointment and promotion committee, there is a risk that such a committee might tend to deviate from central policies; but the main danger would be that it might come under undue pressure from the local barons.

We have already observed that the principle of geographical distribution is administered by UN Headquarters (Office of Personnel Services) in a centralized manner for the Secretariat as a whole. As a result, appointments recommended by Geneva are subjected by the Office of Personnel Services in New York—the watchdog of geographical distribution—and by the appointment and promotion bodies, not only to a scrutiny as to qualifications but also to an examination of the effect of the proposed appointment on the overall geographical composition of the staff. We have also observed, in an earlier chapter, that although in theory the principle of geographical distribution is administered for the Secretariat as a whole, and not separately for every department, it has been the policy of the Secretary-General to have as wide a spread of various nationalities in the departments as possible and, in particular, not to allow the gross over-representation of a particular nationality in a department as a whole or in its upper echelons. The Geneva Office is in a rather special situation for it is a parallel headquarters of the UN and a conglomeration of substantive and administrative departments outside Headquarters in New York. Geneva administrators have expressed the view that the selection of the best available people in Geneva is subjected by Headquarters in New York so strictly to the principle of geographical distribution that qualifications assume a clearly secondary role in relation to nationality. In contacts with the Geneva administration, some delegations, including that of the Soviet Union, have taken the approach that it is not enough if their nationals have reached a certain percentage of the staff of the Secretariat as a whole and that they should represent at least the same percentage in UNOG. In theory at least the administration in Geneva is reluctant to deal with national delegations concerning matters of recruitment of their nationals to UNOG on the basis of claims of underrepresentation in Geneva, and stresses that, as a matter of law, the principle of geographical distribution applies to the Secretariat as a whole. Nevertheless, whenever any delegation finds that the causes of the representation of its nationals would be furthered if if were to stress their underrepresentation in the Geneva Office, it does not hesitate to do so. Given the fact that the administration in Geneva would like to have a wide spread of nationalities there, it cannot be said that such representations do not yield results.

It should, however, be observed that in addition to pressure from states for increased hiring of their nationals in UNOG there may be very good nonpolitical reasons for the differences between the composition of the staff in Geneva and in the Secretariat as a whole. Thus, it is well known that for family, cultural, and educational reasons, nationals of Western European countries have often expressed preference for a posting in Geneva. On the other hand, for a long time, nationals of Latin American, North American, and Caribbean countries have not expressed interest in serving in Geneva and have often preferred Headquarters in New York. It is, therefore, not surprising that the percentage of nationals of states belonging to the Western European region serving in Geneva in May, 1976, was 18.89 percent above the midpoint of the regional desirable range as it existed on 30 June 1975 and 18.99 percent above their actual representation in the UN Secretariat as a whole on that date (see Table 7–1). Nationals of the North American and Caribbean region were, in May, 1976, 9.53 percent below the desirable range as it existed on 30 June 1975 and 11.33 percent below their actual representation in the Secretariat as a

Table 7–1
Percentage of Staff by Region in the United Nations Office in Geneva

	Percentage of Staff by Region in the United Nations Office in Geneva in Established Posts, Including UNCTAD but excluding Language Staff and ECE[a]	Midpoint of Desirable Range	Staff Position in the Secretariat as a Whole
Africa	8.11	7.8	11.1
Asia and the Far East	8.69	19.9	14.5
Europe (Eastern)	11.59	16.2	11.5
Europe (Western)	42.89	24.0	23.9
Latin America	7.24	6.7	8.6
Middle East	2.60	3.7	5.0
North America and Caribbean	12.17	21.7	23.5
Others	6.66		1.8

[a] Based on figures given to the author by the Secretariat in Geneva in May, 1976. The second and the third columns are as presented in A/10184, Annex, Table 2, and reflect the situation as of 30 June 1975.

whole on 30 June 1975. Given the fact that these figures do not include the Economic Commission for Europe which, in accordance with the accepted policy, should be staffed predominantly by nationals of the countries of the region, the percentage of nationals of the Western European region appears to be too high and a concerted effort should be made by the Secretariat to introduce a somewhat more balanced representation. It will, of course, not be easy to attain this objective since Western European nationals continue to prefer to be posted in Geneva.

The Economic Commission for Europe and its "Regionalization"

Let us now turn to the situation that prevails in ECE. It may be recalled that, in 1970, the Secretary-General expressed the view that the secretariats of the economic commissions should be based on a desirable "mix" of 75 percent staff from their own region and 25 percent from other regions.[3] The term "from their own region" is of course ambiguous as illustrated by the case of ECE. States which are members of ECE belong to no less than five regional groups as defined for the purposes of the geographi-

[3] A/8156, 25 GAOR, Agenda Item 82, at 7.

cal distribution of the staff. In addition to Eastern Europe and Western Europe, members of ECE belong to the regions of the Middle East (Cyprus and Turkey), North America and Caribbean, and "others" (Switzerland). If the criterion for the definition of the term "region" in the report of the Secretary-General was not geographical but institutional, that is, membership in a particular economic commission, less than 1 percent of the professional staff of ECE was from countries which are not members of the commission.[4] Even if "region" were to be defined in a broad "European" sense as comprising the Eastern and Western European regions, Switzerland, Cyprus, and Turkey, about 87 percent of the staff of ECE are "European" nationals and about 13 percent are nationals of countries belonging to other geographical regions, that is, North America and the Caribbean, Asia and the Far East. Finally, an observation should be made about the relationship between the Western European and Eastern European nationals on the staff of the commission. At the end of April, 1976, nationals of the Western European countries represented 44.54 percent of the staff of ECE, while nationals of the Eastern European countries represented 34.54 percent of the staff of the commission. What is of particular significance, however, is the fact that both the executive secretary of ECE (a Yugoslav; his predecessor too was a Yugoslav) and his deputy (USSR) are nationals of countries with centrally planned socialist economies. Indeed, it appears that the Soviet Union and other Eastern European countries have made a particularly determined effort to staff the Secretariat of ECE with as many Eastern European nationals as possible, presumably in order to have a greater influence on the substantive work of ECE.

We have already observed that less than 1 percent of the staff of the commission belongs to states that are not members of ECE. Indeed, there have been forces favouring a 100 percent regionalization of the staff of the commission. What are the reasons for this? In the first place, ECE is the most technically advanced and sophisticated of all the regional economic commissions. It operates through branch committees dealing with complex technological questions such as the steel committee, chemical industry committee, or the committee on coal or on gas. This structure of ECE has necessitated the development of a very specialized staff which serves the branch committees. The staff must enjoy the confidence of the Member States represented on the various branch committees. It has been said that in technology, there is more in common between East and West than between North and South. The factor of confidence, the fear of competition with countries such as Japan and Australia, and even the desire to protect technological secrets have been important factors in the reluc-

---

[4] Based on figures prepared by the ECE Secretariat and reflecting established professional posts as of 29 April 1976.

tance of ECE to go beyond the membership of the commission in recruiting staff to its Secretariat. Still the fact that less than 1 percent of the staff of ECE belongs to states not members of ECE is certainly contrary to the spirit of the Secretary-General's statement about "desirable mix" and may be counterproductive in terms of the global interests that ECE should take into account.

Staff-Management Relations

Finally, some remarks about the question of staff-management relations in Geneva. In the UN Headquarters in New York, staff-management relations are good on the whole and the Joint Advisory Committee—consisting of the representatives of the Secretary-General and the representatives of the Staff Council—established by the Secretary-General in accordance with Staff Regulation VIII and Staff Rule 108.2, performs an essential role in the discussion of personnel policies and of general questions pertaining to staff welfare, and in advising the Secretary-General on such matters and especially on proposed changes in personnel policy prior to their promulgation and implementation. In Geneva, however, the Joint Advisory Committee does not appear to fulfill the same useful and constructive role. Not only is it less frequently convened, but moreover, it seems that in Geneva it serves primarily as a forum for airing staff complaints rather than for a joint discussion of personnel policy before it is finally decided upon. Naturally, given the fact that personnel policies are formulated in New York, the Director-General of UNOG has a more difficult role in that he must remain faithful to a policy already decided upon at Headquarters. The area reserved to his competence is, of course, limited. Nevertheless, even after all due allowance is made for these considerations, it appears that the tensions which prevail in Geneva between staff and management are at least in part due to formal, hierarchical, even patronizing, attitudes on the part of the administration and perhaps also to a more politically oriented attitude on the part of some members of the staff. It would be interesting to speculate to what extent the malaise in staff-management relations is affected by the rather more formal Geneva environment. A greater psychological effort is needed on the part of the Director-General and his senior aides to establish a constructive dialogue with the staff.

The problem is further complicated by lack of proper coordination, in negotiations with the staff, among the United Nations and the various specialized agencies in Geneva. A militant group of staff which advocated active trade union tactics, including a strike of the general service category in spring, 1976, has contributed towards radicalization of the "official" staff bodies in Geneva. In the past, trade union tactics had not been acceptable to many staff members as incompatible with their obligations as international civil servants. The experience of the strike in Geneva suggests that the administration will have to learn how to deal with the trade union type of bargaining.[5]

---

[5] The Joint Inspection Unit proposed that a sole negotiator with unqualified powers (except that any decision having financial implications exceeding the existing budgetary provisions should be subject to approval by the General Assembly and the general conferences of the various organizations) should be appointed by the United Nations and the specialized agencies in Geneva to conduct negotiations with staff representatives. See JIU REPORT ON SOME ASPECTS OF THE STRIKE AT THE UNITED NATIONS OFFICE AT GENEVA FROM 25 FEBRUARY TO 3 MARCH 1976, JIU/REP/76/6 at 18–19 (1976). Regarding the crisis in communication and in confidence as well as the absence of any real dialogue based on understanding and mutual trust between the heads of UNOG and the staff, see *ibid.*, at 21–25. JIU suggested that official recognition be granted (in addition to the official staff association) to such other associations or unions that the staff has freely decided to form. See *ibid.*, at 24.

8   Equality of Women

Even a cursory look at the statistics contained in the 1975 report of the Secretary-General on the composition of the Secretariat shows that the situation of women in the Secretariat is unsatisfactory. That year, women comprised 54.2 percent of the staff in the general service category,[1] but only 19.4 percent of the staff in the professional category and above.[2] The proportion of women in senior grades is even lower. There was one woman assistant-secretary-general for 15 men at that grade, 2 women at the D–2 level for 69 men, 7 D–1 (for 196 men), 41 women at the P–5 level (for 415 men).[3]

That the situation of women is now recognized as being unsatisfactory, even intolerable, and has become a public issue, is due in no small part to the growing awareness of women, the impact of the women's liberation movement in the United States, the raising of the consciousness of women in the Secretariat and—following that—in the national delegations as a result of the work done by the (staff) Ad Hoc Group on Equal Rights for Women [4] and the important UNITAR studies on women in the United Nations.[5] The author will not address the material already covered in these studies, but concentrate on the current situation and problems.

The Charter basis for the equality between sexes in the Secretariat is, of course, Article 8, according to which the United Nations shall place no restrictions on the eligibility of men and women to participate in any capacity and under conditions of equality in its principal and subsidiary organs. Under Article 7, the Secretariat is one of the principal organs of the United Nations, to which Article 8 applies. We have already alluded to the intention of the Founding Fathers to have full equality for women in the employment of the United Nations.[6]

Elimination of "Statutory" Discrimination

Nevertheless, equality of women in the Secretariat has been slow in com-

---

[1] A/10184, Annex, Table 20(B).

[2] *Ibid.*, Table 19.

[3] *Ibid.*, Table 20(A).

[4] See Tsien, *The Struggle for the Improvement of the Situation of Women in the United Nations Secretariat*, WOMEN AND THE UN, 7 UNITAR NEWS 22 (No. 1, 1975).

[5] SZALAI, THE SITUATION OF WOMEN IN THE UNITED NATIONS, UNITAR RESEARCH REPORT No. 18 (1973); WOMEN AND THE UN, 7 UNITAR NEWS (No. 1, 1975).

[6] See *supra* Chapter 1, note 4.

ing, not only in practice (this, as will be seen, has not been achieved as yet), but also even in statutory provisions, in the staff regulations and rules. This was made obvious by the case of *Mullan v. The Secretary General*,[7] decided by the Administrative Tribunal of the United Nations in October, 1972. This case involved an appeal by a woman staff member against the practice, established under Staff Rule 107.5(a) consistently with Staff Regulation 7.1, whereby a woman staff member could claim payment of her husband's travel expenses on home leave only when the husband was dependent on her, while a male staff member could claim such payment for his wife whatever her total occupational earnings. The tribunal observed that Staff Rule 107.5(a), applying a traditional sociological and economic yardstick, assumed that the wife is always dependent, departing from the legal criterion used in another rule for a dependent husband. The tribunal noted that Article 8 of the Charter, on which the applicant relied, was of great historic scope, marking an orientation towards equality of sexes. It contains a rule that is legally binding on the organs of the United Nations, but the responsibility for its implementation falls upon those who are competent to make rules applicable to the staff. While rejecting the claim of Mrs. Mullan, the tribunal made the following statement which had a major impact on the subsequent establishment of equality between sexes in the various staff rules and regulations:

In any event, by making a distinction between wife and husband for the payment of travel expenses in connexion with home leave, the Staff Rules establish a distinction by reason of sex between staff members, and this distinction would appear contrary to the principle of equal conditions of employment enunciated in Article 8 of the Charter. While it is the responsibility of the Secretary-General to implement that principle with regard to payment of a spouse's travel under Staff Regulation 7.1 and while he possesses a wide discretion in this respect, his discretion must be exercised in accordance with Article 8 of the Charter.[8]

Soon after the adoption by the Administrative Tribunal of the decision in the *Mullan* case, the General Assembly expressed, in Resolution 3007 (XXVII) (1972), the desire to ensure that, in accordance with Article 8 of the Charter, no restrictions are placed on the eligibility of men and women to participate in any capacity and under conditions of equality in the work of the Secretariat. The General Assembly requested the Secretary-General to submit a study of those provisions of the staff rules and staff regulations, which, if applied, might give rise to discrimination between staff members on grounds of sex. The Secretary-General did submit such a study to the twenty-eighth session of the General Assembly in 1973.[9]

He reported that the staff rules and regulations contained a number of

---

[7] Judgment No. 162.

[8] At 394.

[9] A/C.5/1519.

distinctions based on sex in regard to the conditions of service under which the staff members of the United Nations are appointed. Such differentiation related to travel entitlements and separation payments. With the sole exception of maternity leave, the distinctions arose out of the traditional concept of the husband as the breadwinner in the family. A different treatment was thus applied to men and women with regard to the determination of the dependent spouse. The Secretary-General concluded by observing that, in the light of contemporary thinking on the relative values to be attached to equality of men and women under the law as compared to other notions, there was "a compelling reason for eliminating present distinctions based on sex from the statutory provisions governing the employment of the staff of the United Nations."[10] Following agreement in the Administrative Committee on Co-ordination (ACC), the Secretary-General presented to the twenty-ninth session of the General Assembly (1974) specific proposals for the elimination of differential treatment based on sex in staff regulations and rules.[11] The suggested amendments to the staff regulations were adopted by the General Assembly in Resolution 3353 (XXIX), which also took note of the corresponding changes made by the Secretary-General in the staff rules.[12]

Another area where differentiation was made between the benefit entitlements of male and female participants was in the Joint Staff Pension Fund. The main differentiation was in the survivor's benefits, in that in the case of male participants the entitlements were automatic but, for women, proof was required that the surviving widower was without means to support himself and was unable by reason of age or infirmity to engage in substantial gainful employment.[13] The Joint Staff Pension Board proposed in 1974, as a first step, to eliminate this differentiation in circumstances where the staff member died in service or retired because of disability.[14] Subsequently, in furtherance of the implementation of the principle of equal treatment of male and female staff, the board proposed in 1975 to the General Assembly an amendment to the fund's regulations designed to provide to widowers benefits identical to those payable to widows. It also proposed to the General Assembly to remove the differences in entitlement to residual benefits.[15] The board also decided to abolish all differences, based on the sex of the participant, in the amounts pay-

---

[10] *Ibid.*, at 10.

[11] A/C.5/1603.

[12] See also *infra* note 16.

[13] See REGULATIONS AND RULES OF THE UNITED NATIONS JOINT STAFF PENSION FUND, JSPB/G.4/Rev. 7, Articles 35–36.

[14] REPORT OF THE UNITED NATIONS JOINT STAFF PENSION BOARD, 29 GAOR, Supp. No. 9 (A/9609), at 15.

[15] See REGULATIONS AND RULES OF THE UNITED NATIONS JOINT STAFF PENSION FUND, JSPB/G.4/Rev.7, Article 39; REPORT OF THE UNITED NATIONS JOINT STAFF PENSION BOARD, 30 GAOR, Supp. No. 9 (A/10009), at 6–7 and Annex VII.

able under the regulations and resulting from applying different actuarial factors to the calculations. Since the longevity of women is calculated to exceed that of men, this is one of the instances where complete equality might not be beneficial to women.

By Resolution 3526 (XXX) (1975), the General Assembly approved the amendments to the regulations of the United Nations Joint Staff Pension Fund proposed by the board. With this resolution, the principle of equality between the male and female staff members was finally established on the "statute" books of the United Nations, some 30 years after the founding of the Organization.[16]

Equal Opportunity for Employment: Legislative Background

Let us now turn our attention from entitlements and benefits under the various regulations to equal opportunity for employment in the Secretariat.

For some 25 years the General Assembly, representing the Member States of the United Nations, did not devote any attention in its resolutions on the composition of the Secretariat to the situation of women staff members. Had the General Assembly given the situation of women but a small part of the loving care it gave the principle of geographical distribution, the situation today would have been far better.

For the first time, in 1970, the General Assembly adopted a resolution, the text of which had been proposed by the Economic and Social Council (in Resolution 1510 [XLVIII]), concerning employment of qualified women in senior and other professional positions by the secretariats of organizations in the United Nations system (Resolution 2715 [XXV]). The resolution was a positive step and an urgently needed one. Recalling the Universal Declaration of Human Rights and the Declaration on the Elimination of Discrimination against Women, the resolution expressed the hope that the United Nations would set an example with regard to the opportunities afforded for the employment of women at senior and other professional levels, urged the United Nations to take appropriate measures to ensure equal opportunities for the employment of qualified women in such positions, and requested the Secretary-General to include in his re-

---

[16] In pursuance of the policy to eliminate differential treatment based on sex in the staff regulations and rules—see ST/SGB/Staff Rules/1/Rev. 2/Amend. 3—detailed amendments have been incorporated in the 1976 revised edition of staff rules. See ST/SGB/Staff Rules/1/Rev. 3. These amendments have substituted in the English text all references in the masculine gender by pronouns of both the masculine and feminine gender or by common terms that would be suitable in the context. Other consequential amendments concern travel expenses and repatriation grants. See also A/C.5/31/4(1976).

port to the General Assembly on the composition of the Secretariat data on the employment of women, including their numbers and the positions they occupied. The General Assembly adopted additional resolutions on the employment of women in 1972 (Resolution 3009 [XXVII]), and in 1974 (Resolution 3352 [XXIX]). The latter resolution noted that the UNITAR [SZALAI] Report had confirmed that an imbalance existed in the proportion of women at the higher levels and showed the unequal progress of women and men staff members in terms of promotion in the Secretariat. The resolution expressed concern at the lack of an equitable balance between men and women at senior levels including those of under-secretary-general and assistant-secretary-general and requested the Secretary-General to make efforts to achieve an equitable balance between men and women staff members before the end of the second United Nations Development Decade (end of the seventies) and to give increased attention to the recruitment and promotion of women and to the assignments given to them. It did not, however, define what was meant by "equitable balance."

In 1975, the World Conference of the International Women's Year, held in Mexico, adopted a resolution on the situation of women in the employ of the United Nations and specialized agencies, which we have already discussed in Chapter 3.[17]

The Secretary-General reported to the General Assembly in 1975 that, although some progress had been made in the recruitment of women in terms both of numbers and of levels and although the absolute number of women in professional and senior posts was somewhat higher than in the preceding year, the proportion of women was somewhat lower. Given the disparity between various countries and regions concerning the availability of women candidates, the Secretary-General expressed the belief that no real progress would be possible so long as the recruitment of women was subject to the guidelines of geographical distribution. The Secretary-General drew the attention of the Assembly to a number of relevant factors: there was a scarcity of qualified women candidates in certain professions; in some geographical areas there were cultural inhibitions to the candidacy of women; governments put forward very few names of women; family considerations intervened when both spouses were professionals; and there were competing priorities, such as geographical distribution.[18]

It was against this background that a group of countries, several of them overrepresented, led by Australia and Iran, presented to the thirtieth session of the General Assembly (1975) an important draft resolution (A/C.5/L.1257) establishing a desirable initial goal of 30 percent for the proportion of women in the professional grades by 1980. The draft introduced a regional, rather than a purely national, approach to the recruitment of women in that it requested the Secretary-General to set aside during each of the next two (budget) biennia 1976–77 and 1978–79 a number of posts subject to geographical distribution equivalent to 5 percent of the midpoint of the desirable range of each region for the appointment of qualified women, with special attention being given to candidates from underrepresented and unrepresented countries.

In the course of the debate in the Fifth Committee, the draft resolution was progressively watered down. Underrepresented countries expressed strong suspicions about the proposed application of the principle of geographical distribution on a regional basis. Thus, the delegate of the Federal Republic of Germany argued that the need to appoint a growing number of women must not lead to a change in the desirable range of Member States and that the first priority must be to do away with underrepresentation. Similarly, the delegate of Japan spoke against a special quota for women. He regarded the proposals as designed to circumvent the principle of geographical distribution. The delegate of the German Democratic Republic emphasized that women must be recruited in full equality with men candidates in application of the principle of equitable geographical distribution. The delegate of the Soviet Union disagreed with the suggestion made in the report of the Secretary-General that a real breakthrough in the employment of women in professional posts would not be possible so long as the recruitment of women was subject to the guidelines of geographical distribution. To believe that was, in his opinion, tantamount to attempting to evade the Charter principle of equitable geographical distribution. Such an approach would favour overrepresented countries. The procedure used in recruiting women must remain compatible with the principle of geographical distribution and be applied within the limits of the desirable range established for each Member State. Other delegates, however, were willing to give priority to the need to give preference to female candidates (for example, Norway), to a positive discrimination in favor of women (for example, the Netherlands), to affirmative action.

While watering down the original draft resolution, the goal of 30 percent for the proportion of women in the Secretariat by 1980 was dropped. Resolution 3416 (XXX) reaffirmed that the equitable distribution of positions between men and women in the Secretariat was a major principle governing the recruitment policy of the United Nations, urged Member States to recommend qualified women candidates for professional posts, requested the Secretary-General to intensify recruitment missions in order to increase the number of women candidates for such posts, and recommended that the Secretary-General pay special attention in the staff development programme to training that would assist women in increasing their career opportunities. The central provision of the resolution, operative paragraph 3, was considerably weaker than in the original draft. The Secretary-General was requested to make every effort during each of the next two biennia, that is through 1979, to fill a number of posts subject to geographical distribution equivalent to 5 percent of the midpoint of the desirable range of each region by appointing qualified women. Priority was to be given to candidates from unrepresented or underrepresented countries, "while not adversely affecting opportunities for the recruitment of qualified men" from those countries. The resolution thus establishes a desirable regional target for the appointment of women. The stress on the priority to be given to candidates from underrepresented countries reflects, of course, the anxiety of these countries that overrepresented countries from their regions would take advantage of the emphasis on the recruitment of women in order to increase still further their own participation in the Secretariat. It is, however, often the overrepresented countries from various regions that have a large supply of qualified candidates, including women. (Women candidates are usually found in Western Europe, North America, and in overrepresented developing countries such as Iran, the Philippines, Egypt, India, Pakistan, and Sri Lanka.) The emphasis that the target established should not adversely affect the opportunities for recruitment of qualified men greatly weakens this resolution. How is the Secretary-General supposed to act when he has a qualified woman candidate from an overrepresented country whom he could, however, recruit within the "regional quota," and a qualified man or even a somewhat less qualified man from an unrepresented or underrepresented country within the same region? Given the strong likelihood that he will give preference to the man from the underrepresented country, the effectiveness of the resolution appears to be questionable.

The Reality

We have seen, so far, that the United Nations has eliminated from its statute books provisions that discriminated against women. We have also seen that the General Assembly committed itself to improving the situation of women staff members in practice and that it accepted the principle that an equitable balance between men and women staff members should be established by the end of the present decade. The thirtieth session of the General Assembly also approved a regional recruitment target for women for the next two budget cycles. But what is the situation in practice? Let us look at recent statistical data gathered by the Joint Advisory

Committee's Standing Committee on the Employment of Women in the Secretariat[19] (hereinafter "standing committee"). Unless otherwise indicated, the statistical data used in this chapter have been collected by or for the standing committee. (These data also include staff on special missions.)

Let us first look at the breakdown of the professional Secretariat staff by sex and department, as it existed on 15 December 1974. On that date women constituted 19.55 percent of the professional staff members. In many departments and offices, the percentage of women was much lower (for example, in the regional economic commissions, UNEP, UNCTAD, UNIDO, and several offices in Headquarters, such as the Office of Legal Affairs).

The situation of women was even more discouraging if we look at the distribution of staff members by grade and by sex. Women represented about one-quarter of the staff at the P–3 level, but in higher grades the proportion dropped sharply. At the P–4 level, women represented about 14 percent of the staff, at the P–5 level less than 10 percent, and at the D–1 and D–2 levels less than 4 percent.[20]

If such is the situation, it is obvious that tremendous efforts would be required to bring about a significant improvement in the proportion of women in the professional grades and especially in higher grades. It would be necessary to ensure that a great number of the net yearly additions to the professional category should be women. But the standing committee's recruitment figures for the period July, 1973 to June, 1974, indicate that no improvement has occurred in the number and in the percentage of women recruited to professional posts and that those who were recruited during that period were recruited only up to and including the P–3 level.

Women were also at a considerable numerical disadvantage in the appointments to occupations in which qualified women are not scarce (for example, sociology, administration, information).

The fact is that the number of women appointees is only slightly higher

[19] This standing committee was established by the Joint Advisory Committee following a proposal made in the Fifth Committee during the twenty-ninth session of the General Assembly and accepted by the Secretary-General. A/9980, paras. 72–74. The committee is headed by a chairperson, designated by JAC, and consists of three persons designated by the representatives of the Secretary-General and three persons designated by the representatives of the Staff Council. Its mandate is to recommend measures to end any employment policies or practices that discriminate between men and women and to ensure equality of opportunity. Specifically, it is to make recommendations on concrete administrative steps to be taken in order to achieve an equitable balance between men and women staff members at all levels before the end of the second UN Development Decade, on measures to encourage and promote the employment of women in the professional and higher categories, including policymaking positions, on improvements in recruitment, training, career development, promotion, and on other relevant matters.

[20] As regards the situation on 30 June 1975, see A/10184, Annex, Tables 19–20.

than that of women separated from the Organization. According to data prepared by the Secretariat (unpublished), in the period June, 1974, to July, 1975, 51 women were separated from the Organization, 17 from language posts and 34 from posts subject to geographical distribution (the latter included 5 on secondment to other organizations who therefore may or may not return to the Secretariat). During the period July, 1974, to June, 1975, only 64 women were appointed to the Secretariat, 27 to language posts and 37 to posts subject to geographical distribution.

The appointment of a woman—in September, 1972—to the post of assistant-secretary-general (in charge of the Centre for Social Development and Humanitarian Affairs) resulted to a large extent from the growing pressure for the appointment of a woman to the rank of under-secretary-general or assistant-secretary-general. Though a positive step, this appointment represents only a token gesture which means little in terms of the overall improvement of the situation of women in the Secretariat. So far, this appointment has not been followed by the appointment of women to other senior positions.

Let us now look at the (standing committee's) data pertaining to promotions. An analysis of the grades reached by male and female staff members who were P–1s and P–2s in 1954 and were still on the staff as of 30 June 1974 reveals that about 64 percent of the women had stayed in grades up to and including P–4, while only about 39 percent of the men had remained in these relatively low grades. Thus, women in the Secretariat have been promoted much more slowly than men. The promotion figures are also disappointing if we look at the more recent trends in the years 1970–1974. The proportion of women promoted to the P–5 level has in fact declined during this period. During these five years, 62 men were promoted to D–1 as against only 2 women. It is difficult to imagine that there could have been such a disparity between the availability of men and women candidates qualified for promotion. It should be pointed out that the higher percentage of women up to and including the P–3 level results *inter alia* from many promotions of women from the general service category (where there are more women to begin with) to the professional category, usually to P–2. They then get usually one longevity promotion to P–3, where they remain, sometimes for lack of full professional qualifications.

The Causes of the Disadvantaged Position of Women

What are the causes of the disadvantaged position of women in the Secretariat?

In the first place, it should be observed that there is a scarcity of women candidates in various highly technical and specialized areas, in which there is a considerable demand for recruits. According to the information provided to the Fifth Committee by the Secretariat on 1 December 1975, the percentage of women candidates varied substantially according to occupation, ranging from 39 percent in library sciences to 4 percent in economics and 0 percent in natural sciences and engineering.[21] There are, of course, countries where women can be found in such professions, but these countries are either overrepresented (certain Western countries, or some overrepresented developing countries), or, if underrepresented (for example, the Soviet Union), they appear reluctant to send career women abroad, except in a very few cases. The recruitment of women is thus hampered by the need to apply the principle of geographical distribution and by national attitudes, often traditional and retrogressive, concerning the employment of women. It is more difficult to obtain women candidates where both spouses are professionals; while a woman professional often agrees to interrupt her own career in order to enable her husband to take up employment abroad, husbands are seldom willing to make similar concessions. Indeed, even when it comes to the employment of women within their own countries, there are cultural and social inhibitions in many countries. The UNITAR study observed, with respect to data from 53 countries, that there did not seem to be any country where women had an even approximately equal share with men in professional administrative posts. The United Nations Secretariat ranked very high in the UNITAR listing (it occupied the second place, below France and above Hungary).[22] If the United Nations is a reflection of its Member States, the percentage of women employed in the United Nations and also possibly their distribution by grade would not be unsatisfactory. But the United Nations has to live up to the high standards set by Article 8 of the Charter and is supposed to set an example to national societies. The United Nations has set such an example in the establishment of a complete legal equality between the sexes and in giving women in the Secretariat liberal maternity leave entitlements.[23] This is in line with liberal leave entitlements granted in general to United Nations personnel.

The United Nations must now exert greater efforts to also set an example in recruitment and promotion practices. Cultural, social, and political attitudes of countries with regard to the employment of women in general and with respect to the employment of women abroad in particular

[21] A/C.5/XXX/CRP.13.

[22] SZALAI, *supra* note 5, at 4–5 (1973).

[23] A 1976 REPORT OF THE SPECIAL COMMITTEE ON EQUAL OPPORTUNITIES FOR WOMEN WITHIN THE UNDP recommended that mothers who wish to remain at home and look after their newborn infants be granted parental leave without pay for a maximum of two years, but saw no reason why such an entitlement should not be extended to fathers. Attachment to UNDP/ADM/FIELD/429, UNDP/ADM/HQTRS/249, at 18–19.

are reflected in the distribution by nationality of women candidates in the roster of candidates maintained by the Secretariat (see Table 8–1, prepared by the Secretariat). As of 1 November 1975, out of a total of 4,525 candidates, there were 239 women on the roster, that is, less than 6 percent. Even more significantly, although the candidates on the roster were from 118 countries, women candidates were only from 52 countries.[24]

The roster contains a good many candidates who have applied to the United Nations directly. Since, however, states play a very important role in facilitating the actual recruitment of their nationals, it is of particular interest to examine the composition of the staff by sex and nationality. According to data of the standing committee reflecting the composition of staff as it existed on 31 December 1974, in the region of Africa, out of 37 states, there were no female staff members from as many as 24 states (64.86 percent); in the region of Asia and the Far East, out of 19 states, there were no female staff members from as many as 12 states (63.15 percent); in the region of Eastern Europe, out of 10 states, there were no female staff members from as many as 6 states (60 percent); in the region of Western Europe, out of 18 states, there were no female staff members from 4 states (22.22 percent); in the region of Latin America, out of 20 states, there were no female staff members from 5 states (25 percent); in the region of the Middle East, out of 11 countries, there were no female staff members from 5 countries (45.45 percent); in the region of North America and the Caribbean, out of 7 countries, there were no female staff members only from 1 country (14.28 percent).

The above data confirm that a great disparity exists between the various regions as regards the proportion of women among the staff members belonging to each region. In some regions, such as Africa and Asia and the Far East, there may be serious difficulties in finding qualified female candidates, although such difficulties cannot entirely explain or justify the fact that there is not a single woman staff member from so many countries in these regions. Of course, there are cultural and social difficulties, but, although these could explain the persistence of an unsatisfactory ratio between the number of men and women staff members from certain countries, they cannot be accepted as an explanation for the total absence of female staff members from some countries. The situation as regards Eastern Europe is even more deplorable, for, in that region, there is no scarcity of highly qualified women in almost every field. Despite some improvement, the situation continues to be discouraging even with regard to those states of the Eastern European region that have some women on the staff of the United Nations. Thus, according to these data, on 31 December 1974 only 3.2 percent of the nationals of the Soviet Union in the Secretariat were women (1.3 percent of the Soviet nationals in posts subject to

[24] See *supra* note 21.

Table 8–1
Women Candidates on the Roster by Region and by Number of Nationalities

Region	Totals		Women			
	Number of Candidates	Number of Nationalities	Number of Candidates	Number of Nationalities	% of Candidates	% of Nationalities
Africa	330	35	12	8	3.6	22.8
Asia and Far East	800	17	31	8	3.8	47.0
Europe (Eastern)	488	10	12	5	2.4	50.0
Europe (Western)	1,389	18	64	12	4.6	66.6
Latin America	365	19	24	13	6.6	68.4
Middle East	109	11	6	3	5.5	27.3
North America and Caribbean	1,007	8	89	3	8.8	37.5
Others	37	–	1	–		
	4,525	118	239	52		

geographical distribution). Since the recruitment from the Soviet Union and other Eastern European countries is arranged through the governments, these governments bear a special responsibility for putting their own houses in order so as to make possible the implementation of Article 8 of the Charter.

In a recent letter sent by the chief of the Secretariat Recruitment Service (SRS) to resident representatives of UNDP and to the United Nations Information Centers in order to secure their assistance in reaching women candidates, it was pointed out that approximately 300 professionals, excluding language specialists, are recruited each year, that recruitment within each occupational category is small, except in the case of economists (40 percent of the total recruitment) and statisticians and demographers (10 percent of the total recruitment). Given the occupational breakdown of the skills most required in the Secretariat, the constraints imposed by the principle of geographical distribution, and the passive or even negative attitude of many states towards the recruitment of women to the Secretariat, it is obvious that a real improvement in the present situation will require a far greater cooperation on the part of Member States and a more flexible application of the principle of geographical distribution.

In May, 1974, the Secretary-General addressed a letter to non-governmental organizations (NGOs), asking for help in finding qualified women candidates. In March 1975, the director of the Division of Recruitment in the Secretariat addressed an individual letter to countries whose delegates spoke in the Fifth Committee in favour of the increased participation of women in the work of the United Nations asking for their governments' active cooperation in finding qualified women candidates and for more names of women candidates for the candidates' roster. States were thus asked to follow up their rhetoric with action. These letters do not appear to have brought about tangible results, although it is possible that at some point in the future the efforts made by the Secretariat will start producing a snowballing effect. Yet, this writer feels that far greater pressures on states are needed to ensure that they actively present and support candidatures of women.

Appeals alone just will not do. But, if countries interested in getting their nationals into the Secretariat would be convinced that the prospects for the recruitment of their nationals would be much higher if the candidate were a woman, better results would be attained. The Secretariat's efforts and pressures should be focused on countries that have no women on the staff and on those that have a very low percentage of women in the Secretariat. Groups concerned with the equality of women in the Secretariat should regularly publish the list of states that have poor records for the employment of their female nationals in the Secretariat. The writer is rather pessimistic about the immediate prospects and fears that many years will pass until we witness a real improvement in the situation. Few women candidates have applied for employment in the United Nations even in those areas where the principle of geographical distribution has not been a major inhibiting factor, namely, in the area of technical assistance.

Indeed, in the aforementioned letter of March, 1975, the director of the Division of Recruitment, in asking for cooperation in finding qualified women candidates, drew the attention of governments to the fact that recruitment in the area of technical assistance was not limited by considerations of geographical distribution. It may be observed that the Technical Assistance Recruitment Service of the Secretariat (TARS) has played a positive and active role in fostering candidatures by women and in hiring qualified women. The International Recruitment Reader issued by TARS pointed to the evident need for increasing the participation of women in programmes of technical cooperation. TARS invited national recruitment services to nominate women for vacancies in technical cooperation programmes. In addition to appealing to governments to nominate women candidates, TARS has sent letters to various organizations and individuals requesting their cooperation in this matter and has given wide publicity to its search for women to work as technical experts in developing countries. Yet, despite all such attempts, it appears that this recent campaign to bring women into the technical cooperation work of the United Nations has so far produced meager results. Although the Secretariat was flooded with applications, most of these came from just one country (Philippines) and few applications revealed significant qualifications. This indicates, of course, that, even when the Secretariat makes determined efforts to recruit women, and even where the geographical distribution is not a formal requirement (although naturally, TARS is trying to attain a good geographic spread among its experts), the scarcity of qualified women in various technical areas combined with hesitations on the part of women about working in developing countries (work in the Secretariat proper is likely to involve fewer anxieties) resulted in difficulties in recruitment even in such progressive countries as the Netherlands.

Although the results of the 1975 survey conducted by the Ad Hoc Group on Equal Rights for Women are not conclusive on many questions and do not necessarily represent the majority opinion of the professional staff, they indicate that the bulk of women respondents in the Secretariat felt that their sex adversely affected their prospects for promotion.[25]

From talks with professional women in the Secretariat, the author

---

[25] AD HOC GROUP ON EQUAL RIGHTS FOR WOMEN, SURVEY OF STAFF ATTITUDE ON SEX DISCRIMINATION IN THE UNITED NATIONS SECRETARIAT: ANALYSIS AND RECOMMENDATIONS FOR ACTION; STATISTICAL TABLES.

gained the impression that many felt that a lot of lip service was being paid to the equality of sexes but that little change had occurred in the actual situation of women in the Secretariat. Insofar as there had been improvements, they consisted primarily in the greater efforts made by the personnel department in the area of recruitment. He heard complaints of bias against women in various departments, on the part of various supervisors—practically always men—whose recommendations are necessary for promotion. There were also complaints concerning the reluctance to assign women to positions of greater responsibility necessary for career advancement. Some women appear to suffer from the fact that they serve in small units, such as those in the Centre for Social Development and Humanitarian Affairs,[26] where they find it particularly difficult to be assigned to more senior posts. The increasing stress put on the new economic order and the decreasing importance of social development have not improved the lot of women in the Secretariat.

Remedial Action Needed

Women—possibly more than men—appear to suffer from the fact that vacancies to be filled by promotion from within the Secretariat are not announced publicly and women often do not know about the openings and the opportunities available. On the other hand, an argument often heard against assigning a woman to a position of responsibility is that she lacks the necessary experience. This vicious circle must be broken by a determined policy of assigning women to responsible posts and by a more vigorous programme of career development and of training of women for managerial positions, including training on the job.

There is another aspect in recruitment that requires remedial action. In the past, applications received from women (or men) from overrepresented countries were administratively filtered out by the Office of Personnel Services and were not passed on to the substantive departments. It remains to be seen how such applications will be handled by the Office of Personnel Services following the adoption by the General Assembly of Resolution 3416 (XXX). The administration should regard this resolution at least as a sufficient mandate for not filtering out applications from women from overrepresented countries so as to enable the consideration of such applications by the departments concerned and eventually by the appointment and promotion bodies.

---

[26] There is in the Secretariat, within the Centre for Social Development and Humanitarian Affairs, a Promotion of Equality of Men and Women Branch. This branch is not directly concerned with the improvement of the situation of women in the employment of the United Nations and other international organizations. See ST/SGB/Org., Section K, at 6–9 (Feb. 1976).

156

A problem that must cause considerable concern is the poor representation of women in some departments of the Secretariat. The Ad Hoc
Group on Equal Rights for Women published on a number of occasions in
the *Secretariat News* the sex and grade profiles of departments, so as to
create leverage of public opinion on the heads of the departments with
poor employment records of women.[27] The Secretary-General now pub-
lishes tables pertaining to the distribution of staff by sex for all the departments in his annual reports on the composition of the Secretariat.

What can and should be done in order to create equality of opportunity
for women in the Secretariat?

First, as regards Member States, effective pressure should be exerted
by the Secretariat in order to ensure that states submit more candidatures
of women for vacancies in the Secretariat. Given the social, cultural, religious, and economic attitudes towards women in many countries, it
would not be realistic to expect a dramatic change within a few years, but
pressure can accelerate the processes of change, at least to the extent that
all Member States would present women candidates. Insofar as states
with no professional women in the Secretariat or with an unreasonably
low percentage of such women are concerned, the Secretary-General
should give priority to the recruitment of women from those countries.
Bodies such as the Ad Hoc Group on Equal Rights for Women in the Secretariat should publish nationality and sex profiles of the staff of the Secretariat in order to create a greater public opinion pressure on recalcitrant
states. As to possible action to be taken within the Secretariat, given the
difficulties regarding the recruitment of women and the possibility that
qualified professional personnel could be found, among the large number
of women now serving the the general service category, persons serving
in that category should be allowed to sit for competitive examinations for
junior professional posts rather than only for posts with special language
requirements, as in the past. Persons who would successfully pass these
examinations for junior professionals would become eligible for promotion to the professional category. Such a measure might cause difficulties
in operation of the principle of geographical distribution, but, as we have
already indicated, some flexibility in the application of that principle is, in
any event, required if progress is to be made in redressing the imbalance
that now prevails between women and men in the Secretariat.

In addition to already existing practices such as the sending of recruitment missions, it is necessary to establish the principle that all vacancies
must be announced, including those to be filled by promotion from within
the Secretariat. Vacancy announcements should be circulated not only to

[27] Regarding the composition of the Office of Public Information, see SECRETARIAT NEWS,
30 Sept. 1975, at 8; regarding the composition of the Office of Personnel Services see *ibid.*,
31 Oct. 1975, at 3; regarding the composition of the Department of Conference Services see
ibid., 16 Dec. 1975 at 11.

Member States and UNDP resident representatives, but also to nongovernmental organizations, women's organizations, professional associations, academic institutions, and so on, *even* in overrepresented countries.

The Secretariat should intensify training and career development programmes in order to enable women to prepare more rapidly for managerial positions. There appears to be progress in this direction. Beyond that, the crux of the difficulty in the Secretariat with respect to the promotion of women appears to lie in the area of their assignment to supervisory or managerial positions. The fact that a woman has successfully participated in a senior managerial course does not guarantee that she will be assigned to a position of responsibility. Given the present system whereby grades are linked with specific posts, it is obvious that, without a determined policy of assigning women to positions carrying greater responsibility and higher grades, little progress can be made.

Assigning women to such positions should become a priority objective of the Office of Personnel Services and of the various departments. In order to achieve this, it would become necessary to give women greater mobility throughout the Secretariat.

It is the impression of the author that the Office of Personnel Services is making efforts to improve the situation of women in the Secretariat, but that such efforts are not adequately made in the various departments. Pressure should therefore be exerted on the departments.

As regards the allegations often made concerning *de facto* discrimination against women in assignment and promotion, the author would like to reiterate a suggestion already made by him in a wider context, that is, that it would be desirable to establish in the Secretariat an office of ombudsperson to deal with the grievances and complaints of the staff, including those of women.

In conclusion, a clear program of affirmative action is necessary in order to provide women with equality of opportunity in the Secretariat. It is the view of the author that the establishment of a clear numerical target would be a helpful measure that would assist the Secretary-General, Member States, and all those who are interested in equality for women in the Secretariat. Even with such a target, the establishment of a fair and equitable balance between women and men in the Secretariat will be an uphill struggle requiring considerable time. Success will depend, in large measure, on the emancipation of women in the national life of Member States.

One of the questions occasionally raised is whether it would be right, given the principle of nondiscrimination established under Article 8 of the Charter, to resort to affirmative action in order to advance the situation of women, and thus, in effect, create a certain discrimination against men. Indeed, it may well be that, in recruitment, where a man candidate and a woman candidate have equal qualifications, the woman may now have a certain edge over the man. A similar situation does not, however, exist yet in the area of promotion, where the question of assignment to positions of responsibility is crucial and where departments have a decisive influence. This author believes that, given the fact that throughout the years women have suffered from discrimination in recruitment and in promotion and that, as a result, a considerable imbalance has been created, affirmative action is entirely proper. The "conditions of equality" mentioned in Article 8 of the Charter do not exist as yet and only by positive action will it be possible to create them. Of course, given the clear language of Article 101 (3), the author is not suggesting that a woman candidate should be preferred over a man with clearly superior qualifications. But, whenever the qualifications are similar or comparable, women must be given an advantage, or else the present situation will not be radically changed.[28] Those who complain that this would constitute illegal discrimination against men should consider the constitutional developments in the United States, where positive action has become the norm as regards various disadvantaged minorities. In the United Nations women are such a disadvantaged minority. Such legalistic doubts are particularly suspect given the policy of the General Assembly and the Secretariat to give distinct preference in recruitment to candidates from underrepresented countries, not always consistently with the principle of merit.

One final observation is called for: in the ongoing debate on the recruitment of women to the Secretariat, the General Assembly has insisted that such recruitment must be subject to the principle of geographical distribution. Little attention has been paid to the fact that, according to the explicit language of Article 101(3) the principle of merit is paramount, while the principle of geographical distribution of the staff is only secondary. It is questionable whether the provision according to which due regard must be paid to recruiting the staff on as wide a geographical basis as possible should prevail over the clear principle of equality of sexes established under Article 8. If strict compliance with the secondary principle of geographical distribution prevents the establishment of conditions of equality in employment, the clear norm of equality, pronounced in Article 8, should prevail.

---

[28] For a view that "benign discrimination" or "discrimination in reverse" "might do more harm than good," see SZALAI, *supra* note 5, at 27–28 (1973).

9   Due Process

The Introduction of Due Process by the Case Law of the Administrative Tribunal

Under the regime of the Charter and of the staff regulations and rules, the Secretary-General has a discretionary authority in applying the criteria established by Article 101(3) of the Charter with regard to the appointment and the promotion of the staff. In practice, however, the absolute authority of the Secretary-General is tempered by various political and administrative realities, by the resolutions of the General Assembly, and by many other factors. Legally the appointment and promotion bodies have only an advisory competence, and on a number of occasions Secretaries-General have chosen to disregard their recommendations.[1] The Secretary-General has also appointed bodies to deal with staff grievances, claims, and so on. These bodies, too, only have advisory powers.[2] In practice, of course, the authority of the Secretary-General in matters pertaining to the administration of personnel policy has been delegated to various officials.[3] In the multinational context in which the personnel policies of the Secretariat operate, it is essential to combat discriminatory practices and institute procedures challenging decisions taken under the influence of "extraneous" considerations. And yet, there is no general "statutory" provision subjecting the decision-making process of the Secretary-General and the various administrative bodies and officials that advise him and act on his behalf to the requirements of due process.[4] Nevertheless, in certain areas of administration of personnel policy, the United Nations Administrative Tribunal (UNAT) has developed and applied

---

[1] Regarding the advisory competence of the Appointment and Promotion Board, see Staff Rule 104.14.

[2] Regarding the Joint Disciplinary Committee, see Staff Regulations 10.1 and 10.2 and Staff Rules 110.1-110.5. Regarding appeals by staff members against an administrative decision alleging nonobservance of their terms of appointment, including all pertinent regulations and rules, or against disciplinary action, see Staff Regulation 11.1 and Staff Rules 111.1-111.4. The Administrative Tribunal has, however, a broader authority. Under Staff Regulation 11.2, it may, under conditions prescribed in its statute, hear and pass judgment upon applications from staff members alleging nonperformance of their terms of appointment, including all pertinent regulations and rules.

[3] See ST/SGB/151 (7 Jan. 1976) and ST/AI/234 (7 Jan. 1976).

[4] For suggestions to apply "due process" to the decision-making process of the political organs of the United Nations, see Sohn, *Due Process in the United Nations*, 69 AJIL 620 (1975), *Enabling the United States to Contest "Illegal" United Nations Acts, ibid.*, at 852.

concepts of due process which have had an important and salutary impact on the administration and contributed to filling an unfortunate *lacuna* in the system. Although due process of law is "a basic principle of all well-balanced legal systems,"[5] albeit under different names, it was not introduced to the United Nations Secretariat by either the Charter of the United Nations or the staff regulations and rules but only gradually and somewhat hesitantly by the Administrative Tribunal. In this chapter we shall examine the development of concepts of due process by UNAT pointing out areas in which progress has been made and areas where inroads made by due process concepts have so far been insignificant.

Before proceeding further, one other preliminary observation may be appropriate. Although the substance of due process is known in most legal systems, it has gained greater prominence and sophistication in the legal system of the United States, where the concept of due process of law is part and parcel of the Fifth and the Fourteenth Amendments to the Constitution. In the United States, due process of law implies the right of the person affected to be present before the tribunal that pronounces judgment upon the question of life, liberty, or property, the right to be heard by testimony or otherwise, and the right to controvert, by proof, every material fact. Daniel Webster defined due process to mean a law that hears before it condemns, that proceeds on inquiry, and renders judgment only upon trial.[6] It was probably inevitable that the development of concepts of due process by UNAT should have benefitted from the influence of the legal system of the country where the headquarters of the United Nations is situated. Although UNAT has introduced the language of United States due process, it may well be that in the beginning it did not fully understand its substance.

In the United Nations Secretariat, the analogous concepts of due process must have a broader applicability, so as to cover not only the procedures of judicial bodies and quasi-judicial administrative bodies, but also at least some administrative acts and decision-making processes.

The Reach and the Influence of Due Process

The first area in which UNAT has made considerable impact in developing and in applying concepts of due process is that of the procedure followed in cases of termination of a permanent appointment for unsatisfactory service. Although review of appointments of staff members holding permanent appointments, upon the completion of the first five years of service, has always been a function of the Appointment and Promotion

---

[5] Sohn, *Due Process in the United Nations*, 69 AJIL 620 at 621 (1975).

[6] BLACK'S LAW DICTIONARY 590 (Rev. Fourth Ed., 1968).

Board whose procedure and composition should provide a guarantee of due process, this was not the case where the Secretary-General terminated permanent appointments on grounds of unsatisfactory service. In a series of judgments, UNAT laid down that a permanent appointment cannot be terminated except under the staff regulations, which enumerate precisely the reasons for the termination.[7] The tribunal went, however, beyond the letter of the staff regulations in that it determined that permanent appointments can be terminated only upon a decision that has been reached by means of a complete, fair, and reasonable procedure that must be carried out prior to such decision. The case of *Gillman v. The Secretary-General* (1966)[8] involved the termination of a permanent appointment by the Secretary-General on the recommendation of the Appointment and Promotion Board (which endorsed the recommendations of a working group set up in pursuance of Staff Rule 104.14[d]) for unsatisfactory performance (services) and record of attendance. Given its composition (it comprises members representing the staff and members representing the Secretary-General) and its procedure, the review by the group of the services of a staff member represents, in principle, the complete, fair, and reasonable procedure that must be carried out prior to the termination of a permanent appointment. If the board or working group, however, reached its conclusions in the light of inadequate or erroneous information and the Secretary-General subsequently relied on these conclusions in giving reasons for the termination of a permanent appointment, the review would not secure the validity of the Secretary-General's decision. In this particular case, the working group stated that the staff member's performance had gone steadily downhill, thus disregarding a periodic report covering a two-year period that pointed out that the applicant maintained a high standard of efficiency. Moreover, as regards the applicant's record of attendance, the group added annual leave to sick leave. In these circumstances UNAT held that the report of the group had failed to take into account all the facts of the case. The applicant was thus deprived of the complete, fair, and reasonable procedure that must be carried out before the termination of a permanent appointment. The tribunal decided, therefore, that the case shall be remanded for correction of procedure.

In the case of *Restrepo v. The Secretary-General* (1969),[9] another case of termination for unsatisfactory service, it was found that the deputy-director of personnel had informed the applicant of the Secretary-General's decision to terminate her appointment, in accordance with Staff Regulation 9.1(a), without explicitly indicating the reasons for the termination. The tribunal held that there was a duty to indicate to the staff member

[7] See Staff Regulation 9.1(a) and Staff Rules 104.13(c) and 104.14(d) and (f).
[8] Judgment No. 98.
[9] Judgment No. 131.

concerned both the provision on which the termination was based and the facts that constituted grounds for termination. Allowing the staff member concerned to be kept in ignorance of the reasons for the termination would at the outset be depriving her of the right to file an appeal with full knowledge of the facts. Since the applicant was, however, in fact aware— though not officially— of the grounds for the termination of the appointment, and exercised her rights of appeal, the tribunal held that this procedural irregularity (as well as another procedural error made in not communicating to her the conclusions of the Appointment and Promotion Board in the letter informing her of the decision of the Secretary-General to terminate her appointment) did not justify the rescission of the contested decision. The tribunal noted that the applicant did not allege that the procedure before the working group of the Appointment and Promotion Board involved an element of prejudice or any other extraneous motives. As regards contentions relating to the applicant's services, these would not be considered by the tribunal, since the Secretary-General had full discretion and authority to make the final judgment.

In the case of termination of probationary appointments, the problem was rather different, namely, of proper procedures of a competent body. The case of *Peynado v. The Secretary-General* (1970)[10] involved a decision by the Secretary-General to terminate the applicant's probationary appointment under Staff Regulation 9.1(c), on the grounds of failure to meet standards of performance and unsuitable conduct. The tribunal noted that the purpose of probationary appointments was to grant career service on satisfactory performance and that procedures were prescribed for a proper assessment of the suitability of staff members on probation for the grant of a probationary appointment. Safeguards for a fair review of suitability for the grant of permanent appointments have been provided by the staff rules and their observance constituted "due process." Although the tribunal could not substitute its judgment for that of the Secretary-General concerning the standard of performance of the staff member concerned, if the conclusions of the Appointment and Promotion Board had been reached in the light of inadequate and erroneous information and the Secretary-General had relied on them for the termination of the appointment, the fact of the review did not ensure the validity of the Secretary-General's decision. In the case in point the board had before it a periodic report questioning the judgment and the quality of work of the applicant who— however—contested these negative findings. The relevant administrative instruction required that, in the case of a contested periodic report, the head of the department should conduct an investigation, the report of which would be filed together with the periodic report and the staff member's statement in rebuttal.[11]

---

[10] Judgment No. 138.
[11] ST/AI/115, para. 13 (11 Apr. 1956).

Here such an investigation was not conducted, and the appointment and promotion body had before it "an incomplete document." The absence of such an investigation was particularly important in view of the allegation of prejudice against the second reporting (appraising) officer. The tribunal also noted that two positive periodic reports had been retroactively reappraised (negatively) thus affecting prejudicially the protection to which staff members were entitled. As regards the ground of unsuitable conduct, it was based on confidential and privileged statements made before the Joint Appeals Board. The decision to terminate the appointment on this ground was thus founded on a misuse of information confidentially presented. A letter of reprimand was improperly introduced into the applicant's file and could have prejudiced the recommendations of the Appointment and Promotion Board. Furthermore, it appeared that, on the strength of two (positive) periodic reports, the applicant had been recommended for a permanent appointment, which recommendation was approved by the Secretary-General, although no notification to the applicant followed. Subsequently this recommendation was changed to one for an extension of the period of probation by one year. Despite the extraordinary nature of this case, and the fact that the applicant's superior was afforded an opportunity for oral presentation to the board, such an opportunity was denied to the applicant. The tribunal made the comment that justice should not only be done but also seen to be done and that denial of the right of presentation of his case, especially when an earlier favorable decision was sought to be reversed, could not have satisfied the applicant that justice was being done to him. The tribunal concluded that the applicant had been denied the protection afforded by the administrative instruction, [12] and thereby deprived of a fair and reasonable procedure before termination of his appointment, and awarded monetary compensation for the injury suffered.

The case of *Lane v. The Secretary-General* (1975)[13] involved the termination of a probationary appointment, after the expiry of an extended period of probation. The tribunal held that the applicant, having completed his probationary period, was entitled to due process for the assessment of his suitability for a permanent appointment. The tribunal observed that no periodic report was prepared for the period covering 1 year and 10 months after the expiry of the extended probationary period and that the applicant had no opportunity to offer his comments for that period. Even if it were assumed that certain confidential cables—which, during the period not covered by the periodic reports, reported that there was no improvement in the applicant's shortcomings—were a substitute for a periodic report, there was nothing to show that those cables were brought to the attention of the applicant. The tribunal reached the conclusion that the applicant

---

[12] ST/AI/115.
[13] Judgment No. 198.

was deprived of due process since the termination decision was reached without providing the Appointment and Promotion Committee with the most recent information on the applicant's performance and without affording the applicant an opportunity to state his case.

The case of *Nelson v. The Secretary-General* (1972)[14] involved the termination of the permanent appointment of the applicant on the ground of unsatisfactory service. The periodic report on the applicant and his rebuttal of it had been reviewed by a three-man panel consisting of three senior officials designated by the Secretary-General. The tribunal held that neither in the composition of this panel nor in the procedure followed by it nor in its terms of reference did the panel provide the complete, fair, and reasonable procedure contemplated by the tribunal. The tribunal ruled that such a procedure, to ensure the substantial rights of a staff member with a permanent appointment, must be provided prior to the termination of such appointment either by the Appointment and Promotion Board where the staff rules so provide or by a similar joint (that is, including representatives of the staff) review body in the absence of such a provision. This was required by "due process." Since the applicant was not accorded such a procedure, the case was remanded for correction of procedure.

In the case of *Mila v. The Secretary-General* (1974)[15] the applicant had been warned of the unsatisfactory nature of his services, but did not receive a written warning, nor was there in his personal file any record of any oral warning. Neither was there evidence that any oral warnings contained any hint or threat of action if the staff member's work did not improve. A favourable periodic report contained no mention of such warnings. This the tribunal considered to constitute a serious irregularity. A second irregularity was that no investigation was conducted by a head of a department—under administrative instruction ST/AI/115—in relation to a periodic report contested by the applicant. The Appointment and Promotion Panel was thus sent an incomplete document. In addition, as the panel did not make a sufficiently thorough, searching, and balanced review of the applicant's standards, the decision to terminate his appointment was not preceded by a procedure meeting the requirements of a complete, fair, and reasonable procedure. The case was remanded for correction of procedure.[16]

In view of the above judgments of the Administrative Tribunal, an administrative instruction was issued,[17] setting out procedures to be fol-

---

[14] Judgment No. 157.

[15] Judgment No. 184.

[16] See also *Mila v. The Secretary-General* (1975), Judgment No. 204. Under ST/AI/115, where a staff member makes a written statement in explanation or in rebuttal of a periodic report, the head of the department must investigate the case and record his appraisal in writing.

[17] ST/AI/222, 10 Dec. 1974. Reference to this procedure is contained in the new Staff Rule 104.14(f) (C) (ST/SGB/Staff Rules/1/Rev. 3).

lowed in cases of termination of the permanent appointment of a staff member under Staff Regulation 9.1(a) (other than in the course of the five-year review). The procedure lays down that, to satisfy the requirements of due process, the proposal for a termination must be referred to a joint review body for advice before the Secretary-General takes a decision on it. A copy of the proposal for termination together with supporting evidence, submitted to the joint review body must, at the same time, be provided to the staff member concerned. The staff member concerned would have to have not only an opportunity to comment on the proposal for termination but should be heard by the review body in person, whenever the review body considers this to be feasible. The report of the joint review body shall be transmitted to the Secretary-General through the Appointment and Promotion Board. The report shall include its considerations, conclusions, and recommendations. The Appointment and Promotion Board must remand a case to the joint review body if it concludes that an error in procedure has been committed. Should the Secretary-General decide to terminate a permanent appointment, the staff member shall be given in the notice of termination a statement of the reasons for the decision.

The new procedure is not an unmixed blessing. For, despite a provision that the joint review body shall act on the proposed termination with the maximum dispatch consistent with a fair review of the case, the procedure appears too lengthy and complicated and it makes the termination of appointments extremely difficult even in the case of completely ineffective staff members. But this may be a price worth paying in the interests of due process and justice that must be seen to be done in a multinational context!

It may be mentioned, in passing, that UNAT applied similar concepts of due process in cases involving termination of regular appointments under Staff Regulation 9.1(c),[18] and in cases pertaining to nonextension of fixed-term appointments.[19] It should be observed that decisions of UNAT

---

[18] In the case of *Quemerais v. The Secretary-General* (1973), the evaluation of the applicant's work was entrusted to a personnel committee of UNICEF. The tribunal observed that it could not regard as proper an evaluation of a staff member's work that might lead to the termination of his appointment when it was entrusted to a body comparable to the Appointment and Promotion Board and that body was not put in a position to be informed of the observations of the staff member concerned as well as the complaints about him. The personnel committee did not make a real evaluation of the applicant's work. The participation in the committee of staff representatives could not remedy the fact that the committee was not in a position to carry out an evaluation in accordance with the elementary principles of due process and in fact made no attempt to do so. The tribunal concluded that the applicant was not afforded the guarantees of due process before the committee. Judgment No. 172. See also *Quemerais v. The Secretary-General* (1974), Judgment No. 187.

[19] The case of *Sehgal v. The Secretary-General* (1975) concerned a decision by the Secretary-General not to renew the applicant's fixed-term appointment. One of the issues before the tribunal was whether the requisite procedures to deal with the rebuttal by the applicant (a local staff member of the Office of UNDP in New Delhi) of adverse comments contained in a certain periodic report were complied with. The tribunal observed that an investigation of a rebuttal by a head of department called for a balanced regard for the conflicting views of

complicating the nonrenewal of fixed-term contracts go far towards contradicting the argument that fixed-term appointments assure prompt removal of ineffective staff members.

The second area where UNAT made a substantial contribution in developing concepts of due process—in this case the principle of equal protection of staff members or, more precisely, the equal right of all members of the staff to proper defense—is that of disciplinary proceedings. It should be recalled that, under Staff Rule 110.3(a), staff members serving at Headquarters or at the United Nations Office in Geneva cannot be subject to disciplinary measures until the matter has been referred for advice to the Joint Disciplinary Committee (comprising representation of the staff). But staff serving away from New York and Geneva was subject to disciplinary measures without the safeguards of the procedure of the Joint Disciplinary Committee.

The leading case of *Zang-Atangana v. The Secretary-General* (1969)[20] involved disciplinary measures imposed on a staff member holding a fixed-term contract and serving in a United Nations field office. The tribunal confirmed that it was clear, under the staff rules, that referral to the Joint Disciplinary Committee of the disciplinary measures taken against the applicant was not required, but the tribunal had the right to ascertain whether a procedure respecting the rights of the defense was followed. For a disciplinary measure to be valid, the reasons for it must be stated with a reasonable degree of precision and with due regard for the facts of the case. This was particularly important in the case of a staff member who was not assured of the guarantees provided by referral to the Joint Disciplinary Committee. Noting that the procedure of that committee ensures an objective examination of the case and contributes to the formulation of equitable decisions, the tribunal went on to lay down the principle that whatever the historical reasons that have limited this procedure to New York and to Geneva "it is necessary to establish an equivalent procedure for other staff members, so that all staff are given equal protection."[21] The tribunal decided that the applicant should be compensated for the injury that he had sustained.

UNAT returned to this question in the case of *Linblad v. The Secretary-General* (1974)[22] which involved the application of disciplinary mea-

---

the staff member and his supervisor, a dispassionate approach to the issues standing between them, a search for additional evidence or opinions that may throw further light on their respective viewpoints, and a clear and reasoned determination. The tribunal observed that the investigation of a rebuttal in this particular case was distinguished by a singular lack of objectivity, resulting in the applicant being denied due process. Judgment No. 203. See also *Sood v. The Secretary-General* (1975), Judgment No. 195.

[20] Judgment No. 130.
[21] At 164.
[22] Judgment No. 183.

sures against a field service security officer of UNTSO on grounds of misconduct (disposing of tax-free liquor). The applicant alleged that the decision to dismiss him was contrary to the norms of due process. The tribunal observed that the applicant had not been given an adequate opportunity to explain certain purchases (of liquor). Having regard to the summary manner in which his statements were taken and the absence of any provision for the rebuttal by him of any specific formal charges, the tribunal concluded that he had not been accorded a fair opportunity to give his version of all the relevant facts or to explain his conduct in its entirety. The tribunal expressed the view that a staff member against whom disciplinary proceedings are taken should be furnished with a specific charge and accorded the right to be heard before a sanction is imposed on him. This right includes the opportunity to participate in the examination of the evidence. Since such a right was not explicitly stated in the relevant personnel directive, that directive did not provide adequate protection for staff members away from Headquarters or Geneva involved in disciplinary proceedings and did not establish an "equivalent procedure" (to the Joint Disciplinary Committee's procedure) as envisaged in the *Zang-Atangana* judgment.

In 1976, the administration issued a new personnel directive laying down a detailed procedure to be followed in disciplinary cases involving staff members serving in offices other than Headquarters or Geneva.[23] This new directive was apparently intended to constitute the "equivalent procedure" upon which UNAT had insisted.

The third area in which the tribunal has successfully applied concepts of due process is that relating to the proceedings of the Advisory Board on Compensation Claims.[24]

The case of *Azzu v. The Secretary-General* (1966)[25] involved a request by the applicant that the tribunal rescind a decision whereby the Secretary-General approved a recommendation made by the Advisory Board on Compensation Claims, on the ground that the procedure followed by the board did not meet the requirements of due process. The tribunal noted that, since the relevant decision of the Secretary-General was taken on the recommendation of the board, the latter must observe the requirements of due process in arriving at its recommendation. The tribunal recalled that the requirement of due process, providing adequate safeguards for the rights of the individuals, is a generally recognized principle that the

---

[23] PD/1/76.

[24] See rules governing compensation in the event of death, injury, or illness attributable to the performance of official duties, on behalf of the United Nations, see Staff Rule 106.4 and ST/SGB/Staff Rules/Appendix D/Rev. 1 and Amend. 1.

[25] Judgment No. 103.

Secretary-General must respect. In the present case, due process would have required that the applicant be informed of the specific facts (warranting the reopening of the case) and be granted the right to give explanations that could be brought to the attention of the organ competent to make recommendations to the Secretary-General. The tribunal found that the procedure followed by the advisory board failed to meet the requirements of due process. The case was remanded for correction of procedure.[26]

In the recent case of *Dearing v. The Secretary-General* (1975),[27] the tribunal stated that the discretion of the Secretary-General whether to reopen a case related to compensation, as requested by the applicant, must not be exercised unjustly or unreasonably. Due process required that an authority competent to make recommendations or decisions should arrive at its conclusions without factual errors or prejudice. In the case in point, since there was a difference between the Medical Director of the United Nations and the applicant's physicians over the latter's medical reports, the requirements of due process involved recourse to an impartial medical examination of the applicant. Since this was not done, the tribunal held that the recommendation of the advisory board to reject his request for the reopening of the case was vitiated by lack of due process, and that the decision of the Secretary-General not to reopen the case based on such recommendations suffered from the same weakness.

So far we have looked at areas where the application by UNAT of concepts of due process had a real impact on the official personnel policy of the Secretariat.

But the influence of such UNAT decisions is apparent even beyond the specific areas to which concepts of due process have been applied. Thus, in an (unpublished) opinion (1971), the Legal Counsel of the United Nations emphasized that certain administrative instructions (relevant to the eligibility for promotion of the staff member concerned) were incorporated in an internal document, of which the staff member could not have any notice. The Legal Counsel expressed the view that the policy expressed in the internal instructions could not be applied to that staff member, given the fact that throughout the entire promotion procedure everyone concerned was unaware of that policy. The Legal Counsel concluded that in such circumstances it was very doubtful that the Administrative Tribunal would uphold the denial of the promotion of the staff member concerned. The administration accepted the view of the Legal Counsel that the staff member concerned should be promoted from the general service to the professional category. Although the Legal Counsel did not mention due process *expressis verbis*, it appears that such concepts were involved in his opinion.

[26] See also *Khederian v. The Secretary-General*, Judgments No. 114(1968) and 120(1968).
[27] Judgment No. 200.

But what about the areas where concepts of due process have not, so far, had an impact on personnel procedures?

So far staff members concerned have not been allowed to make presentations in person before appointment and promotion bodies and have thus been denied the right of oral rebuttal of the case made against them, although representatives of departments are allowed to make oral presentations to such bodies. In the case of *Peynado*, which we have already considered, the tribunal observed that the denial to the staff member concerned of the right to present his case to the Appointment and Promotion Board did not—in the circumstances—satisfy the requirement that justice should not only be done, but should also be seen to be done. Despite the *Peynado* case, the policy regarding the denial of the right of oral presentation continues unchanged. The *Peynado* decision does not suggest that due process requires an oral, adversary hearing before the *ordinary* termination of a probationary appointment. Many administrators feel that such a requirement would encourage the unit chief to let the unproven probationer pass rather than get caught up in litigation. The author believes that there is room for considerable tightening of the procedures pertaining to termination of probationary appointments.

Another area of concern is that in the present practice it is not uncommon that positive written recommendations of the staff members' supervisors—such as those contained in the periodic reports—are contradicted by them through derogatory comments transmitted orally to the Office of Personnel Services and/or to members of the appointment and promotion bodies. In such cases the staff member is denied the elementary right of due process of knowing what charges or allegations have been made against him, and consequently of the right to defend himself.

A particularly delicate general question is that of the right of access of a staff member to confidential documents and memoranda pertaining to him. A staff member may examine his "official status file,"[28] but has no access to confidential memoranda relating to him which are placed in privileged-confidential files. Although the official status file of a staff member is accessible to the staff member in proceedings before UNAT, this is not the case with privileged-confidential files. By deciding whether to put certain documents in the official status file of a staff member or in the confidential file, the administration may prejudice ("load") the case against him. In the case of *Sood v. The Secretary-General* (1975),[29] where termination of a fixed-term appointment involved a denial of due process, the tribunal observed that there were in the applicant's file confidential memoranda that should have been removed when the charges that they contained failed to be substantiated.

[28] ST/ADM/SER.A/1934 (30 Jan. 1976).
[29] Judgment No. 195.

In view of the multinational character of the Secretariat it would be desirable to have in the United Nations clear and fair regulations providing for fuller access to the material pertaining to a staff member.[30]

The author does not wish to suggest that the confidential-privileged file should be made available to the staff member. In theory such a file should protect the staff member from nosy colleagues and contain material (such as references) received under an explicit or implicit assurance of confidentiality. The administration must, however, make sure that the confidential-privileged file does not contain information that could be adduced by the staff member in any proceedings. Thus, due process would not be involved.

The entire area of recruitment and promotion is within the administrative discretion. Persons who complain that they have not been recruited for lack of due process cannot seize UNAT's jurisdiction because no contract with the Secretary-General has been concluded.

Even in a case where a recommendation to include a member of the staff in the promotion register was suppressed by the regional director (at the South Central Asia Regional Office of UNICEF), the decision not to promote him was not considered by the tribunal as "an abuse of discretion," and the suppression of the recommendation only as "not in keeping with good administrative practice."[31] It should, however, be observed that only three months remained until the expiration of the fixed-term contract of the applicant.

Indeed, the procedure of recourse available to members of the staff who have not been included in the promotion register appears to be inadequate.[32] The staff member concerned may bring to the same reviewing body only new information that will be examined with a view to determining whether, had it been known at the time of the initial review, it would have warranted the inclusion of the staff member in the promotion register.

The Secretary-General has recently approved a new administrative instruction (ST/AI/240) concerning the performance evaluation system that will supersede the 1956 instruction (ST/AI/115). The future procedure pertaining to the right of a staff member to rebut comments made about him in a periodic report will include the establishment by the head of a department or an office of a list of five senior officers, from among whom the staff member would choose a panel of three to investigate the case. The panel must hear the interested parties.

We have seen that the tribunal has performed an important task in in-

---

[30] Compare, the (United States) Privacy Act of 1974, 5 U.S.C. §552a.

[31] *Nath v. The Secretary-General of the United Nations* (1974), AT/DEC/181, at 10.

[32] See ST/ADM/SER.A/1934 (30 Jan. 1976).

troducing concepts of fair procedures, of equal rights to protection and to proper defense, and of the right to be heard (*audi alteram partem*).

The Administrative Tribunal does not, however, appear to have been able to implant concepts of due process in many areas of personnel policy that continue to fall within the ambit of administrative discretion. In Chapters 4 and 8 the author has already expressed the view that it is important to appoint in the United Nations an ombudsperson, empowered to deal with allegations of discriminatory practices. An ombudsperson should be a person of impeccable integrity and expertise in law and in personnel problems. It may not be easy to find such a person (a *retired* international civil servant might be considered for the post involved). He should not be selected on a political basis and he should have a right of access to the Secretary-General and to his senior aides. It would not be easy to draft his terms of reference,[33] but, by his very presence, by his availability to members of the staff having legitimate grievances, by his ability to approach the most senior officials of the Secretariat, and by his power to report on violations and irregularities, an ombudsperson could perform a major role in applying to the administration concepts of due process.

Finally, a comment about the consequences of a determination by UNAT that due process has been denied. Such a determination may lead to a remand for correction of procedure or it may lead to a decision on the merits rescinding the decision of the Secretary-General. Under Article 9(1) of its statute, however, UNAT when rescinding a contested decision also fixes the amount of compensation to be paid for the injury sustained should the Secretary-General, within 30 days of the notification of the judgment, decide, in the interest of the United Nations, that the applicant should be compensated without further action being taken. It is exceedingly rare for a staff member who has been terminated to be reinstated in the service and to return to the *status quo ante*. The choice between reinstatement and compensation belongs to the Secretary-General and not to the tribunal. Financial compensation and moral satisfaction is all that one can normally look forward to.

---

[33] For a potentially useful precedent, see the terms of appointment of ombudsmen for the UNDP, in UNDP/ADM/PER/26. See also UNDP/ADM/PER/60 and UNDP/ADM/PER/63.

10 Critique of the Appointment and Promotion Process

We have already alluded on a number of occasions to the fact that, given the intense political pressures within and without the Secretariat, the integrity of the appointment and promotion process needs to be protected by as many safeguards, checks, and balances as possible. Existing safeguards are for the moment weak and ineffective. It must be recognized that despite 31 years of experience, the United Nations lacks a real tradition of management, common to modern organizations.

In view of the well-justified mistrust of senior officials, who in many cases are selected on the basis of criteria other than administrative excellence and who must be impeded from showing political preferences, whimsical favouritism, or capricious dislikes, it is important not to leave things to their untrammelled discretion and to develop and strengthen a system of checks and balances and of fair and objective procedures.

The Role of the Office of Personnel Services and the Role of the Substantive Departments

Under the Charter, all authority and all responsibility are vested in the Secretary-General and are mostly delegated by him down the "chains of command" to subordinate officials who have coextensive authority and responsibility in their own fields. They are answerable to the Secretary-General for the performance of the functions of the Secretariat in their fields. The appointment and promotion bodies are legally only advisory bodies, and they must also constantly bear in mind that no board or committee could, for practical reasons, take the place of the responsible administrator (however inept or corrupt he may be) in seeing that the work gets done.

An argument can be made that appointment and promotion bodies and also the Office of Personnel Services would go beyond their legitimate sphere of action if they attempted to decide that Mr. Y, instead of Mr. X who has been recommended by the substantive department or office, should perform particular functions. When dealing with a new appointment, they can in general interpose a veto (unless the Secretary-General is willing to exercise his authority and go against their advice, as the last three secretaries-general have occasionally done); but in matters of promotion or assignment they can only advise, warn, or delay. If the head of the department continues, however, to insist that Mr. X is the man he wants to perform particular functions, neither the promotion bodies nor the Office of Personnel Services (OPS) can indefinitely refuse to give Mr. X the grade that goes with those functions. The hierarchical principle on which the Secretariat is and must continue to be operated, tempered though it may be by advice, warnings, and delays, cannot be changed, and this means that letting politics outweigh competence, integrity, and efficiency in the choice of high officials is a sure road to demoralization and inefficiency.

A comment is called for concerning the role of OPS in relation to the role of the substantive departments which, of course, cooperate in the presentation of proposals to the appointment and promotion bodies. Although it would be foolish to suggest that proposals of the substantive departments regarding appointments and promotions do not often have a strong political component, it is nevertheless a fact that it is OPS, more than the substantive departments, which have to have qualified personnel for the fulfilment of their functions, even if these persons are nationals of overrepresented states, that constantly stresses the importance of compliance with the principle of geographical distribution—desirable ranges—as established by the General Assembly. Indeed, OPS can properly be regarded as a watchdog for geographical distribution. This is not surprising, since OPS rather than the substantive departments, is regarded by the General Assembly, and especially by the Fifth Committee, as responsible for strict compliance with the principle of equitable geographical distribution of the staff. Indeed, OPS is also under the obligation to see to it that common standards are applied and that justice is done to all the departments.

The Role of the Appointment and Promotion Bodies and the Role of the Staff

Let us now look in greater depth at the role of the appointment and promotion bodies, established under Staff Rule 104.14. All these bodies, the board, the committee, and the (general services category) panel are based on "joint" representation. (In Chapter 7, pages 139-140, we have already discussed the role of the staff in JAC.) Not only are members of these bodies appointed by the Secretary-General after consultation with the Staff Council, but also three members of the board as *now* composed are appointed by the Secretary-General upon nomination by the Staff Council.[1] In theory, this active participation of the nominees of the staff should

---

[1] Regarding the composition of the Appointment and Promotion Board and Committee, see ST/ADM/SER.A/1940 (17 Feb. 1976). Under Staff Rule 104.14(b)(i), the board consists of

have proved an important safeguard against the politicization of the appointment and promotion process.

Members of the Appointment and Promotion Committee and Board are sometimes approached by members of national delegations and by members of the staff in order to persuade them to support particular appointments and promotions. The reaction to such overtures depends on the moral integrity and the standing in the Organization of each member of these bodies.

In fact, the Appointment and Promotion Committee, which recommends to the board appointments and promotions up to and including the P–4 level, is more insistent on the observance of the rules. The committee itself consists of relatively junior officers, at the P–3 level and above.

The Appointment and Promotion Board—as a body of first instance—recommends to the Secretary-General appointments and promotions to the P–5 to D–1 level. It consists of officers at the P–5 level and above. In the past the members of the board included persons at the assistant-secretary-general level, but now, owing to efforts made by the Staff Council to combat the politicization of the board, except for the chairman, an under-secretary-general, and a nonvoting *ex officio* member, the assistant-secretary-general for Personnel Services, all the members of the board are officials up to the D–2 level. Such officials are, however, senior executives of the Secretariat. There is no doubt that there does go on among the members of the board a fair amount of horse trading involving primarily departmental but also political *quid pro quos*. It appears that the nominees of the staff on the appointment and promotion bodies have not, on the whole, taken positions different from those taken by other members. For a staff member to be appointed and to be reappointed to one of the appointment and promotion bodies is an important status symbol. It appears that the nominees of the staff do not wish to criticize too severely the recommendations of OPS, possibly out of fear that if they are too far out of step their reappointment to the appointment and promotion bodies and even their own career prospects might suffer. Whether such fears are justified or not is not important. What matters more is that it is difficult to discern in the appointment and promotion bodies distinct attitudes of the nominees of the staff. In this respect several additional factors should be noted. In the first place, all the members of these bodies, including those nominated by the staff regard themselves—and correctly so—as appointees of the Secretary-General. Second, senior officials who sit in the Appointment and Promotion Board regard themselves as senior executives of the Secretariat rather than as defenders of the interests of the staff.

---

seven members and seven alternates. The assistant-secretary-general, Personnel Services, is an *ex officio* nonvoting member. At least two members and two alternates are appointed from among nominees submitted by the Staff Council.

Third, the principle of secrecy, which is strictly applied to the proceedings of the appointment and promotion bodies, has prevented concrete discussion in the staff bodies of questions arising in the appointment and promotion bodies and of positions taken by the nominees of the staff. Rules pertaining to the procedures of the Appointment and Promotion Board, as amended in 1962, provide that the deliberations of the board and the recommendations resulting therefrom should be treated as strictly confidential and should not be disclosed to anyone by the participants in the work of the board. There is, of course, full justification for secrecy to be observed in evaluating individual staff members. In contrast, the policy decisions should be made known and be subject to consultation. Fourth, it appears that some members of the Staff Committee as well as some nominees of the staff often do not possess enough expertise in staff regulations, rules, personnel directives, and so forth, to be a strong interlocutor for senior administrators from the Office of Personnel Services or from among members of the appointment and promotion bodies not nominated by the Staff Council.

The author holds the view that a conceptual and practical change in the role of the staff on the appointment and promotion bodies is essential in order to prevent further politicization of the system and as a safeguard of the merit principle. A more active and more informed attitude on the part of the staff, more in the spirit of trade union expert representation as it is known in the United States, should not be interpreted as being in conflict with the obligations of the staff as international civil servants. Indeed, opposition by staff to candidates put forward for political or other extraneous considerations could be effectively used by senior administrators who prefer a commitment to the merit principle as a justification for the rejection of such candidates.

In the light of the comments already made about the role of the appointment and promotion bodies, let us now look at the actions taken by the Appointment and Promotion Committee and by the Appointment and Promotion Board in the years 1974–1975. The following data are based on material given to the author, but he himself has not been able to examine the actual files or decisions of the appointment and promotion bodies.

The Appointment and Promotion Committee puts its recommendations to a vote. The board, however, operates on the principle of consensus. In both bodies, reservations are sometimes voiced to proposed appointments and promotions.

In 1974, in the Appointment and Promotion Committee, reservations or negative votes against appointments and promotions proposals presented to the committee were entered in about 10 percent of the cases dealt with (including rejections of the recommendations). In about 4 percent of the cases, the reservations related to geographical distribution (overrepresentation of the candidate's country). Other reservations or objections were voiced—*inter alia*—on the following grounds: undergrading, overgrading, qualifications not relevant to the job description or to the post, inadequate qualifications, improper recruitment practices, improper use of *ad hoc* promotion procedure, Staff Council should have been consulted (in the case of an appointment to a joint body), correction of entrance level unjustified, too many nationals of the candidate's country in the relevant department, performance of a staff member not justifying promotion, and accelerated promotion not justified. In about 1 percent of the cases the committee recommended rejection.

Of the cases that went directly to the Appointment and Promotion Board, reservations (including rejections)[2] were made in about 7 percent of the cases. In three cases (two of them coming from the committee), the board expressed disapproval of the Secretary-General's preemption of the function of the body by merely "taking note." The board rejected the proposals in about 5 percent of the cases that came before it. It is of interest to note that in two cases in which the committee recommended rejection because of overrepresentation, the board, reversing the committee's decision, recommended approval.

In 1975, in about 19 percent of the cases that came before the Appointment and Promotion Committee, reservations and objections (including rejections) were voiced. In about 13 percent of the cases the objections were on the grounds of geographical distribution (overrepresentation of the candidate's country). Other grounds for reservations included: alternative candidates had not been provided or a more extensive search for qualified candidates should have been made, *ad hoc* promotion procedure unjustified, qualifications not relevant to job description, qualifications inadequate, job description not circulated, proper recruitment practices not followed, correction of entrance level unjustified, staff member on secondment from his government should resign before the grant of a probationary appointment, reservations as to the procedure to be followed in the appointment to a political mission, and lack of integrity of the candidate in his application.

The rejections by the committee amounted to about 1 percent of the cases. In one case the committee reversed its negative decision, after the case was remanded to it by the board. Certain rejections were reversed by the board.

In the cases that went directly to the board, there were about 7 percent of reservations and rejections. The board rejected proposed appointments

---

[2] Including cases where the committee was divided and could not reach a decision, and where the rejection was therefore by the board.

and promotions in about 4 percent of the cases. In one case, the board expressed a reservation to the Secretary-General's preempting the process by merely taking note of the intention of the Secretary-General to make the appointment.

In one case where the committee's vote was 3 in favour of an appointment and 3 against on the ground of geographical distribution (overrepresentation), the board approved the appointment.

It is of interest to observe that reservations have been voiced more often in the Appointment and Promotion Committee than in the Appointment and Promotion Board. Even in cases where reservations were voiced or negative votes were cast, with very few exceptions, the committee went along with the proposals that were presented to it. The Appointment and Promotion Board voiced reservations in relatively few cases but rejected proposals to a greater extent. The board appeared to be less reluctant than the committee to grant appointments to nationals of overrepresented and even grossly overrepresented countries. This may be related to the fact that in quite a few cases such appointments were given to politically "advantaged" nationalities.

As regards the cases where the board expressed disapproval by merely "taking note," these were the more obvious cases in which the Secretary-General preempted the function of the appointment and promotion bodies because of his interest in a favorable action being taken, either in an appointment or in a promotion. The influence of high Secretariat officials on the process is normally exerted more subtly and does not bring about such adverse reactions on the part of the appointment and promotion bodies. Normally, the appointment and promotion bodies would, of course, not express reservations about cases in which the Secretary-General has a special and legitimate interest. One must assume, therefore, that the reservations of the board were called forth by proposals that were out of the ordinary.

Obviously, the power of appointment belongs to the Secretary-General who, as a matter of law, may intervene in the appointment and promotion process. Although the Secretary-General has a legitimate interest in senior appointments, his intervention in relatively junior or middle-level appointments is all the more inadvisable, as it may cast doubt on his sincerity in supporting the Charter principle of merit, it weakens and even discredits bodies appointed to advise him on appointments and promotions, and it sets a dangerous example to the many officials who are only too keen to exert political pressures on the appointment and promotion bodies.

The impression of the author is that, although the appointment and promotion bodies perform a useful function in focusing on irregularities and in subjecting proposed appointments and promotions to a review by a body that includes nominees of the staff, these bodies are not sufficiently strict in insisting on the compliance with the Charter principles regarding recruitment and promotion. The board, especially, can be singled out for criticism, for rather too often reversing negative recommendations of the committee, for too often going along with recommendations made by the administration, and for not voicing reservations often enough.

It is noticeable that rejections of actions proposed by the administration are extremely rare. It would be difficult to imagine that only such a small percentage of recommendations for appointment or promotion deserves to be rejected. Given the inadequate role of the staff and the political and departmental trade-offs that go on around the board, it appears difficult to suggest that the board is fully realizing its role of advising the Secretary-General on appointment, promotion, and review of staff.

The Role of the D–2 Special Review Group

In our discussion of the appointment and promotion machinery in this chapter, we have confined our comments, so far, only to appointment and promotions up to the D–1 level. As regards appointments to the D–2 level, such appointments are not within the competence of the Appointment and Promotion Board. The Secretary-General appointed the Special Review Group to advise him on appointments and promotions to the D–2 level.[3] The group comprises all under-secretaries-general occupying regular budget posts at Organization Headquarters, together with Mrs. H. Sipila, Assistant-Secretary-General, Center for Social Development and Humanitarian Affairs, and the assistant-secretary-general for Personnel Services as an *ex officio* member. It should be observed that the Special Review Group is a political body *par excellence* composed of political appointees of the Secretary-General, rather than of international civil servants. This composition reflects the growing acceptance of the political character of appointments at and promotions to the D–2 level. It is appropriate to observe that, although there has been talk for some time now of establishing specific terms of reference for the Special Review Group, such terms of reference have not yet been issued by the Secretary-General. Despite some dissatisfaction articulated by various members of the Special Review Group, it is generally accepted that the group continues to be a rubber stamping body recommending to the Secretary-General appointments and promotions that have already been decided upon by the Secretary-General and the head of the department concerned.

---

[3] Bohdan Lewandowski of Poland, under-secretary general for Conference Services and Special Assignments, was appointed in 1975 as its chairman.

The guidelines for the group raise several difficult questions. For instance, should preference be expressed for the existing staff, so as to stem the tendency towards increasing recruitment from outside the Secretariat at the D–2 level? Should the group be governed by explicit staff rules? In the past, the approach appeared to be against making this body into a statutory one. And what to make of the relationship between appointments to the D–2 level and career service?[4]

As of now, the Special Review Group is not conducting an annual review of the staff at the D–1 level with a view to possible promotions. Promotions to the D–2 level are arranged on an *ad hoc* basis, mostly on the initiative of a head of department, without any attempt to consider systematically other persons at the D–1 level who may deserve promotion. A similar lack of systematic screening applies to appointments from the outside to the D–2 level that are not subject to a vacancy announcement.

Bertrand Proposals for Reform of the Appointment and Promotion Bodies

We have already mentioned, on several occasions, the analysis of the appointment and promotion process made by Inspector Bertrand of the Joint Inspection Unit in his report of 1971 and the proposals he made for the reform of the system. Following the Bertrand report, the Administrative Management Service conducted a review of management and manpower utilization in the Office of Personnel Services in 1972, and made its own analysis and suggestions. In 1975, the Joint Advisory Committee appointed a working group on appointment and promotion procedures to review the procedures for the appointment, promotion, and review of staff in the light of the aforementioned JIU and AMS reports.

The main proposal put forward by JIU and AMS and now under active consideration in JAC is that some of the functions of the appointment and promotion bodies should be exercised by career planning committees composed of persons belonging to the same occupation or profession as the prospective appointee or promotee. Although supporting this suggestion in principle as a possible means of insulating the appointment and promotion process from undue political pressures, from which it suffers at the present time, the author must enter a note of caution. If the precise definition of "the same occupation or profession," extends over more

[4] Persons appointed from the outside to D–2 posts are given fixed-term contracts. Only those officials who have been promoted from inside the Organization and who obtained permanent contracts before being promoted to the D–2 level have permanent status. In one recent case, however, a person belonging to an advantaged nationality was promoted to D–2 while on a fixed-term contract and was given a permanent contract at the D–2 level.

than one department, it will rapidly be found that considerable intra-Secretariat snobbery exists; lawyers employed in the Office of Legal Affairs might not do justice to lawyers in Human Rights, the Law of the Sea, and so on. Much worse, the bulk of the committee members will of necessity be drawn from the unit in which members of the particular profession are the most numerous; they must go on living with their director, assistant-secretary-general or under-secretary-general, and their proceedings are unlikely to remain secret. This means that the committees will be more subject to pressure from above than the present appointment and promotion bodies, which have a Secretariat-wide composition, and in which one under-secretary-general can scarcely control more than one or two members. Breaking down the consideration of promotions along the lines of separate professions may thus mean that even the present right to advise, warn, or delay (exercised by the appointment and promotion bodies) might be impaired to a considerable degree.

This writer himself has proposed the creation of panels of outside experts to advise the recruitment division and the appointment and promotion bodies. He has, however, to admit, that, if—in the highly political context of the United Nations—the outside experts were to be chosen on the advice of delegations, this might cause a further politicization of the process and perhaps add yet other political games.

Geographical Distribution and Grossly Overrepresented States

What about the criteria applied by the Appointment and Promotion Board? A directive on recruitment policy issued by the assistant-secretary-general, director of personnel on 28 July 1969, interprets Staff Rule 104.14(a) (ii) as requiring the board to consider both the professional qualifications of the candidates for recruitment and the geographical distribution. The same criteria were to be applied when dealing with conversions of temporary appointments into permanent appointments and in cases of extensions of appointments. Thus, at least insofar as the policy of the Office of Personnel Services is concerned, an extension of a fixed-term appointment would not only be subject to considerations regarding the qualifications of the person concerned, availability of a post, and so on, but also would depend on whether at the relevant time the staff member's nationality is not overrepresented in the Secretariat. Another feature of this personnel directive is that it does not point out that personal qualifications are, under the Charter, the *paramount* consideration. The policy laid down by the Office of Personnel Services was to refrain from proposing for appointment candidates from overrepresented countries, save in the following "exceptional circumstances":

(a) A suitable candidate from another country cannot be found within a reasonable period of time, despite extensive and vigorous efforts; in this case, the Office of Personnel Services considers it appropriate to grant very short-term contracts.

(b) A candidate of a particular nationality is desired in the interest of establishing or maintaining an internal geographical balance within UNCTAD or UNIDO; this effort towards a better balance should be carried out to the extent possible, within each department or organization.

(c) The candidate, although a national of a heavily "overrepresented" country, comes from a region which is itself substantially "underrepresented," the term region designating, for example, a political [sic!] or linguistic unit.[5]

(d) The candidate is an outstanding university graduate, willing to take up a career or long-term appointment and thus falls under the category of future replacements for experienced officials who will be retiring in the years ahead.

The directive stated further that, when a candidate from an overrepresented country is submitted by OPS to the board, this is done in the belief that the case falls within one of the above exceptions, but that it is within the competence of the board to weigh all the considerations.

Some of the "exceptions" stated in the directive raise certain difficulties. Can underrepresentation of a particular region justify the preferential recruitment of an individual from an overrepresented country within that region over a more qualified candidate from another region? In practice, such a formula has been used to continue recruiting candidates from heavily overrepresented countries on the ground that they belonged to an underrepresented region and sometimes even to an adequately represented region. Moreover, there is no legal authority for interpreting the term "region" as including a linguistic unit. The interpretation of a unit in the political sense is not correct either, since, for the purpose of geographical distribution, regions are considered from a geographical rather than political viewpoint, although in some cases geography may coincide with the political system (Eastern Europe).

In 1966, in a case concerning the proposed appointment of a national of a grossly overrepresented Member State, the Appointment and Promotion Board gave an interpretation of policy whereby nationals of such

---

[5] Compare the 1969 report of the Secretary-General to the General Assembly which referred only to geographical or linquistic regions. A/7745, 24 GAOR, Annexes, Agenda Item 83, at 3.

states could be appointed only where the candidate offered a particular combination of qualifications and experience difficult to find elsewhere. This criterion was to be applied with the greatest strictness in the appointment of candidates at the intermediate and higher levels, but at the P–1 and P–2 levels some relaxation of these standards might be warranted.

In practice, however, candidates from grossly overrepresented countries have been appointed to intermediate and higher levels, especially if they belonged to one of the political advantaged nationalities.

Thus, between 1 July 1974 and 30 June 1975, nationals of the following states whose overrepresentation in the Secretariat on 30 June 1975 reached at least twice the midpoint of their desirable range were appointed at the P–5 or higher level: Algeria, Egypt, Ghana, Nigeria, Tanzania, India, Nepal, Colombia, Cyprus, Lebanon, Syria, Turkey. Nationals of many other overrepresented countries were appointed at the P–4 or lower levels.[6]

In 1959, the administration laid down, for the Appointment and Promotion Board, the policy on the conversion of fixed-term appointments to probationary appointments. It was stated that the principal considerations leading the Office of Personnel Services and the department concerned to recommend such action were the quality of the staff member's performance, the knowledge that the Organization will have a continuing need of his specialization if he is a specialist, and the "attractiveness of his nationality." We have already observed that the policy on conversion of fixed-term contracts into probationary appointments is inspired largely by the desire to improve the geographical distribution of the staff.

In the course of our discussions, we have referred to continued recruitment from grossly overrepresented states. Table 10–1 gives a list of countries that are grossly overrepresented in the sense that the number of their nationals on the staff of the Secretariat on 30 June 1975 was at least twice that of the midpoint of their desirable range. The sign plus or minus indicates increase or decrease in the number of staff members between 30 June 1974 and 30 June 1975.

The above data[7] indicate in the first place that no country belonging to the regions of Western and Eastern Europe is grossly overrepresented. Gross overrepresentation of the "North" is therefore only a myth. Certain developing countries, not the developed countries, are grossly overrepresented. Nevertheless, recruitment has continued, in 1975, from some of the grossly overrepresented states. These facts are not surprising, given the fact that the guidelines that we have already singled out for criticism allow for recruitment of nationals of overrepresented countries

---

[6] See A/10184, Annex, Table 8 and Table 10.

[7] Based on A/10184, Annex, Table 8.

184

Table 10–1
Overrepresentation Ratio

Region	Country	Overrepresentation Ratio (Number of Staff: Midpoint of Desirable Range)	Increase or Decrease
Africa	Algeria	2.8	+
	Dahomey	2.3	+
	Egypt	4.5	−
	Ethiopia	4.0	+
	Ghana	3.1	
	Kenya	2.9	−
	Mali	2.8	+
	Nigeria	2.8	+
	Sierra Leone	3.1	+
	Sudan	2.6	−
	Togo	2.6	+
	Tunisia	4.6	
	Uganda	3.7	+
	U. Rep. Tanzania	3.7	+
Asia and the Far East	Burma	2.5	
	India	2.2	−
	Indonesia	2.0	−
	Malaysia	2.2	−
	Nepal	3.1	+
	Pakistan	3.0	−
	Philippines	4.5	+
	Sri Lanka	4.0	+
	Thailand	3.6	−
Latin America	Bolivia	3.4	+
	Chile	4.8	+
	Colombia	2.6	−
	Haiti	2.8	
	Peru	2.2	+
	Uruguay	3.1	−
Middle East	Afghanistan	2.0	+
	Cyprus	2.6	+
	Iran	2.3	+
	Iraq	3.3	+
	Jordan	2.6	+
	Lebanon	4.5	+
	Syria	3.7	+
	Turkey	2.3	+
North America and Caribbean	Guyana	2.0	+
	Jamaica	3.4	−
	Trinidad and Tobago	2.8	+

from underrepresented regions, and, given the political prominence of some of the grossly overrepresented countries, it appears that the application of restrictive recruitment to nationals of overrepresented countries is therefore stricter with regard to countries of the North than to the countries of the South. This is, of course, a reflection of the growing political prominence, in the United Nations, of the developing countries. Indeed, we should expect that in the future the strength of developing nations in the Secretariat will increase because of favourable recruitment policies, especially if the formulae for the determination of desirable ranges (which, at the present, give a considerable advantage to the larger contributors while the desirable range of many small contributors is only 1–6, 2–6, 2–7) are further changed to the advantage of the smaller contributors.

Vacancy Announcements

What is the formal policy of the Organization with respect to vacancy announcements? By a circular dated 21 February 1974, the assistant-secretary-general, Personnel Services, advised the executive officers of all the departments that he had decided to discontinue forthwith the issuing of a circular of vacancies, a cumbersome and expensive document often out of date by the time it appeared, and to institute a system for announcement of actual vacancies by distributing job descriptions for every post open for outside recruitment. The system of individual vacancy announcements was designed to make possible a distribution of up-to-date job descriptions not only to governments, but also to other recruitment sources. Each vacancy notice was to include a deadline (two months) for the submission of applications. According to this circular, no recruitment action was to be initiated unless a vacancy notification and the job description had been circulated and no candidate could be presented to the appointment and promotion bodies until after the application deadline had expired. The circular was to govern recruitment to all professional and higher posts, except at D–2 and higher levels, posts filled through competitive examinations and for short-term (that is, less than a year) appointments. The above exceptions do not appear unreasonable, if appointments at the D–2 level are regarded as discretionary and political. If, however, appointments at the D–2 level are regarded as career appointments, the exception would appear unjustified (recently the possibility has been discussed in the Secretariat of making appointments at the D–2 level subject to vacancy announcements). The exception concerning posts filled through competitive examinations appears to be justified.

By a circular of 1 May 1975, the assistant secretary-general, Personnel Services, went back on his broad commitment to the principle of vacancy announcements. According to the new circular, vacancy announcements would *not* be circulated "from time to time as required by special circumstances." "Usually" such circumstances would "include" the availability of a well-qualified candidate from an underrepresented Member State for a technical job that had been difficult to fill. Thus, the principle of vacancy announcements was to be subject to the requirements of geographical distribution. It is obvious that in the absence of a vacancy announcement (and of competitive examinations), it is impossible to ascertain whether the "qualified" candidate from an underrepresented state is indeed well qualified compared to other candidates, who might have applied if a vacancy announcement had been issued.

The circular went on to establish another exception, that is, for posts "with special requirements such as" those of special assistants to department heads. Elsewhere, we have already referred to the practice of appointing assistants to heads of departments possessing the same nationality.

In conclusion, the circular of 1 May introduced vagueness and loopholes to the vacancy announcement system, making illusory the Charter requirement—implied by Article 101(3)—of equal consideration of candidates.

In Chapter 4, pages 57–58, we have already discussed the legal aspects of the present policy pertaining to vacancy announcements.

A second problem relates to the scope and method of publicizing vacancies that it has been decided to announce. The administration has a considerable discretion as to the distribution of the vacancy announcements. If a department already has someone in mind whom it considers to be a good candidate for recruitment, a minimum distribution list is used. The idea is to meet the "obligation" of announcing the vacancy without stirring things up, which might bring a flood of applications. The minimum list includes only governmental addresses and certain international organizations. The regular distribution list already contains a mixture of specialized addresses by nationality and occupation in underrepresented and in adequately represented countries. In the cases of maximum distribution, the regular distribution list is used with the addition of overrepresented countries. Maximum distribution is, however, used primarily in cases of recirculation of a vacancy announcement, that is, where the Secretariat has not succeeded in filling a post following the initial circulation.[8]

[8] Minimum distribution includes: Permanent missions, specialized agencies, overseas offices, Headquarters addressees. Regular distribution includes: 1. regional and international organizations, societies, institutes, etc.; universities; women's organizations. 2. In under- and adequately represented countries: a. United Nations Information Centers, resident representatives, national recruitment services (including UNIDO national recruitment services for a UNIDO vacancy); b. professional bodies, according to the qualifications needed.

In the case of a minimum distribution, candidates from overrepresented countries are filtered out at an early stage (that is, their names are not even forwarded to the interested departments); in the regular distribution, the filtering out is less automatic and more discretionary. The significance of the filtering out is, of course, that the department is not given the possibility to express preference for some candidates. The restricted methods of distribution, taken together with the administrative filtering out procedures, make it difficult for a qualified candidate from a country that is overrepresented and sometimes even from a country that is adequately represented, to be considered for recruitment on an equal basis with candidates from underrepresented countries.

Opponents of the introduction of a comprehensive commitment to the principle of vacancy announcement argue that the decision is inevitably discretionary, guided only by common sense and guarded only by the vigilance of the appointment and promotion bodies. If OPS produces a candidate so appropriately qualified that it seems very unlikely that circulation of an announcement could produce anyone better, and if this judgment of the qualifications is shared by the relevant appointment and promotion body, circulation would only result in a useless waste of two months (the time that has to be left for submission of applications) before the post is filled. If the relevant appointment and promotion body does not agree on the qualifications of the candidate, it can always reject him and make circulation necessary (at least if there is no urgent need that the functions be performed immediately).

In the view of the author, this argument overstates the capability and the willingness of the appointment and promotion bodies to contest the qualifications of a candidate produced by OPS. Qualifications must be considered on a relative basis, in comparison to other candidates. Given the political factor in the selection of candidates, a two-month waiting period is not too high a price to pay for safeguards designed to make it possible to consider all candidates.

We shall return to the question of vacancy announcements in the context of promotions in the section on promotion, pages 192–193.

Competitive Entry

Despite the stress placed by Article 101(3) on the necessity of securing the highest standards of efficiency, competence, and integrity in the recruitment of staff, Staff Regulation 4.3 provides only that "[s]o far as practicable, selection shall be made on a competitive basis." The words "competitive basis"[9] include, of course, competitive examinations, and other

---

[9] The Secretary-General has reported that progress was made in the use of the computerized roster and that in the year covered by his report one candidate (rather than multiple candidates) was considered in only 22 percent of all recruitment actions for professional posts. A/10184, at 5 (1975).

competitive ways of selecting the most qualified candidates. The only area where the Secretariat has consistently and successfully followed the practice of recruiting professional staff by competitive examinations is that of special language skills. Despite their high cost, the examinations have enabled the United Nations to maintain a very high level of efficiency in the language area. Not surprisingly, perhaps, this is also the one professional area where appointments are not subject to the requirement of equitable geographical distribution.

Competitive examinations are also sometimes held for young professionals, to be recruited at the P–1 to P–2 levels.[10] Such examinations have recently been held in a number of underrepresented countries (Japan, Federal Republic of Germany, Italy) and in the United Kingdom. The examinations have produced some excellent candidates for recruitment. The cost of examinations has proved, however, very high. But the principal difficulty concerned the availability of posts for the successful candidates. The examinations were held without a prior and definitive earmarking of posts for the successful candidates. OPS had to work hard to "sell" the successful examinees to the various departments, which often showed grave shortsightedness by preferring more experienced and older candidates. Unless persons who have successfully passed examinations are in fact given, within a short period of time, posts in the Secretariat and unless the departments come to understand the vital need and usefulness of taking in young people for careers in the Secretariat and give them training on the job, the whole system of competitive examinations may fall into disrepute. The fact that only a handful of successful examinees for junior professional posts is already "on board" does not augur well for the future.[11]

In principle, competitive examinations should be the principal way of entering the Secretariat, at least up to a certain level.[12] It accords particularly well with the principles underlying the selection of staff as laid down in Article 101(3). But it is a difficult and expensive method. If an examination is held for nationals of more than one country, it is necessary to overcome difficulties regarding comparability of national educational systems

---

[10] See, in general, *ibid*.

[11] According to the Secretariat, in the course of 1975 the Appointment and Promotion Committee and Board approved 311 appointments to posts subject to geographical distribution. By 1 June 1976, only 25 persons recruited from competitive examinations held in Italy, the Federal Republic of Germany, Japan, and the United Kingdom had actually joined the departments. This constitutes only about 8 percent of the appointments approved by the board and the committee in 1975 alone. Inadequate as this percentage is, one should not disregard the progress which this percentage reflects.

[12] The Advisory Committee on Administrative and Budgetary Questions has not shown great willingness to support the development of a separate examination unit within the Secretariat. 30 GAOR, Supp. No. 8 (A/10008), at 139–40. At the present a small unit is in charge of both training and examinations.

and the relative strength of institutions of higher learning. Beyond and above that, one has to tackle carefully the question of national pride and susceptibilities. In the view of the author, greater stress should be placed on holding examinations on a regional basis, selecting for that purpose countries with similar educational, cultural, and linguistic systems.

Recruitment missions that continue to be used as a means of interviewing groups of candidates in selected locations are helpful. The author believes, however, that by themselves they cannot adequately ensure competitive recruitment. If written and oral examinations cannot be developed in a significant way in the foreseeable future, outside expert panels—already suggested by the author—might be useful in introducing an element of objective expert evaluation of the records of candidates. Such panels might help in weeding out unqualified candidates and conversely in selecting from hundreds of applicants those few who hold a promise of talent. The international character of such a panel may, however, pose major problems.

Determination of Level for Recruits

In 1974, the Division of Recruitment of the Secretariat prepared for the use of the administration rough but useful guidelines for the determination of the grade of a prospective staff member in relation to his academic and professional record. The guidelines were accompanied by details concerning comparability of particular degrees in a number of countries constituting major sources of recruitment (Canada, France, India, Japan, United Kingdom, Soviet Union, Federal Republic of Germany). The final decision regarding the determination of the grade of a candidate rested on the "professional judgment" of the OPS, in other words, remained within the discretion of the administration. In fact, the administration retained a particularly broad measure of discretion in evaluating the past professional experience of a candidate. Allegations have been made that, in practice, different grades have been offered to candidates with roughly similar records coming from different countries. In practice, the grade on initial appointment is often not related to the functions to be performed; it is set on the basis of the candidate's academic degrees and the length of his relevant experience. Thus, it may happen that a P–4 vacancy may be filled at the P–3 or even the P–2 level, if the candidate is young.

Obviously, the system imposes disadvantages and career impediments on staff members, especially brilliant ones, who, if they are appointed young, will not receive a level that corresponds with their real usefulness, and who, as we shall see, may be blocked from attaining that level not only by the required minimum period of service in grade but also by the absence of vacancies.

Promotion

In 1958, the directives of the Appointment and Promotion Board laid down criteria to be applied in promotion cases. These included professional qualifications, seniority of service (a minimum period of service in each grade was to be a normal requirement for promotion),[13] and personal qualities.

In 1962, additional procedures were laid down by the board for officers who show exceptional ability in the performance of their duties but who have less than the normal minimum seniority.

We have already alluded to the fact that the policy of the Organization is not to promote talented young people too quickly on the basis of conspicuous merit, so that they would not arrive too early at the top level. Thus, in considering recommendations for "accelerated promotions" (that is, promotion of persons with less than the minimum period of service in grade),[14] the appointment and promotion bodies generally insist on evidence that the promotion is required by some interest of the Organization, apart from the merit of the candidate. Staff representatives, as such, are more interested in promotion on the basis of seniority, rather than in promotion on the ground of exceptional merit. This factor tends to encourage mediocrity in the Secretariat.

Indeed, as shown by Table 10-2 prepared by the Secretariat (unpublished), not many cases are placed each year on the promotion registers as a result of accelerated promotions.

Accelerated promotions are decided upon within the framework of the regular review by the appointment and promotion bodies of staff eligible for promotion, but there are cases in which a staff member is promoted outside the regular review, which provides at least some assurance of comparability.

One such case is a correction of the entrance level within the first year of service on the ground that a person was recruited at a lower level than he or she deserves or as a result of an error in evaluating his or her qualifications or because of the absence of a post at a higher level at the time of recruitment. In the years 1971–1975, only 18 persons were promoted through the correction of entrance level.[15]

In the same years, however, as many as 73 persons were promoted outside the regular review through the procedure of *ad hoc* promotion under Staff Rule 104.14(f) (iii) (B) which provides that, in the event that a particular vacancy cannot by reason of the nature of the work be appro-

[13] See Staff Rule 104.14(f) (iii) (C).

[14] Two years from P–1 to P–2, three years from P–2 to P–3 and P–3 to P–4, and five years from P–4 to P–5 and P–5 to D–1.

[15] Data obtained from the Secretariat.

Table 10–2
Promotion Registers–1974–1975
Accelerated Cases

Register	Recommended by Dept.	Accepted by Reviewing Bodies
I–1974		
D–1	6	6
P–5	14	12
P–4	14	9
P–3	13	8
P–2	7	5
P–1	2	2
II–1975		
D–1	7	5
P–5	20	9
P–4	24	21
P–3	13	10
P–2	13	9
P–1	2	2

priately filled from a promotion register, the board may recommend exceptionally, in advance of the next regular review, the promotion of a staff member considered by it to be best qualified "after review of a relevant group of staff." An OPS memorandum (1975) explained that the procedure of *ad hoc* promotion is used in cases where a staff member does not have the necessary seniority in grade but because of his special qualifications has to be assigned to a post at a higher level to which other staff members with equal or greater seniority could not be promoted.

A note by the assistant-secretary-general, Office of Personnel Services, (1972) interpreted the rule as applying to cases where, because of the particular nature of the post, and the required qualifications, the post could not be filled by staff members already on the promotion register, and the promotion was urgently needed and its delay could hamper the work of a particular office. As regards the meaning of the term "relevant group," this would normally include a selected number of staff whose qualifications and experience are relevant to the particular post and who possess the same—or greater—seniority in grade as the candidate recommended. The note further stressed that the *ad hoc* promotion procedure should not be used as a circumvention of the regular review of staff for promotion and that it must not become a device for promoting staff members who have failed to be included in the promotion register because of factors such as seniority, qualifications, and potential. Moreover, the staff member is judged to be best qualified in the relevant group of staff.

Despite the above exhortations, the author has gained the impression that the *ad hoc* promotion has in some cases been used to promote persons who would have been rejected in the course of the regular review. The lists of "relevant groups of staff" appear to have been prepared with considerable selectivity.

It should be observed that the normal promotion procedure, that is, through the inclusion of a name in a promotion register, does not guarantee the actual promotion of the staff member concerned. The actual promotion may depend on the availability of a post. The author has found that considerable dissatisfaction prevailed with regard to the periodic reports which should carry considerable weight in evaluating staff members for promotion. In practice, however, it is customary for supervisors to give members of their staff very high marks, *inter alia*, in order to avoid personal difficulties in the daily working relations. This makes the job of comparing qualifications of various staff members very difficult. Moreover, the positive evaluation is sometimes counterbalanced by derogatory comments of which the staff member is not informed. A new administrative instruction (ST/AI/240) approved by the Secretary-General will, it is hoped, improve the procedures of performance evaluation.

Given the difficulties in implementing the principle of promotion on the basis of merit, it may be worthwhile giving consideration to supplementing the present system with promotion by dint of seniority, so that every professional with a decent service record would become a P–4 after a given number of years of service, regardless of the vacancy situation. Some certainty of a career—of advancement in rank as the official advances in age—is desirable, because, without it, morale decays. If grading penalties are imposed on youth, age should receive grading rewards.

A few comments about vacancy announcements in the context of promotion procedures may be necessary.

As already mentioned, the circular of 21 February 1974 which enunciated the policy of vacancy announcements applied it only to posts to be filled by outside recruitment. Thus, as regards posts to be filled by promotions, no vacancy announcements are circulated at all. Obviously, unless forthcoming vacancies are brought to the notice of members of the staff, they cannot actively present their candidatures and Staff Regulation 4.4 may be rendered academic. The opposition to the introduction of the vacancy announcements in the context of promotion comes primarily from the managerial establishment which is anxious to maintain control over promotions and placements.

One of the disadvantages of the promotion register system is that it leaves too little scope for the effective use of the vacancy announcements. This writer does not feel that there is a necessary conflict between the continuation of the promotion register system and the introduction of a vacancy announcement system to promotions. Indeed, a comprehensive vacancy announcement system could protect persons already on the register as against preferred candidates for *ad hoc* promotions. Although the present system of *ad hoc* promotions requires an examination of the relevant group of persons already on the register, such an examination might at times be rather perfunctory. Moreover, persons already on the register are not able to present their own case. When the Secretariat is not expanding as it was, the prospects for a speedy promotion through promotion register have declined, while the importance of *ad hoc* promotions has increased, especially to more senior posts. Announcements of vacancies may also be helpful to persons on the register, even outside the context of *ad hoc* promotions, in that they could press their claims more effectively. At the very minimum, no *ad hoc* promotions should be allowed except after a mandatory posting of an announcement for a certain period of time. By allowing applications from persons already on the register and from those that have been left out, safeguards would be introduced against abuse of the *ad hoc* promotion procedure.

Finally, we have already referred to the problem concerning the promotion of staff serving on fixed-term contracts. In 1962, the Appointment and Promotion Board observed in a report to the Secretary-General that, although staff rules did not differentiate in respect of promotion register between career staff and staff under fixed-term contracts, promotion was, as a rule, appropriate only with regard to the career staff. Staff members on fixed-term appointments should, therefore, be promoted either in order to correct an obvious error in the initial grading, or at the time of the renewal of the contract (or according to the procedure on *ad hoc* promotions). Despite the views expressed in the above report, staff members on fixed-term contracts, including those serving on secondment, have been promoted during the lifetime of their contracts.

Classification

The United Nations does not have any system of classification of jobs, that is, no system for relating the duties of the post to the grade levels, and no administrative machinery for uniformly implementing and maintaining such a system. Thus, the same responsibilities are often performed by staff members who carry different grades and titles. This, of course, is closely related to recruitment, selection, placement, and promotion. In the absence of a uniform and effective post classification system, it is possible to tailor job descriptions and vacancy announcements in such a way as to make virtually certain that a candidate preferred by the department will be recruited; it is possible to give a favourite candidate a higher grade, and to reclassify (upgrade) the post, so as to promote the incumbent for *ad hominem* considerations, without any change in the real content and duties involved. Despite Staff Regulation 2.1, serious work began only in 1976 in the Secretariat on the preparation of a comprehensive job classification system, an effort likely to require a number of years. And yet, without a proper job classification system, reforms of the appointment and promotion process cannot be effective.

The absence of common post classification standards means that the rank of a new post may be adjusted in response to particular pressures exerted by the candidate or by a government. It may also mean that it is relatively easy for the administration to claim that a post should be upgraded (reclassified) in recognition of the increased responsibilities attached to the post. In some cases this justification, which is advanced by the Secretary-General in his budget proposals, is a mere fiction. Moreover, there is no doubt at all that some recent reclassifications of posts, including to the D–2 level, were politically motivated. (Although the incumbent of an upgraded post has to pass through the promotion process, cases in which he is not promoted to the grade carried by the post are rare.)

The Advisory Committee on Administrative and Budgetary Questions has repeatedly observed that the reclassification of posts was an essential element in the process of promotion; although it was not opposed to the promotion of staff in recognition of increased responsibilities, it could not agree that a post should be reclassified primarily for the purpose of promoting its incumbent.[16]

The Hammarskjöldian consolidated manning table made it possible to shuffle posts around among the various departments—and facilitate the promotion of talented staff members—but now such mobility is permitted only within the same section of the budget. Reclassification of posts may thus be viewed as a safety valve, tempering the rigidity of the system. But it is far from being a desirable way of doing so.

There are areas in the Secretariat (for example, Conference Services) where grades are closely linked with functions. In many areas this is not the case, however. People do not change from one kind of work to another as they advance in grade; they generally go on doing the same kind of work, but with less and less close supervision.

All professional units tend to have a "journeyman level," that is, a grade whose occupants are considered to be mature, fully competent offi-

[16] 28 GAOR. Supp. No. 8 (A/9008), at 27; 30 GAOR, Supp. No. 8 (A/10008), at 25. Meron, *The United Nations "Common System" of Salary, Allowance and Benefits: A Critical Appraisal of Coordination in Personnel Matters*, 21 INT'L. ORG. 284(1967).

cials who can be relied on, in the general run of the work, to do their jobs in a way that is a credit to their units. Their competence gives them a claim to promotion to the next higher level after the normal minimum period in grade, if there is a vacancy, but their functions sometimes have very little to do with their grade.

The realities are thus very different from the theory that every post has fixed, immutable functions listed in the job description attached to it, and that promotion should occur only when the staff member moves to a higher post that encompasses broader functions than the one he has been occupying.

11 Future Directions

If no major reforms are introduced and implemented we may expect the recent trends to continue and even intensify. In particular, it is probable that recruitment and promotion processes will become increasingly politicized and that the criteria of efficiency, competence, and integrity will be regarded more and more as secondary. We may expect a growing "Balkanization" of the Secretariat and the parcelling out of major posts to powerful countries and blocs. The institution of international career service is likely to decline gradually. More officials are likely to serve on fixed-term appointments, often on secondment from their governments.

In the next few years, after the old-timers and particularly the first generation of international civil servants will have retired from the service, the pace of change is likely to increase as the restraints resulting from tradition and the outlook of the old-timers will fade away.

The Secretariat of the future is therefore likely to resemble more a multinational, rather than an international, body. It is likely that, as less and less heed is paid to merit both by the Secretariat and by Member States, the staff will be technically less efficient and that, with the increasing politicization, Secretariat officials will be less independent of their governments and less impartial. The staff would probably be suspected of lacking neutrality and would lack the confidence of some Member States. The national, regional, and group loyalties of the officials are likely to grow concurrently with their increasing dependence on their governments. The result might be a paralysis of the Secretariat, which would be unable to play an effective role, in situations of crisis.

In order to reduce the impact of such tendencies, the author has suggested that the role of law in the Organization be reinvigorated and that proper procedures, counterbalances, safeguards, and due process be developed.

The problem, however, is not only, or even primarily, technical. The competiton between states and groups of states for the staffing of the key Secretariat positions by their nationals and supporters is not primarily a manifestation of patronage or nepotism, but it reflects a real power struggle, an attempt to control the Organization and its activities. Few states have not participated in this race, and most states share the blame—although in differing degrees—for the results. Among the groups that have been particularly active in advocating the primacy of geography in recruitment has been the group of developing countries. Although their claims for a more equitable participation in the Secretariat are understandable, and their struggle to make the Secretariat more responsive to their developmental needs is both legitimate and increasingly successful (in the view of the author these objectives could have been better accommodated with the merit principle), it is they who, more than the larger contributors, are likely to suffer if the Secretariat becomes technically less efficient and politically discredited.

It is unreasonable to expect that reforms can come from within. The Secretariat, which inevitably reflects and mirrors many national and group attitudes and which is headed by secretaries-general who may run for reelection, cannot reform itself on its own momentum. Although more effective staff action is both desirable and feasible, it is only the Member States that can force effective reforms on the Secretariat.

As long as many states appear to be happy with the ongoing game of musical chairs and with the fight for larger slices of the pie, as long as a common will is lacking, reforms are unlikely to be implemented. Only when a sufficiently large number of states, including the major contributors, realize that it is in their urgent interest to bring about reforms that such reforms will come about. Let us only hope, in the broader long-term interest of the Organization, that this happens before it is too late.

Index

Index

About the Author

Theodor Meron has combined a career in the Israel Ministry for Foreign Affairs with academic activities. He served for several years as a Representative on the Fifth (Administrative and Budgetary) Committee of the General Assembly and has participated in many diplomatic conferences. From 1967 to 1971 he served as Legal Adviser to the Ministry for Foreign Affairs and was subsequently Ambassador to Canada. He studied at the Hebrew University (Jerusalem), the Harvard Law School and Cambridge University, and was Visiting Professor of International Law at the Faculty of Law of the University of Ottawa.

This book was written during Professor Meron's leave from the Foreign Service as a Rockefeller Foundation Fellow and Visiting Professor of Law at New York University.

Professor Meron's publications include many articles on international law and organizations as well as a book entitled *Investment Insurance in International Law*.